A FIELD GUIDE TO
Selma's Architectural Legacy

A FIELD GUIDE TO
Selma's Architectural Legacy

SUSAN BESSER

A Field Guide to Selma's Architectural Legacy

© 2025 Susan Besser

ISBN 13-979-8-218-61128-6 (hardcover)
ISBN 13-979-8-218-61129-3 (paperback)

Cover by Jackie Brown.

Published by Franklin Preservation Associates

franklinpreservation.com

CONTENTS

Acknowledgments

CHAPTER 1

The Architectural Influences and History of Selma   1
   Architects and Craftsmen   4
   Evolution of Selma's Commercial Districts   8
   Significant Churches   12
   Pattern Books and Mail-Order Houses   14
   Apartment Dwellings   15
   Notable Queen Anne Examples   16
   Influences of Ornamental Cast Iron   17
   Spanish Eclectic and Mission Revival in Selma   18
   African American Neighborhoods   20
   Early History of Selma   22
   Selma's Transition from Frontier Town   24
   Industrialization of Selma   25
   Pre–Civil War Politics   26
   Selma's Role in the Civil War   27
   Reconstruction Politics   29
   Reconstruction Infrastructure   31
   Selma at the Beginning of the Early Twentieth Century   34

The Depression Era	38
Selma During World War II	40
The Civil Rights Movement and Selma Architecture	41
Linking Selma's Architecture and Selma's History	42

CHAPTER 2
Old Town Historic District — 45

Broad Street	47
Broad Street Residential	75
Lauderdale Street	86
Church Street	106
Tremont Street	120
Furniss Avenue	134
Mabry Street	136
J. L. Chestnut Boulevard	164
Union Street	164
Abbot Street	175
Lapsley Street	176
Old Live Oak Cemetery	196
Pettus Street	201
Dallas Avenue	202
McLeod Avenue	222
Parkman Avenue	225
Washington Street	231
Franklin Street	239
Selma Avenue	243
Alabama Avenue	269
Arsenal Place	296
Lamar Avenue	306
Notable Buildings	307

CHAPTER 3
Water Avenue Historic District — **315**
    Water Avenue — 318
    Martin Luther King Street — 333
    Lafayette Park — 336

CHAPTER 4
Boyntons Street — **339**

CHAPTER 5
African American Historic Sites — **353**

CHAPTER 6
Lost Buildings of Selma — **389**

CHAPTER 7
Looking to the Future of Selma — **419**

Glossary — 427
Bibliography — 433
About the Author — 439

ACKNOWLEDGMENTS

This book began with an invitation by Trina Binkley of the Alabama Historic Commission to resurvey Old Town Historic District and Water Avenue Historic District in Selma, Alabama. I decided to make the journey to Selma to explore the town. I was guided by Patty Sexton of the Selma Planning and Development Department on a tour of Selma and was so impressed with the level of architecture and by the encouragement of Elizabeth Driggers, director of the Selma Planning and Development Department, that I felt compelled to accept the project. Jean Martin, with the Selma Times-Journal was most valuable for providing me with the local culture. Early on I felt Selma had the potential to feature in a book of architecture sites and local history.

I began writing about ten years ago. Jackie Brown was instrumental in solidifying my introductory chapter overview.

As I delved more into the book Dr. Carroll Van West and I brainstormed about the format of the book and how to make it engaging.

Jen Rogers has been guiding me through the process of publishing. Becky Nichols, Director of the Selma Dallas County Library and Stephen Posey, librarian, assisted with local history research. Rachel Metcalf was most helpful with local preservation research. Sarah Aghedo has assisted in keeping me informed of the local preservation activity.

I want to thank the O'More College of Architecture and Design of Belmont University students from the Historic Preservation Class who studied historic photographs and the current condition of the details of the buildings and created drawings of the buildings that show promise of being rehabilitated. While doing the survey Rena' Taurman explored Selma with me on one occasion and assisted in the documentation.

Bill Tomey of the Selma Times-Journal assisted with photography, as did Dr. Carroll Van West, particularly with the African American sites.

Tom Headley, who was the administrator of the Selma Alabama History Facebook page connected me with preservationists in the area.

I am very grateful for everyone's assistance and most of all for the support of my husband, John Besser, throughout this endeavor.

CHAPTER 1

The Architectural Influences and History of Selma

Selma is a surprising city architecturally. Set among the canopies of live oak draped with Spanish moss, this city is comparable to Savannah and Beaufort in terms of architectural richness and yet is vastly unknown by the general public. Selma is also rich in history, most notably the Civil Rights era. By exploring the history of this vast storehouse of high-style architecture, one can trace how this forgotten town was once a bustling city and yet today struggles to keep its historic resources and maintain a strong economy.

The architecture of Selma indicates a high level of expertise. Many local craftsmen and builders, both white and African American, are responsible for the fine architecture of Selma. These masters created a vast architectural legacy, both high-style and vernacular, which tells the story of the ebb and flow of history, interwoven with economic booms and downturns. For Selma has history that traces from the Antebellum era to the Civil War to Civil Rights. All properties listed in this book are on the

National Register of Historic Places except for those listed on Boyntons Street. Most were part of a resurvey done in 2002; a number of properties were designated separately as noted by "NRHP" and the date following the name of the property.

Imagine it is 1940 and the newly opened Edmund Pettus Bridge is ringing in a new era of prosperity into a prominent downtown Selma streetscape with buildings of the Italianate era, as well as Romanesque Revival, Second Empire, Gothic Revival, and Art Deco. Traveling through the center of town and into the residential district, one notices the magnificent churches with four-story bell towers and a Gothic Revival church replete with gargoyle downspouts. The residential districts reveal an abundance of two-story residences of every style including Georgian Revival, Queen Anne, and Italianate.

FIGURE 1-1, Downtown Selma Circa 1940s, Old Depot Museum Archives

Even today, despite the loss of significant buildings such as the Hotel Albert, the Gillman Building, and grand Queen Anne dwellings, this architecturally rich city retains much of the 1940s-era building stock. One will note that photographs from the Historic American Building Survey, known as HABS, are incorporated in this book. These photographs were taken by noteworthy photographers and were one of President Roosevelt's programs to provide work during the Great Depression.

It is a journey worth exploring as Selma's history and architecture weave together a compelling story of a forgotten city. Use this guide to explore the storied streets of Selma and experience this rich architectural history for yourself.

A city's growth is evidenced in the architectural periods that correspond to national trends in architecture. In the 1860s, Selma was one of the largest cities in the south, being the center of cotton production and war munitions. The Battle of Selma on April 2, 1865, left the city in ruins. Selma's resilience after this setback was remarkable, and by the 1880s new houses such as the Queen Anne Koenigstahl-Williamson-Luker House were a testament to the success of its business district and the ability to attract architectural talent to the area.

FIGURE 1-2, Koenigstahl-Williamson-Luker House, 730 Dallas Avenue, Photograph by Susan Besser, 2002

This guide will explore some of the more significant and well-maintained architectural structures from the 1800s through the 1980s in Old Town Historic District and Water Avenue Historic District as well as

African American resources. Selma's churches are legendary, and this work also includes the churches built before 1925, several of which have African American congregations and have nationally significant connections to Civil Rights history, such as Brown Chapel, designed by African American architect A. J. Farley.

FIGURE 1-3, Brown Chapel A.M.E. Church, 410 Martin Luther King, Jr. Street, Photograph by Susan Besser, 2011

Architects and Craftsmen

Selma is significant for the local and regional architects and builders who worked in the area, such as Thomas Helm Lee and Andrew Jackson Mullen. Practicing before the Civil War, Thomas Helm Lee designed Sturdivant Hall, also known as Watts-Parkman-Gillman House, and the Lee-Bender-Butler House, no longer extant. Lee is held in high regard for his interpretation of the Greek Revival in these buildings.[1] Grace Hall, an Italianate dwelling, is also attributed to Thomas Helm Lee.

---

1. Ralph Hammond, *Ante-bellum Mansions of Alabama* (Bonanza Books, 1978), 140-141.

FIGURE 1-4, Lee-Bender-Butler House, 401 Church Street (no longer extant), Photograph by Susan Besser, 2002

Another fine craftsman of the late nineteenth century was Andrew Jackson Mullen, who built Dallas Academy, circa 1889, designed by Chisolm and Green, and the Wilby Theater, no longer extant, as well as other buildings in Selma and Marion.

Michael J. Miller, an Englishman, practiced architecture in Selma in the 1880s. He is noted in the *Selma Times-Journal* as designing William Weaver's house, also known as The Castle, on Lauderdale Street.[2] Miller had high-profile projects in Florida, one of which was the Belleview-Biltmore in Belleair, Florida, with Francis J. Kennard, also from England.

Charles Henry Hopson, an architect who left his mark on Selma with the Carnegie Library, married a Selma native and made his home in Selma from 1900 to 1913. Hopson was English born and practiced in Nova Scotia and Washington, D.C., in the post office division, before moving to Selma, and he left Selma in 1913 to reside and practice in Atlanta. He achieved national and international recognition for his ecclesiastical architecture, creating churches in Atlanta, Indianapolis, Birmingham, and Nova Scotia,

---

2. "An Elegant Mansion," *Selma Times-Journal*, September 14, 1882, 4.

as well as the towers on the Cathedral in Guelph, Canada, shown here with before and after images. Notable among his churches is the Peachtree Christian Church in Atlanta, a National Register of Historic Places property.

FIGURE 1-5, Guelph Cathedral, http:www.basilicaofourlady/about/history

FIGURE 1-6, Guelph Cathedral, Photograph by Susan Besser, 2019

Hopson recruited architect John W. McKeil from Nova Scotia. McKeil designed commercial and residential buildings in Selma, chiefly the Selma Buick Company building at 901 Selma Avenue, and in the surrounding region, moving to Birmingham in the late 1920s. McKeil designed another automobile-related building, Central Alabama Motor Car Co., which appears on the 1913 Sanborn map and is no longer extant. Showing his affinity for this type of structure, he wrote an article in 1919 for *Motor World for Jobbers, Dealers and Garagemen* regarding the design of a two-story showroom/garage that featured the actual plans. It was innovative for that time period. McKeil is buried in Selma's Old Live Oak Cemetery.

Frank Lockwood, a regionally recognized architect with strong classicist leanings, designed an addition to the Alabama State Capitol in Montgomery. He is also responsible for the Alabama Baptist Hospital in the Italian Renaissance style and Selma Junior High School, as well as additions to St. Paul's Episcopal Church and King's Hospital. Lockwood designed a particularly exquisite dwelling of the Georgian Colonial Revival located at 725 Dallas Avenue.

Raymond Sizemore based his practice in Montgomery and designed many projects in Selma. Chief among these is the city hall building done as a Public Works Administration project in the Neoclassical style. He is credited with the design of R. B. Hudson Middle School, which is a simple modernistic design. As evidenced by his handling of these buildings, Sizemore had the capability to design within any style, with an impressive list of projects including a movie theater in Centerville, Alabama. Sizemore worked with Frank Lockwood early in his career.

Two nationally recognized architects of the nineteenth century, Edward Tuckerman Potter, who designed the Commercial Bank of Alabama at 132 Broad Street, and Richard M. Upjohn, who designed St. Paul's Episcopal Church on Lauderdale Street, also left their mark on the Selma architecture legacy.

FIGURE 1-7, St. Paul's Episcopal Church, 210 Lauderdale Street, Photograph by Susan Besser, 2016

In the late nineteenth century and early twentieth century, African Americans were making strides in their education, and Selma architecture has much visible evidence of that in their building stock. Notable architects include David T. West, credited with Tabernacle Baptist Church on Broad Street. Robert Robinson Taylor and Leo Persley designed buildings on the Selma University campus. Taylor was the first African American to attend Massachusetts Institute of Technology. Taylor's work showed his ability to innovate by varying the fenestration to achieve his own unique interpretation of classic architecture. In the 1890s Taylor developed a curriculum of architectural drawing at Tuskegee Institute that would offer opportunities for young African Americans.[3]

Wallace Rayfield was the architect for several residences of notable Selma African American civic and religious leaders. He apprenticed with A. B. Mullet and Company in Washington, D.C., before attending Howard University and Pratt Institute and then graduating from Columbia University. Rayfield also taught at Tuskegee Institute.[4]

Less is known about A. J. Farley, of Beloit, Alabama, credited for his design of Brown Chapel, a National Historic Landmark. George Wilson, a local architect and builder, designed residences for the rising middle class of African Americans and most notably the Dallas County Colored Community Center on Franklin Street.

Evolution of Selma's Commercial Districts

Surveying the city after the Civil War it was evident that most of the commercial area of Broad Street and Water Street was damaged. Rebuilding began soon after the war, creating an opportunity for expression of architectural form such as the Italianate, the Renaissance Revival, and the rare Gothic Revival. The architecture of Broad Street is reflected in the brick

---

3. Ellen Weiss, *Robert R. Taylor and Tuskegee: An African American Architect Designs for Booker T. Washington* (Montgomery: New South Books, 2012), 45-48.

4. Allen R. Durough, *The Architectural Legacy of Wallace A. Rayfield: Pioneer Black Architect of Birmingham, Alabama* (Tuscaloosa: University of Alabama Press, 2010), 2-3.

and stone commercial-block buildings with early historic wood storefronts, circa 1870–1880, and cast-iron-supported storefronts that were constructed from 1880 to 1910, as well as the myriads of architectural details of the time, such as corbel tables and arched hood molds. Selma's Broad Street resonates with the late nineteenth-century commercial architecture that is celebrated with modern-day Main Street revitalization efforts.

FIGURE 1-8, 6 Broad Street 1870s-Era Storefront, Photograph by Susan Besser, 2002

John Hardy, who was the founder and editor of the *Selma Sentinel* as well as mayor from 1873 to 1875, in writing of Selma in 1879 lists the business categories and business owners illustrating the level of prosperity that Selma experienced during that time. Grocer Griel & Kohn occupied 6 Broad Street, S. F. Hobbs, a jeweler's establishment at 40 Broad Street (now 113 Broad Street), was located in a fine Italianate commercial building designed by W. K. Ball. Beautiful Italianate detailing such as the bracketed cornice embellished with a modillion course and a semicircular pediment graced with brackets and modillions creates a distinctive façade for a high-end jeweler.

FIGURE 1-9, 113 Broad Street, Photograph by Susan Besser, 2002

M. Meyer & Co. at 109 and 111 Broad operated a dry goods establishment. In the first decades of the twentieth century, specialization of services superseded the general store.[5] This trend had become evident in Selma before that time. Separate businesses existed for millinery and shoes, such as A. Meyer, milliner, and I. B. Howard, shoe store. Specialty shops such as confectioneries and cigar shops were also on Broad Street.

The most dramatic change in the downtown commercial district was the appearance of businesses owned or operated by African Americans. The city directory of 1880–1881 lists numerous African American merchants within the commercial directory, and many of these are cross-referenced

---

5. Carole Rifkind, *Main Street: The Face of Urban America* (New York: Harper Colophon, 1978), 64.

from Hardy's list. As with many towns African Americans initially owned or were represented in all manner of occupations: restaurateurs, upholsterers, butchers, cooks, barbers, carpenters, livery stable owners, and teachers. Alfred Wilson was a local African American contractor who managed his practice in the basement of the Hotel Albert, no longer extant; R. Johnson operated a barbershop at the corner of Alabama and Franklin; and Stollenwerck & Co. livery stables occupied a site on Washington Street between Selma Avenue and Dallas Avenue.

As higher education became more accessible, African Americans expanded their presence in society as teachers and physicians. Dr. L. L. Burwell, a graduate of Selma University and Leonard Medical College in Raleigh, N.C., where he graduated as valedictorian, set up his practice in Selma and saw a need for a pharmacy to serve African Americans.[6] L. L. Burwell is acknowledged as an Alabama Pioneer for his work in establishing the pharmacy, which was located on Franklin Street, and also Burwell Infirmary.

FIGURE 1-10, Drug Store of L. L. Burwell, M. D., www.alabamapioneers.com

---

6. Donna R. Causey, "Biography: L.L. Burwell, October 25, 1867, African-American," Alabama Pioneers, https://www.alabamapioneers.com/31173-2/.

An important African American commercial building is the Sullivan Building, located at 1220 Alabama Avenue. Undertaker Horace B. Sullivan and his son, H. Stanley Sullivan, a local dentist, oversaw the construction of this building. During the Civil Rights era it was the headquarters for the Student Nonviolent Coordinating Committee. The Courageous Eight along with J. L. Chestnut Jr., Margaret Moore, and Louretta Wimberly also held Voting Rights meetings in the Sullivan Building in the 1960s.

FIGURE 1-11, Sullivan Building, 1220 Alabama Avenue, Photograph by Dr. Carroll Van West, NRHP 2013

Significant Churches

Within the City of Selma are many handsome churches, four of which dominate the Selma skyline. First Baptist Church, 218 Lauderdale Street, a High Victorian Gothic Revival stone edifice, was constructed in 1904. The church was built in the Akron plan and displays a four-story tower featuring lancet arch windows, gargoyles, and tracery capped with a conical roof flaring to bellcast eaves. Front gabled parapeted entrances feature

Tudor arched doors surmounted by ogee arches capped with a boss. The manifestation of this building early in the twentieth century is an anomaly in Alabama.[7]

In 1893 First Presbyterian Church, 301 Broad Street, a two-story front gable edifice with a sixty-foot tower with turret detailing and slit windows, was executed in the Romanesque Revival style. Architect Reuben Harrison Hunt of Chattanooga was a master of church design as evidenced by his deft use of the Syrian arch, complex massing, and the combination of brick and cut stone.

J. W. Golucke & Co. designed Church Street United Methodist Church, 214 Church Street. Completed in 1901, the church is a late example of the Romanesque Revival. Built in the Akron plan with a front gable, the church features a four-story bell tower with conical copper roof, Romanesque Revival details such as the cushion capital, and foliated banding, all hallmarks of the style.

The fourth of these major churches, St. Paul's Episcopal Church, circa 1875, is the architectural design of the R. & R. M. Upjohn firm of New York, recognized among the foremost ecclesiastical architects of their time. The church displays the Gothic Revival as interpreted in the English vernacular. It is built in the cruciform plan and incorporates a large rose window of stained glass in the front gable. R. M. Upjohn's mastery of design is evident. The English Gothic vernacular, exhibited by the four-story tower with crenellated parapet featuring slit windows and tracery detail, is striking. Tiffany windows by Clara Weaver Parrish, who studied with Louis Comfort Tiffany, were added in the late 1800s.

African American religious leaders undertook similar impressive improvements in church architecture at the turn of the century. East of downtown stands First Baptist Church (1894), a Gothic Revival landmark in a historic African American neighborhood. At the other end of the street is Brown Chapel A. M. E. Church. Built in 1908, and attributed

---

7. Robert Gamble, *Historic Architecture in Alabama: A Primer of Styles and Types, 1810–1930* (Tuscaloosa: University of Alabama Press, 2001), 116.

to architect A. J. Farley, its twin-towered Romanesque Revival design features a recessed three-arch entrance with Byzantine- and Mission-inspired details.

At the north end of Broad Street stands the magnificent Neoclassical-styled Tabernacle Baptist Church, an African American religious and Civil Rights history landmark. Designed by African American architect David T. West in 1922, the church is a Broad Street gateway to the town's historic African American neighborhood, suggestive of the rising Black middle class in early twentieth-century Selma.

The Jewish population had grown steadily since the 1840s with the growth of Selma, having immigrated from Germany to Mobile and then upriver to Selma. Their Romanesque Revival temple with a Star of David window creates a strong presence on Broad Street and is believed to have been designed by Thomas Sully of New Orleans, Louisiana.

The presence of these churches and temple throughout the town symbolizes the priority the Selmians placed on their worship centers as well as the strong economy Selma was experiencing, especially in the late nineteenth and early twentieth centuries.

Pattern Books and Mail-Order Houses

Pattern books, such as those popularized by George F. Barber, played a significant role in the development of national trends. One of Barber's designs has been identified within the city. Located at 520 Selma Avenue is a stucco-exterior dwelling. It is identified as House No. 599 in George F. Barber's designs and known as "A Plastered House." This dwelling displays Barber's deft handling of the Queen Anne vernacular.

Mail-order houses were sold across the country along with the molds to fabricate rock-faced block houses. In addition to the popularity of pattern books, major retailers packaged house-building kits. One such house in Selma has been classified as a Sears & Roebuck Co. house. The dwelling at 707 Selma Avenue appears to have been based on a Sears house, Design 52 from a 1908 general catalog. There are modifications from the original design, such as paired windows and a flat-roof porch with balustrade, which would have been done by John McKeil, architect with Chambers, McKeil & Co. The most notable feature is the rock-face block exterior, which would have been made on-site. Sears produced the machines that manufactured the blocks and boasted that the "concrete houses can be erected at one-third less cost than any other kind of stone structures."[8]

Apartment Dwellings

A nationwide trend in apartment dwellings beginning in New York in the late nineteenth century became evident in Selma early in the twentieth century. Apartments became a popular alternative to single dwellings in Selma in the 1920s and 1930s, offering the latest in technology such as hot and cold running water. Architectural historian Gwendolyn Wright has noted that apartments indicated a cosmopolitan trend in the acculturation of society.[9] Within Old Town Historic District are six apartment buildings. The oldest surviving apartment building, Georgette, is a three-story Georgian Revival. Noteworthy is the Joe-Ann on Selma Avenue, named for the owners, Joe and Ann Rosenberg, and designed by John W. McKeil. It has four apartments comprising seven rooms in addition to the kitchen and bathroom. Sadly, the Belle-Marie Flats, designed by Charles Henry Hopson, which was located at 100 Alabama Avenue, was demolished in 1978 for the Court House Annex located at the corner of Church and Alabama. The building held six flats that had six rooms each in addition to the kitchen and bathroom. It is described as having "magnificent large reception halls" with the construction being concrete, creating a fireproof building. Hopson

---

8. Daniel D. Rieff, *Houses from Books: Treatises, Pattern Books, and Catalogs in American Architecture, 1738–1950, A History and Guide* (University Park, PA: Pennsylvania State University Press, 2001), 186.

9. Gwendolyn Wright, *Building the Dream: A Social History of Housing in America* (Cambridge, MA: MIT Press, 1981), 141.

incorporated a skylight into the center of the Y-shaped building to give daylighting to the occupants.[10]

FIGURE 1-12, Belle-Marie Flats, Postcard Courtesy of Jonathan Chappelle

The Eagles Nest on Arsenal Place was named after the Eagle family who owned the apartments and was designed by architect H. J. Koski. Siblings of the Eagle family occupied each of the apartments. The Eagles also owned Eagles Department Store on the corner of Alabama Avenue and Washington Street at 1119-1121 Alabama Avenue.

Notable Queen Anne Examples

In the residential area of Old Town Historic District, the Queen Anne period is displayed in an abundance of dwellings. Hallmarks of the style are imbricated shingles in the gable ends, cutaway bays with corner brackets, spindlework detail, and turreted porches. This would indicate that the 1880s–1910s were a period of prosperity for Selma as that was a popular style in the era. The grandest of these is the Koenigstahl-Williamson-Luker at 730 Dallas Avenue, which is technically a Shingle Style but has many elements of the Queen Anne. Noteworthy are other examples such as the Strother House at 510 Tremont Street with its wraparound double-tiered porch and the exquisite dwelling at 613 Parkman Avenue with a turreted porch. In the historic

---

10. "New Flats Now Near Completion," *Selma Times-Journal*, May 1, 1910.

districts there are over 120 Queen Anne dwellings, some of which are in the Folk Victorian vernacular style with spindlework detailing. According to James C. Massey and Shirley Maxwell the Queen Anne was "spurred on by pattern books" with a style that had universal appeal, featuring picturesque exteriors with plans that could be adapted to narrow city lots or larger estates and yet maintained a welcoming human scale.[11]

FIGURE 1-13, 613 Parkman Avenue, Photograph by Susan Besser, 2002

Influences of Ornamental Cast Iron

The French Colonial Revival influence in Selma is illustrated by the incorporation of cast-iron ornamentation and can be attributed to the influences of commerce with Mobile, Alabama. Before the railroads and steamboats, the stage coach made daily rounds to Mobile. There are a great many dwellings detailed in cast iron in Mobile. Many Selmians saw this detail in the

---

11. James C. Massey and Shirley Maxwell, *House Styles in America: The Old House Journal Guide to the Architecture of American Homes* (Dovetail Publishers, 1996), 127-131.

port city and incorporated it into their architectural design. The corner of 2 Broad Street in the early 1900s originally had a two-story gallery of cast iron. Properties such as the St. James Hotel and Berry House at 900 Alabama Avenue retain their cast-iron balconies. Cast iron was a logical choice for fire escapes, which were manufactured at the local Peacock Foundry owned by George Peacock, the metallurgist, hired to work with the Confederate Foundry during the Civil War. After the War he established his business in Selma on Water Avenue. In 1887 he developed the Peacock self-oiling railroad car wheel manufactured in Selma and distributed throughout the country.[12] A photograph of 15 Union Street illustrates the beautiful locally produced ironwork (figure 1-14).

FIGURE 1-14, 15 Union Street, Library of Congress

Spanish Eclectic and Mission Revival in Selma

Within the historic districts are fewer than a dozen Spanish Eclectic–influenced dwellings, with the YMCA at 532 Broad Street originally in the Mission style and Brown Chapel exhibiting Mission elements.

---

12. Walter M. Jackson, *The Story of Selma* (Birmingham: Birmingham Printing Company, 1954), 232.

FIGURE 1-15, YMCA 532 Broad Street (Original Façade), Postcard Collection of Susan Besser

Charles Henry Hopson created a beautiful Spanish-influenced dwelling for his family on 22 View circa 1905 that exemplifies this style. Hallmarks of the style are shaped parapets, tile roofs, crenellation, and a stucco exterior. The 1920s were a boom period for Selma, and several buildings in the style appeared during that period. One in particular, though not in these districts, was built in 1927 by Mrs. W. A. Cobb and is located at 1721 Broad Street. Architects and contractors for the house were R. N. Smyly and Sons.

FIGURE 1-16, 1721 Broad Street, Photograph by Susan Besser, 2017

It was featured in *The Selma Times-Journal* and was open to the public for a week—in essence a modern-day showhouse for the 1920s. Known as Acta Vista, the seven-room dwelling has a red tile roof and stucco exterior with shaped parapets. It was promoted as having all the modern conveniences such as "two-way switches [that] make it impossible to stumble around in the dark."[13]

African American Neighborhoods

Even in the twenty-first century Selma's neighborhoods remain largely segregated, with large historic neighborhoods for African Americans situated north of the downtown business district and north of the railroad tracks that pass through the town, as well as a second large neighborhood east of the railroad depot and old cotton factories and warehouses.

According to Dr. Carroll Van West, "the first steps to asserting their [African Americans'] place not only within the society but also within the actual physical landscape of the town"[14] were establishing schools, churches, and recreation sites that formed the basis for their community and historically have given them purpose and meaning. These selected resources demonstrate those patterns and also inform the town's architectural traditions in Gothic Revival, Renaissance Revival, Neoclassical, Craftsman, and Bungalow styles. Highlighted buildings also are associated with previously mentioned African American architects Wallace Rayfield and David West and architect/builder A. J. Farley.

Selma was known as "The Athens of Black Alabama" due to the creation of four schools, two of them universities, founded by religious groups.[15]

---

13. "The Public Is Invited to Visit Selma's Newest Home," *Selma Times-Journal*, September 7, 1927, 5.

14. Carroll Van West, Amber Clawson, Jessica French, and Abigail Gautreau, "The Civil Rights Movement in Selma, Alabama, 1865-1972," National Register Multiple Property Nomination, 1, https://npgallery.nps.gov/NRHP/.

15. Alston Fitts III, *Selma: A Bicentennial History* (Birmingham: University of Alabama Press, 2017), 140.

Burrell Academy was formed by the North Congregationalist American Missionary Association in 1868. The Reformed Presbyterian Church created Knox Academy in Selma in 1874 led by Rev. Lewis Johnson. Knox Academy grew substantially, necessitating the need for a three-story brick Victorian-style building, built in 1881 and no longer extant, which continued to serve Black students into the 1930s.

The creation of the most important African American school, Selma University, was an auspicious time for the African American community in Selma. Two distinctive buildings of the campus are Dinkins Memorial Chapel, an Italian Renaissance building by Robert Robinson Taylor and Leo Persley, and the Neoclassical Foster Memorial Hall by Wallace Rayfield.

In 1889, the Methodists created the fourth school, Payne University (not extant; the historic location is the site of Payne Elementary School), sponsored by the Alabama A.M.E. churches.[16]

Within these historic neighborhoods are many important community institutions, churches, schools, and lodges, as well as architecturally impressive dwellings associated with significant African American leaders from the 1880s to the present day. Several properties are listed in the National Register of Historic Places or are awarded the prestigious status of National Historic Landmark, for their associations with African American community-building and the Civil Rights Movement in Selma, from the time of emancipation to the 1970s.

On L. L. Anderson Street, north of downtown, stands the impressive Craftsman-styled Burwell-Dinkins House, built in 1889 and expanded in 1909 for noted African American medical leader L. L. Burwell. When W. E. B. DuBois highlighted sixteen African American homes of distinction across the nation in the October 1920 issue of the *Crisis* magazine, he included this impressive house.

There are other African American resources within the existing historic districts, such as the Dallas County Colored Community Center in Old Town Historic District, and these will be noted further elsewhere.

---

16. West et al., "Civil Rights Movement in Selma," 5.

Early History of Selma

There are tales of DeSoto's travel in and exploration of the region in 1540 and exploration of the area by Native Americans. The French are acknowledged to have explored the site of Selma, designating the city as Ecor de Bienville on a map of 1732. The area was known as High Soapstone Bluff in the early 1800s until Thomas Moore, a settler from Tennessee, established a trading post in 1817 and named it Moore's Bluff.[17]

Selma Town Land Company—led by William Rufus King, who would become a United States senator, diplomat, and vice president—was organized in 1818 for the purpose of buying and selling land in Alabama. The sale of lots in Selma was to take place in May of 1819. Nearly all of the lots were laid out for the town plan. Those not purchased were reserved for a public square, a market house, an academy, a Presbyterian church, a Methodist Church, a Baptist Church, and Cumberland Presbyterian Church. The lots for the public square and market house were not used and were divided and sold to the public. With the sale of these lots the company completed its business and terminated the Selma Town Land Company.[18]

William Rufus King is credited with the naming of Selma, a name taken from what was believed to be a translation of the work of Ossian, a Gaelic poet of the thirteenth century. The translation published in 1806, by James McPherson, was later acknowledged as a hoax. The poems depicted a mystical land but were oddly prophetic in their allegorical description of the bluffs and live oaks of Selma.

> "I behold thy towers, O Selma!
> The oaks of thy shaded wall:
> Thy streams sound in my ear;
> Thy heroes gather around."[19]

---

17. Jackson, *The Story of Selma*, 1-2.

18. John Hardy, *Selma: Her Institutions and Her Men* (Spartanburg, SC: Reprint Company), 142.

19. James MacPherson, *The Poems of Ossian*, 37, quoted in Jackson, *The Story of Selma*, 16.

Before the advent of the railroad, the steamboat was the mode of travel throughout the southeast. According to John Hardy, mayor of Selma and author of *Selma: Her Institutions and Her Men*, the first steamboat on the Alabama River was the *Tensas* and it arrived in Selma in 1822.[20] River traffic began on December 7, 1827.[21] The primary cargo was cotton, and steamboat travel was far superior to land. However, this mode of travel had inherent difficulties as steamboats were prone to fires and were affected by adverse water conditions.

John Hardy notes that in 1825 General Lafayette arrived in Selma via steamboat and was met by William R. King for a brief celebration as the guest of honor at a banquet at Woodall's Hotel, formerly at the corner of Green and Water streets.[22] Walter Jackson provides an account from Israel Pickens's journal noting that the citizens of Selma boarded Lafayette's steamboat the *Henderson* and "paid their respects to the guest."[23] Although the accounts differ, it is significant that General Lafayette traveled through the region on his way to Cahawba.

Selma was a prosperous town during the early settlement period, but Cahawba, ten miles away, eclipsed it. In the 1820s Cahawba was the state capital and enjoyed the prestige and enterprise associated with this status for a brief period. Due to flooding in 1825 in the Cahawba region, the legislature moved the capital to Tuscaloosa, although Cahawba remained the county seat for a few more years.[24] Many Cahawba buildings were moved to Selma after this flood.

A harbinger of the permanence of a town is the establishment of a newspaper. In 1827 Philip J. Weaver, an early settler of Selma and prominent merchant, brought Thomas Jefferson Frow, a journalist from Pennsylvania,

---

20. Hardy, *Selma: Her Institutions and Her Men*, 168.

21. Jackson, *The Story of Selma*, 82.

22. Hardy, *Selma: Her Institutions and Her Men*, 142.

23. Jackson, *The Story of Selma*, 24.

24. Alston Fitts III, *Selma: Queen City of the Black Belt* (Selma, AL: Clairmont Press 1989), 14.

to form *The Selma Courier*. The paper had been known as *The Selma Free Press* during the Whig dominance in Alabama and then *The Selma Reporter* when Frow moved to Texas in 1848. It is presently known as *The Selma Times-Journal*.[25]

Selma's Transition from Frontier Town

The following decades were indicative of the untamed nature of the city, where horse racing in East Selma and "bucking the tiger," a gambling card game, drew a large following. The city council headed by Gilbert Shearer attempted to discourage violence by passing a law forbidding drinking on Sunday. With little backing from the community the council lost its support and disbanded. Religious institutions such as the Methodists and Cumberland Presbyterians began to form in the 1830s and rallied against the corruption of gambling. Minister Samuel M. Nelson displayed particular persuasiveness, and the citizens of Selma began to transform the town.[26]

The year 1838 proved to be auspicious for Selma as the town witnessed the beginnings of the Real Estate Bank of South Alabama, the formation of a medical society, and the origins of a library. According to Selmian historian Alston Fitts, the Methodist Church and Presbyterian Church initiated building on their respective lots as set out by the Selma Land Company.[27]

The year 1838 also saw the foundation of Selma's educational system with the formation of the Ladies' Educational Society of Selma, which founded the Masonic Institute and Dallas Academy.[28] Dallas Academy was established in 1844 by Professor L. B. Johnson and his wife, Harriet Johnson; the initial location was 114 Mabry Street, a two-story brick school building of the Federal period built by William Johnson.

---

25. Fitts, *Selma: Queen City of the Black Belt*, 15.

26. Fitts, *Selma: Queen City of the Black Belt*, 16.

27. Fitts, *Selma: Queen City of the Black Belt*, 16.

28. Fitts, *Selma: Queen City of the Black Belt*, 18.

In the mid-nineteenth century Selma was acknowledged as the Queen City of the Black Belt, garnering this designation by virtue of its proximity to the river for steamboat travel, its burgeoning railroad systems, its expanding financial institutions, and its abundant cotton crop.[29] The prosperity of Selma in the antebellum period reflected the elite Southern way of life within the hierarchy of the agricultural planter society. The plantations relied on enslaved labor to bring the most prized agricultural resource, cotton, to the marketplace, tying Dallas County into the national and international market economy. Furthermore, the tangible artifacts such as the antebellum houses and dependencies that survived the Civil War reflect the contributions of the craftsmanship of enslaved African Americans.

Industrialization of Selma

In the decades leading to the Civil War, the technology of the northeast was making its way to the South. In 1840 total capital invested in manufacturing accounted for $20,270, which is equivalent to $641,000 in today's market economy. In 1850 the value of annual product in manufacturing was $194,420, and in 1860 sixty-nine manufacturing establishments produced $492,444 of goods. Dallas County was rich in agricultural resources but also developed a sizable industrial base.[30]

Selma owed its prominence as a growing industrial and distribution city to the foresight of local leaders in establishing a rail system. Selma's civic leaders recognized the importance of the railroad to the prosperity of the city as they witnessed the steamboat-to-rail evolution. As early as 1848 a movement was started to create a rail system in the region. Over the next ten years railway lines were initiated, and by 1858 the Alabama and Tennessee Rivers Railroad had laid a hundred miles of track.

---

29. Fitts, *Selma: Queen City of the Black Belt*, 23.
30. Fitts, *Selma: Queen City of the Black Belt*, 10.

Pre–Civil War Politics

The political climate of Alabama and the South in the decades before the Civil War was particularly affected by the actions of Selmian William Rufus King. King served as U.S. senator from Alabama from 1819 to 1844, when he was appointed minister to France. He witnessed the seeds of secession on his return from France in 1847 and was distressed to learn two factions from the Alabama Democrats had fomented out of the controversy of the Wilmot Proviso—those who were committed to the ideology of the national party and those dedicated to the dogma of states' rights. An 1850 letter to M. P. Blue underscores King's deep convictions: "I am again in the Senate and am engaged in making efforts . . . to protect the rights of the South and save the Union—whether these efforts will prove successful is I fear exceedingly doubtful."[31]

In a letter to William Garrett in 1848 King expressed concern for the future of the Union. "The end none can foresee, and the purest are forced to doubt the permanency of the Union. . . . I for one will be forced to the conclusion that the days of the Republic are numbered."[32] King worked tirelessly to bridge the tensions over "slavery and sectionalism" and was instrumental in creating the ill-fated Compromise of 1850. His involvement in helping to draft the Compromise placed him in the forefront as a potential vice-presidential candidate in 1852, and he was elected on the ticket with Franklin Pierce. Sadly, he had developed tuberculosis and died soon after taking office.[33]

As the nation prepared to elect a new president in 1860 the divisiveness of the state became apparent as those dedicated to keeping Alabama in the Union witnessed the growing tide of secessionist sentiments. On January

---

31. Letter of Rufus William King to M. P. Blue, April 11, 1850, quoted in Fitts, *Selma: Queen City of the Black Belt*, 25.

32. Letter from William Rufus King to William Garrett, 1848, as quoted in Joseph Hodgson, *Cradle of the Confederacy*, quoted in Jackson, *The Story of Selma*, 286.

33. Daniel Fate Brooks, "The Faces of William Rufus King," *Alabama Heritage* 69 (Summer 2003): 14-23.

11, 1860, the Secession Convention held in Montgomery voted to secede. As the nation moved toward war, Selmian unionists joined the secessionists.

Selma's Role in the Civil War

Due to Selma's prominence as a transportation and manufacturing center, the city had a secondary but important support role in the Civil War. The importance of the rail system, and especially the Alabama and Tennessee Rivers Railroad shipments running from Selma to Bibb and Shelby Counties, made it possible for Selma to become a distribution center for coal and iron ore. This would prove fortuitous for Selma for, with the fall of New Orleans and the arsenal in Mt. Vernon, Alabama, Selma became the obvious choice for a new arsenal.[34]

Selma's destiny was tied to its emergence as an industrial and railway center. Selma, the chief market town for the surrounding country, was the main headquarters for artisans, mechanics, and tradespeople, and called for that reason the Pittsburgh of the South. The town had production facilities for cartridges, saltpeter, powder, shot, and shell, and for the assemblage of lumber, coal, and iron. Selma became a center of equipment for troops and fortifications, and for the manufacture of every sort of war material for

FIGURE 1-17, Ruins of C. S. Naval Foundry, warfarehistorynetwork.com

---

34. Fitts, *Selma: Queen City of the Black Belt*, 50.

the Confederacy.[35] Commander Catesby ap Roger Jones recruited George Peacock, an Englishman, to assist in the war effort at the Confederate Arsenal. Peacock was an expert metallurgist, and his system of core-making for shells enabled the foundry to triple production.

Late in the Civil War, mere weeks before Appomattox, Union commanders took action to subdue the Black Belt region and destroy the war-production facilities at Selma. U.S. Gen. James Harrison Wilson in late March began his raid into the Alabama heartland. On April 1, 1865, at Ebenezer Church, approximately twenty miles north of Selma, his forces routed the Confederates, led by C.S. Gen. Nathan B. Forrest, who retreated to Selma to protect the factories there. According to an article included in *Civil War Times Illustrated*, the English engineer Millington, who had been instrumental in the operations and design of the Confederate Foundry, surrendered to U.S. Gen. Emory Upton and divulged plans of the foundry to the Union army.[36] "Mr. George Peacock, the maker of cannons for the Confederate Government, as superintendent of the naval gun foundry, had orders from Confederate officials to sink all cannons on hand into the Alabama River when Wilson's Raiders were advancing upon the city of Selma."[37] C.S. Gen. Forrest ordered that every white male, "no matter what his calling or position, must go into the works or into the river."[38] Union forces led by Generals Eli Long and Emory Upton defeated the Confederates and took control of the city. By April 12, Wilson's troops had occupied Montgomery, the state capitol.

The Battle of Selma devastated the town, with an estimated 150 houses along with the arsenal, naval foundry, and navy yard destroyed. The Union forces also captured valuable cotton and railroad cars and took control of

---

35. Jackson, *The Story of Selma*, 198-199.

36. Jerry Keenan, "Wilson's Selma Raid," *A Civil War Times Illustrated Extra,* January 1963, 37-44.

37. Letter of Mrs. Mamamar Jarvis, quoted in Jackson, *The Story of Selma*, 215.

38. Jackson, *The Story of Selma*, 216.

the bridges throughout the region.³⁹ Confederates decried the losses and looting from the Union troops. "The destruction was fearful," said Elijah Even Edwards, a Methodist chaplain of the 7th Minnesota Volunteer Infantry, who described the dire circumstances of Selma in his journal:

> Their destitution is terrible to think of. Women who have the air of having once lived genteelly and in affluence come to the camp and beg for washings to do to keep them from starvation. Some of the people are defiant in their rags and wretchedness and while they ask for alms, keep up a show of bitterness against the flag that illy comforts them with suppliance. It is a war-waste land. And yet I suspect unconquered.⁴⁰

Enslaved African Americans rejoiced in the end of the Confederacy and rushed to support the occupation forces of the Union army. The presence of the Union troops meant the provisions of the Emancipation Proclamation could now be enforced.

Reconstruction Politics

Political upheaval characterized the mood of the country during the initial period of Reconstruction. The most significant change was the enfranchisement of African American males. Radical Republicans, in an effort to stymie Confederate power, mandated black suffrage, federal assistance for public education, seizure of Confederate plantations, and military occupation of the South. The Reconstruction Act of 1867 separated the ten Confederate states into five military districts governed by Union generals, enfranchised African Americans, and disenfranchised those who held office under the Confederacy. Those who had held political office during the war under the Confederacy were considered traitors to their country and, consequently, only Selma unionists were considered for public office. Selma

---

39. Jackson, *The Story of Selma*, 243.

40. Elijah Even Edwards, journal, May 24, 1875, quoted in Keenan, "Wilson's Selma Raid," 44.

came under the district of Military Governor General Pope. Pope removed the elected mayor and designated Ben F. Saffold to that office and then commissioned loyalist city council members. John Silsby, head of registration for Dallas County, registered both Black and white male voters. The government formed under congressional Reconstruction signaled a divergence from the old order, empowering African American males to have a voice in the new government.

The Southern electorate was vastly changed by Reconstruction legislation because African Americans had gained the "voting majority" in five states. Republican domination remained in South Carolina, Mississippi, Louisiana, and Alabama as these states maintained the highest African American population. Through this new order it became possible for African American men to become elected to political positions in Selma and gain congressional seats in the House of Representatives.

The most noted of these is Benjamin Turner, who had been an enslaved worker for Dr. James T. Gee and managed the St. James Hotel. Turner's leadership is recognized in his formation of the first African American firefighter's unit and his donation of property for a Black church and school. He also assumed a leadership role in the Reconstruction period, serving first on the Selma City Council and then as congressman in the U.S. House of Representatives. Turner ran on a platform of "universal suffrage and universal amnesty." He introduced a bill to provide amnesty to approximately 20,000 Confederates adversely affected by the Fourteenth Amendment. "They may have sinned wonderfully, but they suffered terribly. I have no coals of fiery reproach to heap upon them now. Rather would I extend the olive branch of peace, and say to them, let the past be forgotten and let us all, from every sun and every clime, of every hue and every shade, go to work peacefully to build up the shattered temples of this great and glorious Republic."[41] The ill-fated bill never made it to the floor.

Other Selmians to occupy notable positions during Reconstruction were Roderick B. Thomas, the first African American judge in the history

---

41. Quoted in Jean Martin, "Old Depot Spotlights Black History," *Selma Times-Journal*, February 5, 1989, 17.

of Alabama, and Jeremiah Haralson, the first African American state senator, who was the last African American congressperson of that age.[42]

The end of the Civil War did not mean African Americans were fully enfranchised. The Freedmen's Bureau combined with various white missionary groups to give limited support and encouragement to the newly emancipated African American citizens of Selma. Most of the gains made came from African Americans themselves as they created churches, schools, and cemeteries as "key community-centered institutions."[43] In the latter part of the nineteenth century the advancements of the African American throughout the South and across the nation during Reconstruction were slowly eroded in the aftermath of the *Plessy v. Ferguson* (1896) decision when justices upheld a Louisiana law requiring segregation on railroad passenger cars. Thus began the policy of "separate but equal" facilities for African Americans. Alabamians held a Constitutional Convention in 1901 to review African American suffrage as well as women suffrage. Despite the appeal of African American leaders in Alabama led by Booker T. Washington, the move to limit suffrage continued. Selma delegate P. H. Pitts submitted a proposal that became Article VIII restricting the right to vote to adult males. Regulations that required citizens to pass literacy tests, pay poll taxes, and own property were enforced throughout the nation, eroding the advancements of African Americans.

Reconstruction Infrastructure

Improvements in the transportation system and electrical system not only improved the quality of life for Selma but also brought transportation to the outlying areas. In 1872 the beginnings of the horse-drawn Selma Street Rail Road Company provided essential transport to those living in outlying areas. The City Fathers contracted to install electric lighting in downtown Selma with the Jenney Electric Company.[44]

---

42. Fitts, *Selma: Queen City of the Black Belt*, 77.

43. West et al., "Civil Rights Movement in Selma," 1.

44. "City Council," *Selma Times-Journal*, November 28, 1885, 1.

One of the standard-bearers of the progress of a city is its outreach program. Selma is noted to be the first city in Alabama to form a YMCA, in 1858. Selmian Joseph Hardie was elected president of the international YMCA at a conference in Richmond, Virginia, in 1874. Fundraising for the first YMCA building, a Second Empire, three-and-one-half-story building at 217 Broad Street, began in the mid-1880s after Rev. D. L. Moody inspired locals by his lecture on the importance of molding young Christian men. The President of the Selma Y, W. B. Gill, contributed $5,000 and the remaining $20,000 came from local Selmians. The building with a central Palladian window, elaborate brickwork, and cast-iron balcony is considered to be a fine example of the style and was completed in 1886.[45]

Dallas Academy transformed from a private school to a public school during this period. Professor G. A. Woodward oversaw the school from 1871 until 1882, when he left for the Montgomery school system. After the loss of Woodward, the Academy found new leadership in Professor Richard E. Hardaway from Petersburg, Virginia. Under Hardaway's guidance the city built a new facility for Dallas Academy at 816 Selma Avenue and added Baker School, a Renaissance Revival building at 300 Washington Street, and Clark School. It is significant to note that George Peabody, known for his benevolence to education, donated $2,000 in 1868 to enlarge Dallas Academy.[46]

Burrell Academy, the first African American public school, was staffed with teachers from North Congregationalist American Missionary Association. The two-story frame building was erected circa 1869 according to historian John Hardy and was located at J. L. Chestnut Jr. Boulevard and Maxey. Jabes Burrell of Oberlin, Ohio, donated $10,000 toward the building. The teachers' salaries were paid by the city school system.[47] John Silsby, delegate to the 1867 congressional convention, was instrumental in the effort to establish the school.

---

45. Fitts, *Selma: A Bicentennial History*, 135-136.

46. Fitts, *Selma: A Bicentennial History*, 101.

47. Fitts, *Selma: A Bicentennial History*, 102.

Clark School, an African American public school, named in honor of Dr. Courtney J. Clark, a Confederate surgeon during the Civil War, received $5,000 from the City of Selma toward the building of a six-room brick school located on Lawrence Street (no longer extant) and was dedicated in 1894. R. B. Hudson, a graduate of Selma University, was the principal of the school during its fledging beginning.[48]

Knox Academy, no longer extant, was started under the auspices of the Reformed Presbyterian Church that adjoined the historically African American residential neighborhood. Knox Academy was brought into the public system in 1937. Payne Institute, no longer extant, was sponsored by the African Methodist Episcopal Church.[49]

Most notably Selma University, the historically Black college, began in 1878 with four students at St. Phillip Street Baptist Church.[50] Selma University was sponsored by the Alabama Colored Baptist State Convention with the mission to provide training for pastors and newly freed slaves. The vision of the trustees was one of improving themselves through the elevation of the churches. The African American Baptist State Convention in 1878 approved $3,000 for the purchase of the old county fairgrounds, a tract of thirty-six acres in the northwest section of town. Initially, the land contained an amphitheater and other buildings that were renovated for use as classrooms and dormitories. Notable leaders were Charles O. Boothe, who was president in 1901, and Robert T. Pollard, who added Foster Hall and Dinkins Hall during his tenure.[51]

Dr. Goldsby King sponsored the Goldsby King Hospital, the first private hospital in Selma, in 1896. Starting from a Queen Anne house, King made additions to the house in the Neoclassical style and over time the building grew to its present state, aided by architect Frank Lockwood, who supervised the

---

48. Fitts, *Selma: A Bicentennial History*, 145-146.

49. Fitts, *Selma: A Bicentennial History*, 140.

50. Adam Powell, "Selma University Established 114 Years Ago," *Selma Times-Journal*, January 2, 2019.

51. Wilson Fallin Jr., *Uplifting the People: Three Centuries of Black Baptists in Alabama*, Religion and American Culture (Tuscaloosa: University of Alabama Press, 2007), 84.

additions in the 1920s. The institution was designated King Memorial Hospital on King's death and maintained operations as a hospital until 1953. The building, located at 515 Mabry Street, later served as Dunn Nursing Home.

FIGURE 1-18, Hotel Albert, Postcard Collection of Susan Besser

These institutions provided a foundation for Selma's growth at the turn of the century. By the 1890s Selma was considered a resort city featuring the grand Hotel Albert, no longer extant. In a pamphlet entitled "Selma, Alabama: A Charming Southern Winter Resort," tourists were drawn to "Park City" to "view the Old and the New South, which are exhibited here side by side."[52] The Hotel Albert, which was patterned after the Doge's palace of Venice, was arranged in suites appointed with parlors and bathrooms. The Academy of Music building, also no longer extant, was a venue for theater and opera. It was not uncommon for towns to have an opera house venue.

Selma at the Beginning of the Early Twentieth Century

Selma's citizens enjoyed paved streets by the 1900s and mule cars were replaced by electric cars in April of 1901. Patrons rode free the first day.

---

52. "Selma, Alabama: A Charming Southern Winter Resort" (1893; reprint, Selma Printing, 1999).

This form of mass transportation continued until the mid-1920s when the automobile became more prevalent, creating a marked change on Church Street, where one-story buildings for auto mechanics replaced dwellings. As automobiles became more affordable the nation saw a 150 percent increase in ownership from 1920 to 1930.[53]

The need for a high school within Old Town Historic District was recognized in the 1910s. A special school bond issue for $35,000 passed through the city council and Tremont High School, a Neoclassical edifice designed by William Warren, was subsequently erected. The school system developed to incorporate the movement for having separate middle schools with the Selma Junior High School built in 1925 as a stately Neoclassical building.

Cotton, known as white gold in the Black Belt, was Dallas County's main agricultural product. In 1914, however, the boll weevil threatened the crop. Production of cotton went from 1,751,375 bales in 1914 to 14,230 bales in 1917.[54] Dallas County's larger landowners survived the debacle, but many small farmers, many of them African Americans, were forced to sell their farms. The collapse of the Alabama Penny Savings Bank in 1915 left middle-class African Americans destitute.[55] Industrial workers were needed in the North, and recruitment of African Americans resulted in a marked population shift in Dallas County. From 1910 to 1930 African American population in Dallas County dropped from 43,511 to 40,867.

Selma was the home of Cawthon Cotton Mill Co. and Sunset Textile Mill, formerly Estelle Cotton Mills Co., as well as Mathews Cotton Mills, which ran 20,000 spindles and 650 looms producing 40,000 yards of cloth per day.[56] These mills were equipped with the latest in fire-prevention equipment, such as sprinkler heads and ironclad fire doors. C. A. Praray designed a state-of-the-art building for Sunset Textile Mill, one of five using

---

53. Kenneth T. Jackson, *Crabgrass Frontier: The Suburbanization of the United States* (New York: Oxford University Press, 1985), 187-189.

54. Fitts, *Selma: Queen City of the Black Belt*, 112.

55. Fitts, *Selma: Queen City of the Black Belt*, 113.

56. "Selma, Alabama: A Charming Southern Winter Resort."

this system, which began operation in 1897, the design having recently being patented by Praray in 1894. The Mill featured triangular bays composed of windows that offered superb natural light.

FIGURE 1-19, Sunset Mill, 218 Morgan Avenue, HAER, Library of Congress

The presence of a cotton mill in a Southern town was a boon to the local economy, as noted by an Atlantan to his associate: "The cotton factory means an increase in population with more money in circulation weekly, and means a high price paid to the farmers for the cotton, with an enlarged market for their produce."[57] Using the raw product from the region, the steam-driven Southern textile mills employed the latest in technology and were comparable to mills in the Northeast or Great Britain. The South furnished 60 percent of exported textiles at the turn of the century.[58] It was fortuitous for Selma that cotton made a comeback as a major cash crop in the 1920s.

Other industries made their way to Selma. F. B. Bartlett, maker of ginger pop, was the first bottling works in Selma, and their products were

---

57. Edward L. Ayers, *Promise of the New South: Life After Reconstruction* (New York: Oxford University Press, 1992) 112.

58. Ayers, *Promise of the New South*, 112.

shipped by train to other regions.⁵⁹ Coca-Cola Bottling Co., located on Green Street, was established in Selma in 1903. It was managed by William N. Brown, who revolutionized the industry by developing a system for cooling the syrup before bottling. Lime-Cola Bottling Company was established in 1920, as was Chero Cola Plant, which had a capacity of eighty bottles a minute.⁶⁰ Orange Crush Bottling Co. at 13-15 Franklin within Old Town Historic District provided this popular beverage to the region in the 1920s.

Some of the major industries, in addition to the mills, included American Candy Manufacturing, located on Alabama Avenue. The headquarters for Certainteed Products Corporation, a roofing company out of St. Louis, relocated to Selma.⁶¹ Manufacturing during this period accounted for over $400,000 annual income to Dallas County with 111 manufacturing firms. The lumber industry, with firms such as A. E. Reamer Planing Mill and Schun-Miller, prospered with an annual production of $175,000.⁶² The affluence of the lumber industry as well as the cotton industry meant increased dollars for the building of houses in Selma with the domino effect that the more houses were built the more lumber would need to be produced.

Further illustrating the state of the thriving economy in Selma in the 1920s was a proposal by architects Chandler Cox Yonge and J. E. Davis. After a fire in the People's Bank & Trust building on Broad Street and Water Avenue caused extensive damage in late 1926, Yonge and Davis presented a design for a six-story Neo-Gothic building. The new building was proposed to have cost $200,000 and would have five floors of offices with

---

59. C. C. Grayson, *Yesterday and Today: Memories of Selma and Its People* (New Orleans: Pelican Press, 1948), 114.

60. "Coca-Cola Taught Public How to Drink," *Selma Times-Journal*, November 12, 1922, 40.

61. "Selma Made Headquarters for Big Roofing Firm," *Selma Times-Journal*, February 3, 1920, 1.

62. "Lumber Industry Brings Millions," *Selma Times-Journal*, November 16, 1922, 1.

some 15,000 square feet of space.⁶³ Ultimately, the decision was made to renovate the existing building.

The Depression Era

The Depression affected Selma much as it did the rest of the country. Two primary employers in Selma, Alabama Textile Mills and Sunset Mills, closed. Residential construction came to an abrupt halt. Selmians looked for diversion from the economic scene and frequented the picture shows for entertainment. Football games were the center of the social scene. "Every Friday afternoon on Broad Street we had a football parade with the cheerleaders and the band and the football players walking behind."⁶⁴ In contrast to the lifestyle of conspicuous consumption of the late 1920s, the 1930s-era lifestyle was a day-to-day existence based on obtaining necessities. The rise in unemployment, foreclosure of mortgages, and loss of confidence in banks occurred throughout the nation. Towns such as Selma that relied on the textile industry were particularly affected by unemployment, especially in the African American sector.

FIGURE 1-20, Proposal for 2 Broad Street, *The Selma Times-Journal*, December 26, 1926

New Deal agencies brought work projects to the city, especially with a modern bridge across the Alabama River and an improved federal highway

---

63. "Imposing New Office and Bank Building Planned for City, " *Selma Times-Journal*, December 26, 1926, 2.

64. Jean Martin, interview, September 7, 2001.

to Montgomery, marking the end of one era and a new possibility of economic progress for the city. Several city leaders were wary of New Deal projects, especially those that might create opportunities for African Americans and change race relations. Others understood economic change had to occur as Selma had witnessed the closing of large textile mills and also the loss of Selma Foundry, with a long-standing reputation as a producer of cast iron.

Selma's largest employer was the Southern Railway, a system dependent on steam locomotion in an era of the advent of the diesel engine. The establishment of industry and changing tides in political influence moved toward Birmingham and north Alabama. Selma had enjoyed prominence as the fifth largest city in Alabama with a population of 8,713 in the early twentieth century. In a climate of prosperity of the 1920s a sign on the city limits to Selma proclaimed it the "fastest-growing city in Alabama—50,000 people by 1930."[65] However, the optimism of the 1920s gave way to reality with a population in 1930 of 16,012 and in 1940 of 19,834. Writing of this period Carl C. Morgan Jr. indicates that even though a push to attract industry to the area was needed many resisted, concerned it would bring unwanted changes in areas such as population demographics and local culture.[66]

New Deal programs were ushered into Selma under Mayor Lucien Burns and Commissioner Claiborne Blanton. Under the Public Works Administration in 1941 a new City Building was erected at 1300 Alabama Avenue, on the site of the former city hall. The building was in the Neoclassical style, designed by Raymond Sizemore and built by Forcum-James Co. of Memphis, Tennessee.[67]

Behind the City Building, at 16 Franklin Street, is the WPA–built-and-funded Community Building for the Colored People. Assistant county

---

65. Carl C. Morgan Jr., "Craig Air Force Base: Its Effect on Selma, 1940-1977," *The Alabama Review*, April 1989, 83-84.

66. Morgan, "Craig Air Force Base," 84.

67. Jackson, *The Story of Selma*, 501.

agent Samuel W. Boynton and notary public Charles J. Adams, both African Americans who felt the need for a community building for African American citizens when they made the trip into Selma to buy groceries and supplies from the outlying areas of Dallas County, supported the project.[68] The building had been necessitated by the "separate but equal" policies of the era. The Rev. E. Gamble of St. Paul's Episcopal Church promoted the project to the city council. Completed in 1938, the building is credited to African American architect and contractor George Wilson with an interior enhanced with murals by Felix Gaines of Birmingham, Alabama entitled *Swing Low, Sweet Chariot* and *George Washington Carver Feeding the Masses*. These significant murals were removed when the center closed and now are in the Old Depot Museum.

Selma During World War II

Real change came with World War II. With the expansion of the Army Air Corps the necessity of additional pilot-training facilities became evident. Before World War II, Kelly Field in San Antonio, Texas, was responsible for training of pilots. Craig Field, located approximately five miles east of Selma on Highway 80 and newly accessible by the Edmund Pettus Bridge, was completed in 1940, encompassing 1,700 acres. Built before the United States' involvement in the war, the commencement in May 1941 celebrated the graduation of 39 cadets with the occasion proclaimed as "Selma Flying Cadet Day." Followed by a parade on Broad Street, the cadets filed into the Wilby Theater for the graduation exercises. British and Dutch fighter pilots were trained at Craig Field along with American pilots. The training field commissioned 4,471 pilots by 1943. Of those trained, 1,392 were British and 10 Dutch.[69]

Craig Field provided the necessary stimulus to bolster Selma's economy. Facilities were built adjacent to the base as housing for the officers'

---

68. Fitts, *Selma: Queen City of the Black Belt*, 118.

69. Lou Thole, *Forgotten Fields of America: World War II Bases and Training Then and Now*, vol. 2 (Missoula, MT: Pictorial Histories Publishing, 1999) 127-140.

families. Local merchants experienced a marked increase in business and, most important, were the opportunities for employment. Local Selmians filled many positions once occupied by military men as America's involvement in World War II increased. Ultimately, the base encompassed 2,000 military and 1,400 civilian employees.[70] After the end of the war, Craig Field continued to train pilots, and during the Korean War the 3615th Pilot Training Wing provided single-engine training and pilot-instructor training. An elementary school constructed on base provided classrooms for primary school children. High school students were bused to Selma for their education.

The officers' wives took an active role in the community in the schools and churches. The employment of Selma civilians at Craig Field provided a boost to the economy both in employment and influx of dollars to the local merchants of Selma. Then with the desegregation of the military in 1949 came the prospect of African-American pilots as examples of freedom. The presence of the base also contributed to the continued growth of an African American commercial and entertainment district on Broad Street, along the blocks between Tabernacle Baptist Church and Jefferson Davis Avenue (now J. L. Chestnut Jr. Boulevard), the latter being a traditional dividing line between whites and Black people in Selma. In the 1940s, local Black residents called this area "the Drag." The closing of the field in 1977 calculated as a loss of $35 million to the regional economy.[71]

The Civil Rights Movement and Selma Architecture

Selma gained national prominence due to its association with the Civil Rights Movement in the 1960s, especially the push for equal voting rights in 1964–1965. Within Selma are numerous buildings that figure prominently in the Civil Rights Movement. Some are public buildings—such as the Dallas County Courthouse, which became a nationally recognized site

---

70. Morgan, "Craig Air Force Base," 95.

71. Jean Martin, interview, September 7, 2001.

for the Voting Rights Movement, and the Carnegie Library, now Chamber of Commerce—which were not accessible to Africans Americans before the Movement. Others are buildings constructed by African Americans as businesses and churches.

The 1940s saw the beginnings of the NAACP and Dallas County Voters Association meetings, which first took place in the First Baptist Church located in the middle-class African American neighborhood. "The n ow Rep. John Lewis set up headquarters at First Baptist and held many nonviolent training sessions and youth mass meetings in its historic building."[72] The most important buildings were the churches, with Tabernacle Baptist Church, First Baptist Church, Second Baptist Church, Mt. Zion Primitive Baptist Church, St. John C.M.E. Church, and Brown's Chapel A.M.E. Church hosting important strategy sessions and mass meetings. The march to Montgomery began in Selma, and the first attempt to cross the Edmund Pettus Bridge headed by freedom fighter (later U.S. Rep.) John R. Lewis led to armed violence from Alabama authorities in an event known as Bloody Sunday. Private residences figured prominently in the Movement; for instance, when President Lyndon B. Johnson announced his support for the federal Voting Rights law, the Rev. Dr. Martin Luther King Jr. watched the address at the historic Jackson House, an unassuming bungalow on Boyntons Street now located in Greenfield Village. The house had served Dr. King, Rev. Ralph Abernathy, and others as a primary strategy head-quarters for the Selma to Montgomery march.

Linking Selma's Architecture and Selma's History

Selma's architecture reflects the growth of the city, beginning with the establishment of the town in 1819 to its rise as an industrial center and its perseverance during the Civil War and Reconstruction eras. The city has witnessed the rise and fall of the planter aristocracy. Much of the residential architecture was constructed from the 1880s through the 1920s, a

72. Christine Weerts, "Selma, Alabama's First Black Church Is Still Going Strong: Take a Look at Its Amazing Legacy," *The Federalist*, February 26, 2020, 4.

particularly prosperous time for Selmians reflecting the boosterism spirit that accompanied the Industrial Revolution. Improvements such as landscaping for the Old Live Oak Cemetery and residential areas complement the distinctive architectural styles that span the period from 1825 to 1952. Selma has benefited from its proximity to the Alabama River and the influx of multiple railroad lines into the region.

The tangible artifacts of Selma reveal an architectural timeline that begins in the Federal period with buildings from succeeding periods up to the ranch house of the 1950s. Woven within the history of Selma is the thread of African American involvement: as craftsmen of antebellum houses, leaders of the community during the Reconstruction era, leaders of the black commercial community in the late nineteenth century and the civic community of the early twentieth century, and foot soldiers of the Civil Rights Movement. The construction of the Dallas County Colored Community Center underscored the necessity of a facility offering a respite for African Americans during shopping expeditions into Selma in the era of "separate but equal" politics. Some of Selma's resources are directly tied to the Civil Rights Movement, and Selma is recognized throughout the nation as the birthplace of voting rights for African Americans. Selmians could not have envisioned the Civil Rights Movement would thrust the city into the national spotlight. Nonetheless, Selma retains architecture of the antebellum period and illustrates the manner in which neighborhoods developed from large estates in the southeast as well as the way the commercial district rebuilt in the period from 1870 to 1890.

In the 1960s and 1970s significant buildings such as the Hotel Albert were lost, as was the case in many cities before preservation of historic structures became a priority for citizens. However, that which remains has a high degree of integrity, largely due to the fact that urban renewal and the interstate highway system did not have a significant influence on Selma. A grand tour of Selma to explore its architectural treasures reveals a sense of place that defines Selma, something that many progressive southern cities have lost in the name of urban renewal. History and architecture are intertwined in Selma's past—each defines the other.

CHAPTER 2

Old Town Historic District

Old Town Historic District encompasses the buildings that were central to the early development of Selma and the downtown commercial center. The Battle of Selma, April 2, 1865, witnessed the destruction of Broad Street commercial buildings and two-thirds of the antebellum houses. Some of the larger houses were used as hospitals or housed Union soldiers during the occupation of Selma and thus were spared.

One of the main plantations in Selma was the Wesley Plattenburg plantation. The primary dwelling for this house is located on Washington Street. The plantation encompassed 1,600 acres with the property bordering what is now Summerfield Road. The primary residences of several plantations and small farms were spared in the Battle of Selma. Interspersed within the city are these magnificent residences such as the Greek-Revival raised cottage known as the Philpot House, 603 Alabama Avenue. Greek-Revival examples such as the John Tyler Morgan House at 719 Tremont Street, Sturdivant Hall on Mabry Street, and the Riggs-Morgan House at 816 Alabama Avenue remain.

Having weathered the Civil War, Selma was prospering in the 1870s and 1880s due to its cotton culture. Architecture constructed during this time period reflected this prosperity. Alan Gowans in *Styles and Types of North American Architecture* discusses the commercial architecture with its Italianate detailing and notes that it was known as a "boom-town front."[1] The architectural character of Selma's Broad Street combines the Italianate of most commercial nineteenth-century historic downtown districts with an eclectic mix of late nineteenth-century and early twentieth-century architecture representing a timeline in the evolution of storefronts.

> Main Street was the face of a town, the expression of its identity. The form of each Main Street was a unique configuration: buildings of every size and shape; a skyline silhouette; built forms and open spaces; the rhythm of windows and walls; the texture of wood, iron, glass and masonry; the contours of pediment, cornice, lintel and carved bracket; the shadow of church tower or signpost.[2]

With the advent of cast-iron materials for storefronts, the face of Main Street changed significantly. Developed by James Bogardus in the 1840s, cast-iron storefronts were structural and allowed for large expanses of glass to be installed in the storefront bringing needed light into the interior and display space. Cast-iron–supported storefronts manufactured by Mesker Iron Works and indicative of the 1880s era are evident on 106–108 Broad Street, 110 Broad Street, and 112 Broad. The founder of the company, John Bernard Mesker, began as a "tinner" producing pressed metal façades. His son, George, concentrated his business in cast-iron storefronts and based the business in Evansville, Indiana. Façades could be custom ordered to fit the size of the building with custom cornices and pediments.

---

1. Alan Gowans, *Styles and Types of North American Architecture: Social Function and Cultural Expression* (New York: Icon Editions, 1992), 172.

2. Carole Rifkind, *Main Street: The Face of Urban America* (New York: Harper Colophon, 1978), 63.

Broad Street

Regional Visitors Information Center for the Selma to Montgomery National Historic Trail, Old People's Bank Building

2 Broad Street • *Constructed circa 1880*

FIGURE 2-1, Broad Street, Postcard Collection of Susan Besser

For many years, the original windows were covered. In 2010 the building was renovated and now houses the National Park Service's interpretive museum for the Selma to Montgomery National Historic Trail. Built circa 1880, this three-story component of a two-part commercial block on the corner of Broad Street and Water Avenue exhibits the elements of the Italianate style with its curved corner, parapet, and full arched windows. An historic photograph taken in 1893 shows a two-story wraparound cast-iron gallery, manufactured at George Peacock's local factory, the influence of Louisiana river ports such as New Orleans and Mobile. In 1927 *The Selma Times-Journal* noted that extensive interior renovations were done on the building after a fire with plans done by architects Warren, Knight & Davis and Chandler Cox Yonge.[3]

---

3. "Repair on Bank Building to Start Soon," *Selma Times-Journal*, February 27, 1927, 6.

People's Bank & Trust was the original occupant of the first floor of this building. For a brief period, it was occupied by a hardware store that sold bicycles and willow ware as indicated by the Sanborn map of 1907. People's Bank & Trust was then located at 808 Water Avenue. By 1909 People's Bank & Trust had once again become the main occupants of this building. Archi-tect J. W. McKeil practiced his trade in this building in the 1920s, as did H. W. Gamble, attorney. E. H. Hobbs, an insurance broker representing several companies including Liverpool & London & Globe Insurance Co. LTD. of England, operated from the offices of the building in the 1920s.

4 Broad Street • *Constructed circa 1880*

This early commercial building that retains its historic storefront has seen many occupants including Brooks & Wilkins, druggist, as well as pur-veyors of paints, oils, and glass and Levy Bros., operated by Nathan Levy. Physicians W. H. Johnson, C. D. Parke, and F. F. Gage practiced at this location. In 1907 the San-born map indicates that moving pictures were shown in this building. Cotton buyer Charles Goldstein occupied the second floor for a period. This two-story brick component of a two-part commercial block on Broad Street has a metal standing-seam porch roof supported by fluted, tapered, cast-iron posts with a bell-shaped capital. Typical of wood storefronts are the cen-tered double doors with one-over-one glass above a wood two-panel door surmounted

FIGURE 2-2, 4 Broad Street, Photograph by Susan Besser, 2002

by a two-light transom. The wide availability of glass allowed for fixed-glass windows above a wood bulkhead. Cornice lintels cap the second story six-over-six double-hung windows, each recessed with brick corbelling above. The cornice is embellished with brick dentil molding.

6 Broad Street • *Constructed circa 1870*

The first story has three sets of double doors with two panes of glass enframed by stiles with a wood panel below and a two-pane transom above. Wood cornice lentils surmount six-over-six sash windows. The decorative parapet is detailed with a corbel table. Reflecting the late nineteenth- and twentieth-century trend to provide porches for commercial spaces, this two-story brick component of a two-part commercial block has a metal standing-seam porch which connects with the porch of the contiguous building, 4 Broad Street, and is supported by fluted tapered cast-iron posts. Often merchants took advantage of the shade of these porches by displaying baskets and boxes of wares spilling out onto the front of the store to entice buyers. Ross A. Smith's Selma Commercial Directory of 1880 lists occupants, Griel & Kohn, under the categories boots and shoes, dry goods, and grocers, making them essentially a general store.

FIGURE 2-3, 6 Broad Street, Photograph by Susan Besser, 2002

8, 10, and 12 Broad Street • *Constructed circa 1890*

Tissier Hardware, founded by Charles G. Tissier, was an early occupant of this building, establishing the business in 1885, and according to the *Selma Mirror* of June 28, 1911, "by reason of the pluck, energy

FIGURE 2-4, 8-12 Broad Street, Photograph by Susan Besser, 2002

and enterprise put into it, assumed such proportions by 1895 that it was deemed necessary to incorporate it."[4] R. L. Polk & Co.'s Directory of 1913–1914 lists Tissier as a department store and hardware. In 1924 Tissier was listed under china, glass and queensware, farm machinery, fencing wire, house furnishing goods, automobile tires, and wagons and buggies, illustrating how it was keeping up with the times and offering merchandise to owners of automobiles as well as owners of horses and buggies. This brick façade reflects the late Italianate style and especially that of the Renaissance Revival period. Cast-iron piers from which the segmental arches of the transom spring flank each opening. To the north and south side façade would have been fixed windows with an arched double-pane transom above. Double doors with arched double-pane transom flanked by cast-iron piers flank the doorways. At either end of the façade would have been paired windows with an arched double-pane transom. The original segmental arched hood molds with label stop are intact. The gable front parapet wall is distinctive for its double row of raking molding surmounting the arcaded corbel table.

---

4. *The Selma Mirror*, June 28, 1911, 69.

21 Broad Street • *Constructed circa 1880*

This two-story component of a two-part commercial brick building was modified circa 1970 with a copper mansard ribbed hood. The first story has double-pane display windows enframed in metal flanking the angled displays and plate-glass entry with transom. A signboard is located above the mansard hood. The parapet wall is distinctive for its open brickwork two courses below the coping.

Edgar Cayce, "the Sleeping Prophet," a native of Hopkinsville, Kentucky, came to Selma to establish himself as a photographer. At the age of twenty-three Cayce lost his voice and, in an attempt to cure this affliction by hypnotic suggestion, he discovered his ability to answer questions and recommend cures for others in this dream-like state. Due to his deep religious convictions this new ability disturbed Cayce, and in an attempt to escape his past as a psychic he moved to Selma, residing there from 1912 to 1924 and founding his studio on the second floor of this building.

Kathryn Tucker Windham recalls an incident involving Cayce's son Hugh Lynn, who had been experimenting with the flash powder used in photography, resulting in an explosion. His eyes were severely damaged, and despite the best efforts of two of Selma's finest doctors, Eugene Callaway and S. Gay, his son was in danger of losing one of his eyes. Cayce, using a self-induced hypnosis, was able to prescribe a cure involving the use of tannic acid packs to save the sight of his son.[5]

FIGURE 2-5, 21 Broad Street, Photograph by Susan Besser, 2002

---

5. Harmon Hartzell Bro, *A Seer Out of Season: The Life of Edgar Cayce* (New York: Penguin Books, 1989), 292.

22-24 Broad Street • *Constructed circa 1880, renovated 1919*
John W. McKeil, Architect

FIGURE 2-6, 22-24 Broad Street, Photograph by Bill Tomey, 2024

Early in this building's life Cawthon & Coleman sold cigars, paints, oils, and glass there. Physicians John P. Furniss, who served as an assistant surgeon for the Confederate army, and John H. Henry, who served as Selma's mayor in 1865 when the Union army occupied the town, maintained a practice on the second floor. In the early twentieth century, a succession of jewelers, J. Hirschfeld Jewelry and Louis Kronenburg Jewelry, occupied this two-story brick component of a two-part commercial block on Broad Street. The building retains the defining elements of the late-nineteenth-century commercial building—the historic storefront, cast-iron work, and original porch—and has a metal standing-seam porch roof supported by tapered fluted cast-iron posts with a bell-shaped capital. The second-story windows have cornice window lintels and wood sills. Each of the three windows is recessed with brick corbeling much like 4 Broad Street.

23 Broad Street • *Constructed circa 1908*
Charles Henry Hopson, Architect

A. W. Cawthon of Cawthon & Coleman Drugs contracted with Charles Henry Hopson to design this building, which was completed at a cost of $25,000 in 1908. In addition to the pharmacy business, they sold candies, cigars and tobacco, paints, oil, and glass. This is an Italianate three-story component of a two-part commercial block. The first story retains the cast-iron façade but was altered circa 1930 with display windows and wood porch with round columns resting on a plinth. The second and third stories reflect the original period. The fenestration is composed of two-over-two windows with pressed metal cornice lintel displaying a sunburst motif. A corbel table adorns the parapet.

FIGURE 2-7, 23 Broad Street, Photograph by Susan Besser, 2002

Teppers/Berndorf Bloom/Oberndorf and Ullman • 25 Broad Street
Constructed circa 1865, two-story addition 1904

In 1888 *The Great South*, published in St. Louis and Mobile, spoke glowingly of Oberndorf and Ullman, former occupants of this building, and their mercantile business. At that time the store employed thirty people selling dry goods, notions, clothing, trunks, and carpets. Teppers, also known historically as Berndorf Bloom Building, is a five-story component of a two-part commercial block. The building was long covered in

FIGURE 2-8, 25 Broad Street, drawing by Sarah Engle, 2002

aluminum siding, which has been removed to reveal the stately façade. Dating to the 1850s the Teppers business began as two structures built by Colonel Goldsby. In 1868, after the Civil War, the damaged floor and roof were rebuilt. In 1904 the two buildings were combined; two stories were added, and a new façade updated with an enframed window wall that brought the building into the twentieth century. Max and Ben Tepper purchased the building, and it served Selma as Tepper Bros. Mercantile Company from 1904 until 1967.

26 Broad Street • *Constructed circa 1900*

FIGURE 2-9, 26 Broad Street, Photograph by Susan Besser, 2002

Bewin-Elebash Jewelry Co. (1913) and Bewig Optical Co., which also advertised as a jeweler, (1924) were located at 26 Broad in this two-part, two-story brick commercial component constructed circa 1900. The first story has a large display window, a circa 1940s-1950s alteration, with a marble bulkhead. The entry has a splayed entrance and a wood door with glazing. Within the parapet are two rows of dentil band separated by band molding.

28 Broad Street • *Constructed circa 1890*

The defining characteristics of 28 Broad Street show influences of the classical movement of the late nineteenth and early twentieth century. Part of a two-part commercial block, this two-story building retains the original wood front recessed entry with a glass and wood door flanked by oblique display windows. The classical influences are illustrated by the brickwork, which creates the pilasters with corbeled capital. The parapet has a deep cornice surmounting a shallow cornice with a panel embellished with a swag detail resting on a cyma recta molding.

FIGURE 2-10, 28 Broad Street, Photograph by Susan Besser, 2002

In the 1910s, Rothschild Mercantile provided ladies ready-to-wear clothing. In the 1920s this building was home to Selma Trust & Savings Bank, an institution that began before the panic of 1907, according to reporting by the *Selma Mirror* in 1911. It was known locally as the "Wage Earner's Bank" and was devoted to serving as a savings institution.

30 Broad Street • *Constructed circa 1880*

FIGURE 2-11, 30 Broad Street, Old Depot Museum Archives

In 1904 the Selma National Bank opened their doors in this Gothic Revival–style three-story building. E. Carlisle Melvin managed the bank as president with a capital stock of $2,000,000, succeeding the banking house of Minthorne Woolsey, and was featured in the *Selma Mirror* in 1911. Early occupants of this building include a men's clothing store managed by Alex Rice with Thomas W. Clark. William R. Nelson was president of the Loan Company of Alabama and occupied the building as well. Satterfield & Young law offices were located on the second and third stories. The Gothic Revival three-story stucco exterior building with hipped roof is a component of a two-part commercial block and is the corner anchor of the block. The original gable-roof parapet embellished with a corbel table was altered, date unknown. Distinctive Tudor arched two-over-two windows with stone hood mold and sill define the upper-story windows.

Weaver Building • 101 Broad Street
Constructed 1871 • W. K. Ball, Architect

FIGURE 2-12, Weaver Building, 101 Broad Street, Old Depot Museum Archives

FIGURE 2-13, 106-108 Broad Street, Photograph by Susan Besser, 2002

The building was constructed in 1871 and received a glowing report in the *Selma Morning Times*. "Taken all in all, this is by far the handsomest building, not only in Selma but in the Southern country." Before the Battle of Selma, Col. P. J. Weaver's store was a prominent business in Selma at this site but was lost to fire during the battle. This replacement was built at a cost of $40,000 by Virgil G. Weaver. Messers. Meyer and Company were the first occupants.[6] Philadelphia pressed brick was used for the face of the building and marble and terra cotta for the window sills and cornices. In 1911 occupants of this building were George A. Cunningham & Co. wholesale and retail druggists and Selma Stationery Company offering Victor talking machines, Globe-Wernicks bookcases, and Eastman Kodak cameras and supplies. Henry Plant managed Selma Stationery, which had locations in Chattanooga, Tennessee, and Rome, Georgia. This Second Empire three-story component of a two-part commercial block has a brick exterior with cut stone details, a wraparound attached porch of standing-seam metal on the hipped roof, and cast-iron columns. The original Second Empire roofline was modified, date unknown. The second-story fenestration composed of two-over-two and one-over-one windows is adorned with hood molds with incised leaves supported by acanthus-leaf corbels. A wide overhanging modillioned cornice creates a division between the second and third stories.

---

6. "The Weaver Building, a Magnificent Edifice, an Ornament to Selma," *Selma Morning Times*, March 5, 1871, 3.

106-108 Broad Street • *Constructed circa 1900*

Keeble-McDaniel Clothing occupied this building in 1924 working as tailors, having moved from 110 Broad Street. A two-bay, two-story Italianate component of a two-part commercial block, this brick building retains the historic wood storefront, which has been modified with a marble bulkhead. The awning has a convex roof of standing-seam metal roof supported by slender cast-iron posts. Second-story fenestration is composed of three one-over-one windows with bracketed hood molds with keystone. A modillion cornice is embellished with large decorative brackets.

107-109 Broad Street • *Constructed circa 1910*
Charles Henry Hopson, Architect

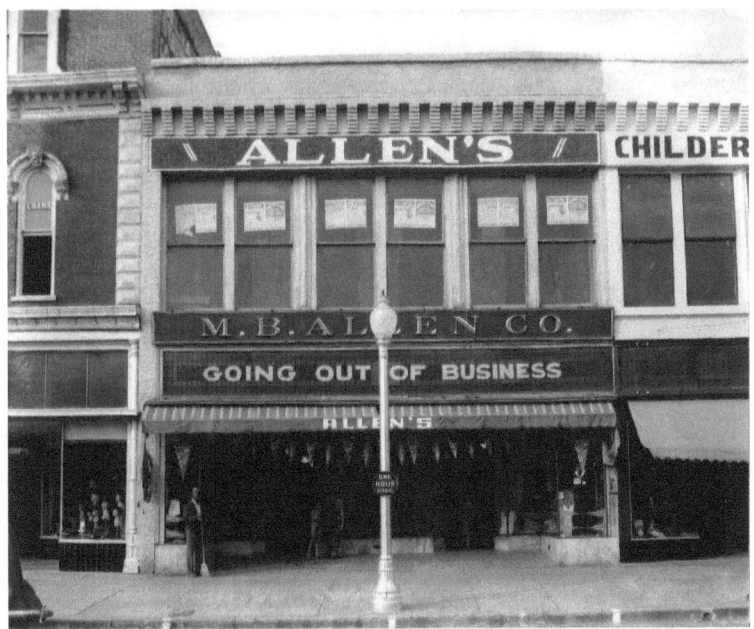

FIGURE 2-14, 107-109 Broad Street, Old Depot Museum Archives

The historic photograph of this building represents an evolution of storefronts that would be considered innovative for its time. In May of 1910, *The Selma Times-Journal* noted that the Eliasberg stores would create a storefront of concrete, plate glass, and copper sash bars. The end result created a store filled with much daylight and maximum display space as all merchants were vying for the customer's dollar. Accordingly, it would be "the handsomest front in Selma."[7]

110 Broad Street • *Constructed circa 1900*

FIGURE 2-15, 110 Broad Street, Photograph by Susan Besser, 2002

P. B. Harrell Drugs occupied this Italianate one-bay, two-story component of a two-part commercial block. The first story retains the cast-iron front encasing an historic wood storefront with original beveled glass and marble bulkhead. Cast-iron pilasters define the entrance with display windows that splay to the central entry covered by a shed roof porch of standing-seam metal. Second-story fenestration is composed of one-over-one windows surmounted by bracketed hood molds with decorative corner blocks with keystone. The modillion cornice is embellished with large carved brackets.

---

7. "New Front for Eliasberg's," *Selma Times-Journal*, May 20, 1910, 1.

111 Broad Street • *Constructed circa 1890*

FIGURE 2-16, 111 Broad Street, Photograph by Susan Besser, 2002

Meyer & Elkan, purveyor of boots and shoes, were longtime tenants of this distinctive Italianate, circa-1890, two-story component of a two-part commercial block with a brick exterior, stone quoins, and parapet. Segmental hood molds with keystone and corbel stop enrich the two-over-two windows. A modillion cornice of pressed tin enriches the parapet wall.

113 Broad Street • *Constructed circa 1870* • *W. K. Ball, Architect*

This Italianate two-story component of a two-part commercial block with stone exterior illustrates the stylistic variations of the period. The first story incorporates the cast-iron elements indicative of the period. Cast-iron pilasters with plinths and square capitals enframe the display windows and opaque glass transoms. This building retains a great deal of Italianate detail

FIGURE 2-17, 113 Broad Street, Photograph by Susan Besser, 2002

such as the bracketed cornice embellished with a modillion course and a semicircular pediment graced with a bracket and modillions. The round opening in the pediment originally contained a clock, a most appropriate adornment for the tenants, E. H. Hobbs Jewelers and Opticians. Mr. Ball, the architect, received high praises for his work in the *Times-Argus* (later the *Selma Morning Times*).[8]

114 Broad Street • *Constructed circa 1880*

Lilienthal Mercantile Co. occupied this building with a Masonic lodge hall in the upper stories indicated by an inset panel between the second and third stories. This brick three-story component of a two-part commercial block is distinctive for the treatment of the one-over-one windows, bracketed hood molds above the second story windows and semicircular hood

---

8. *The Times-Argus,* March 3, 1870, 3.

FIGURE 2-18, 114 Broad Street, Photograph by Susan Besser, 2002

molds, corbel stop, and keystone above the third story. Quoins are of iron. A modillion cornice reflects the influences of the Italian Renaissance.

116-120 Broad Street • *Constructed 1904*
J. G. Barnwell, Architect

FIGURE 2-19, 116-120 Broad Street, drawing by Nora Whelchel, November 2023

McKay Jewelers occupied 116 Broad in the early twentieth century. Kayser & Cammack retailed paints and oil and seeds and operated a soda fountain at 120 Broad Street during this time. An advertisement in the city directory listed this firm as a manufacturer of Liver-Lax "For Lazy Livers, Makes Your Liver Laugh." Constructed in 1904, this three-story component of a two-part commercial block is of the Renaissance Revival period. Although the first story has been altered the building retains the defining elements of the Renaissance Revival style—keystone lintels and the wide overhanging modillioned cornice.

S. H. Kress Building, Butler-Truax Jewelers • 121 Broad Street
Constructed circa 1930 • Edward F. Sibbert, Jr., Architect

S. H. Kress & Co., a dime-store chain founded by Samuel Kress in 1896, was known for its beautifully designed buildings along America's Main Streets and first appears on the Sanborn maps in 1913 as a 10-cent store. Kress began negotiations to enlarge the store in 1928. According to the *Selma Times-Journal* of July 28, 1929, "Kress company had for some time past sought to double the Broad Street frontage, due to the steady growth of its business here."[9] Kress signed a thirty-year lease for the property with two owners for a combined total of $76,000. The Kress Company maintained an architectural division in order to ensure that all facets of the design lived up to the architectural excellence of its reputation. Kress, a fine-art collector, envisioned the stores as "architectural gifts" to the cities. Kress built new stores or updated the façades during the Depression, in order to use the lower construction and labor costs to his advantage. The 1930s stores were often modern in styling; Kress felt continuing construction during this period displayed a sense of optimism for the country's future. The design of each Kress store was specific to the community and oftentimes incorporated references to the area.

Kress's interpretation of this distinctive Art Deco style of this three-story component of a two-part commercial block/enframed window

---

9. "Kress Store Planning Big New Building," *Selma Times-Journal*, July 28, 1929, 7.

FIGURE 2-20, S. H. Kress Building, 121 Broad Street, Photograph by Susan Besser, 2002

building embodies the sense of verticality and stylized decoration typical of the period. Tripartite windows with geometric stylized spandrels contribute to the vertical emphasis. The design incorporates both vertical and horizontal stack-bond patterns. Four polychromed terra-cotta stylized leaf-design tiles embellish the parapet and flank the Kress logo. Since Selma's main crop was cotton, this most likely references the connection to cotton.

In 2002 the Butlers, a long-standing jewelry firm, purchased the Kress Building and renovated it. In doing the renovations the Butlers were sensitive to the historic interior of the store and furnished it with antique mahogany jewelry cases.

S. H. Kress dime stores were the site of sit-ins at lunch counters throughout the South during the Civil Rights Movement, and the Kress store in Selma experienced this as well.[10]

---

10. Carroll Van West, Amber Clawson, Jessica French, and Abigail Gautreau, "The Civil Rights Movement in Selma, Alabama, 1865-1972," National Register Multiple Property Nomination, 32, https://npgallery.nps.gov/NRHP/.

Commercial Bank of Alabama, Southern Hotel, Rosemond Hotel, Hotel Virginia
132 Broad Street • *Constructed 1858*
Edward Tuckerman Potter, Architect[11]

FIGURE 2-21, Commercial Bank of Alabama, 132 Broad Street, Photograph Courtesy Bill Tomey

A local businessperson, William J. Norris, oversaw the construction of the Commercial Bank of Alabama in the late 1850s.[12] George Baker commissioned Edward T. Potter, an architect from New York who had apprenticed in the firm of Richard Upjohn. Potter specialized in the design of ecclesiastical architecture, was the son of Bishop Alonzo Potter of Union College, and is credited with the Mark Twain House in Hartford, Connecticut. The original symmetrical stepped façade of the three-story brick building was designed in a restrained Italianate manner with the windows having bracketed stone lintels. A one-story portico with a cast-iron

---

11. Sarah Bradford Landau, *Edward T. and William A. Potter: American Victorian Architects* (New York: Garland, 1979), 239.

12. John Hardy, *Selma: Her Institutions and Her Men* (Spartanburg, SC: Reprint Company), 192.

balustrade on the second story graced the façade. The south elevation, which was the entrance for the Hotel Virginia, retains elements of the arched hood mold detailing the paneled double-door entry with glazing surmounted by a semicircular transom. The interior retains period details such as ten-foot doors and surrounds and intricate plaster arches indicative of the Italianate period. The Commercial Bank was designed early in Potter's career. Potter is noted for his attention to scale and proportion as evidenced in the Nott Memorial Library in Schenectady, and although the Commercial Bank of Alabama building has experienced alterations, the articulation of Potter's design is still evident.

FIGURE 2-22, Commercial Bank of Alabama,
Drawing by Jaylen Gambrell, November 2023

The bank was tied heavily into Confederate currency and after the war ceased to exist. Completed in 1858, the building later housed the Rosemond Hotel, c. 1900. The hotel operated as the Hotel Virginia, circa 1920, and the *Selma Times* of February 19, 1920, notes that a luncheon given by the Stock Yards Committee took place at the Hotel Virginia. A separate kitchen most likely built to support the Rosemond Hotel and associated with the building is still intact and is to the rear of the building.

Carter Drug Co. • 133 Broad Street
Constructed circa 1880; storefront alterations circa 1950

FIGURE 2-23, Carter Drug Co., 133 Broad Street, Photograph by Susan Besser, 2002

In 1913 LaPorte Café occupied the first story of the Carter Drug Co. Building located at the corner of Broad Street and Alabama Avenue. Shoemakers Green Bynum were located in the rear of the building. The two-story, two-part commercial block building is of the Italianate era. The original hipped roof wraparound porch with flared eaves retains the transom; however, the glass has been lost over time. The storefront was modified circa 1950 with larger display windows of the era. The fenestration is composed of one-over-one double-hung sash windows with cornice lintel and decorative crown. The wide overhanging cornice has a broad frieze band with eave brackets with drop pendants. Four interior brick chimneys with corbeled caps are original to the building.

F. W. Woolworth, Vaughan Building • 201 Broad Street
Constructed circa 1890 • John W. McKeil, Architect, renovations 1912 Skinner-Biedermann Company, Contractor, 1937 renovations

On "the corner where the cars meet," in 1911 the Vaughan Building originally housed G. A. Swift, druggist. Formerly Southern Hotel and

Germania Hotel, the building was remodeled in 1912 with plans completed by architect John W. McKeil adding the plate glass, prism windows, and tile. Featuring a soda fountain, the store offered quick delivery service to its patrons. In 1917 Mr. Swift moved to 215 Broad Street, the Swift Building, especially built for his enterprise. McKeil shared an architecture practice in the Vaughan building with renowned regional architect Charles Henry Hopson. Hopson moved his practice to Atlanta, Georgia, in 1913 while McKeil remained in Selma.

FIGURE 2-24, F. W. Woolworth Co., 201 Broad Street, Old Depot Museum Archives

In 1937 plans were developed for F. W. Woolworth to occupy the entire building with an estimated cost of $22,000 to include exterior and interior renovations.[13] New plate-glass windows were installed on the Broad Street elevation and Selma elevation. The plans called for tearing out all the partition walls on the first floor to "throw the entire first floor of the building into one store."[14]

---

13. "Work Started on New Store Here," *Selma Times-Journal*, December 22, 1937, 1.
14. "New Woolworth Planned for City," *Selma Times-Journal*, November 12, 1937, 1.

The F. W. Woolworth Co. Building is a handsome brick Romanesque Revival two-story component of a two-part commercial block. The first-story storefront splays to two double-door entrances and display windows are enframed in wood resting on a bulkhead of marble. The dramatic second-story fenestration is evocative of the Romanesque use of arches and mixing of brick and dressed stone. Above the transom of the central double window is a lunette with stone-stepped voussoirs. An oculus rimmed in stone is directly above. A stepped parapet surmounts the oculus. To the north and south of the double window are double-sash windows with multi-paned segmental arch-stained glass transoms recessed into Syrian arches composed of dogtooth brickwork. The first-story brickwork is laid to give the effect of rusticated stone while the upper-story corner brickwork has projecting courses and a corbeled terminus. Pilasters accentuate the corners of the building.

F. W. Woolworth Co. • 209 Broad Street
Constructed circa 1912 • B. D. Hoffman, Contractor

F. W. Woolworth Co., one of the first five-and-dime stores, sold merchandise at fixed prices, typically at five or ten cents, and was among the first of these stores discounting and undercutting local competition. Woolworth was also one of the first stores to display merchandise for the buying public to handle rather than have the merchandise behind the counter. Frank Winfield Woolworth began his legacy in 1878. Upon Woolworth's death in 1919 Samuel Henry Kress closed his Kress stores for the funeral, a very unusual business move for the times.

The site had been previously used as a fruit stand. The building was owned by Isidore Kayser & Co. and the new building was contracted to B. D. Hoffman.[15] The two-story gray brick exterior building is a component of a two-part commercial block. The first story has a large five-panel glass storefront with double doors of full glass enframed with wood resting on a wood bulkhead. Above the double doors are a six-light transom and a

---

15. "Hoffman Gets Contract for New Building," *Selma Times-Journal*, December 12, 1912, 1.

FIGURE 2-25, F. W. Woolworth Co., 209 Broad Street, Photograph by Susan Besser, 2002

twelve-light transom. Unique to this building are four-pane casement windows surmounting the storefront. Second-story fenestration, as was typical of the early twentieth century, consists of three pairs of three awning windows. Various brick patterns such as stack bond and diagonally laid brick contribute to the overall distinctiveness and attributes of the building.

Kayser's • 211-213 Broad Street
Constructed 1912

Kayser's Building, an enframed window wall with exterior of brick and stone, is distinctive for its prismatic glass–pane transom. Introduced in the 1890s, prismatic glass was an innovative method of directing daylight into building interiors. The tiled threshold bearing Kayser's name that greeted the shoppers of the early twentieth century conveys the sense of permanence that merchants created when building such an establishment. Constructed in 1912, it was built on the site of J. N. Montgomery Marble Yard.

FIGURE 2-26, Kayser's, 211-213 Broad Street,
Photograph by Susan Besser, 2002

The building was to "be equipped with all the modern conveniences. . . . On the second floor there will be a lady's writing room, rest and lounging room for the comfort of the patron of the firm."[16] Owing to its Neoclassical influences the first story has two square columns in the center and a pilaster on either end. The fenestration of the second and third stories consists of brick piers creating the illusion of pilasters and brick spandrels.

Swift Building/Swift Drug Co. • 215 Broad Street
Constructed 1916

The Swift Building is an excellent example of the understated elegance of early twentieth-century commercial building and is a three-story component of a two-part commercial block with a stone exterior and a shed roof with parapet. Fenestration of the second and third stories resonates with the adjacent Kayser's building and is indicative of the early twentieth-century treatment. Piers divide the six one-over-one double-hung wood

---

16. "Selma Again Steps Forward," *Selma Times-Journal*, April 21, 1912, 2.

FIGURE 2-27, Swift Drug Co., 215 Broad Street, Photograph by Susan Besser, 2002

sash windows into three pairs of two windows. Neoclassical influence is displayed in the simplicity of the piers. A sign bearing the name "Swift Building 1916" is mounted above the spandrels.

First YMCA, 217 Broad Street • *Constructed circa 1887*

One of the standard bearers of the progress of a city are community outreach programs. The YMCA movement had its genesis in 1844 in London, England. Selma is noted to be the first city in Alabama to form a YMCA in 1858. Selmian, Joseph Hardie, served as president of the international YMCA selected by fellow members in Richmond, Virginia, in 1874. Fundraising for the first YMCA building, segregated white only, included plans for a Second Empire styled, three-and-one-half story building at 217 Broad Street began in the late 1880s after Rev. D. L. Moody inspired locals by his lectures on the importance of molding young Christian men. The building

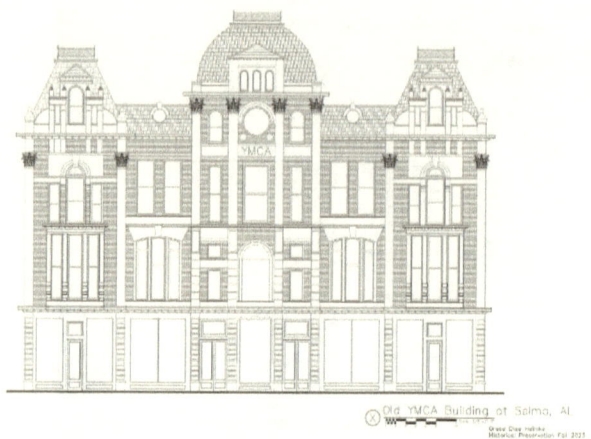

FIGURE 2-28, First YMCA, 217 Broad Street,
Drawing by Elise Heimke, November 2023

with a central Palladian window, elaborate brickwork and cast-iron balcony is considered to be a fine example of the Second Empire. According to the Selma Times Journal of June 19, 1933, the towers were removed at that time. The building has the potential for adaptive use and is considered a pivotal landmark building of Selma's downtown historic district.

Selma City Hall, 222 Broad Street • *Constructed 1976*
Ed Neal of Bigger, Neal & Clark, Architect

The French Colonial vernacular architecture of Selma provided the model for the Selma City Hall, a two-story free-standing building constructed on the site of the Hotel Albert. Built in 1976, the brick building with Italianate details has seven bays with a hipped roof covered with asphalt shingles and brick foundation. The building gives the appearance of a central-passage plan with the central double doors with six lights and four-light transom. The first story has six six-over-six double-hung sash windows surmounted by triangular pediments. Second-story fenestration is composed of seven six-over-six double-hung windows with triangular ped-iment. Indicative of the local vernacular influences is the two-story entry

FIGURE 2-29, Selma City Hall, 222 Broad Street,
Photograph by Susan Besser, 2002

portico with cast-iron balustrade. Paired brackets embellish the flared eaves, and a brick course defines the frieze. There are two interior brick chimneys. One-story lateral additions with a hipped roof and six-over-six double-hung sash windows are on either side of the building.

Broad Street Residential

Cornerstone Presbyterian Church, First Presbyterian Church
301 Broad Street • *Constructed 1893*
Reuben Harrison Hunt, Architect

Designed by Reuben Harrison Hunt, a Chattanooga architect, Cornerstone Presbyterian Church is a pristine example of the Romanesque Revival period inspired by eleventh- and twelfth-century ecclesiastical architecture and popularized by H. H. Richardson with his landmark Trinity Church of Boston. With its grounding in medieval architecture this style is evidenced by heavy use of arches and arcading and incorporation of a tower or turret in the overall design.

FIGURE 2-30, Cornerstone Presbyterian Church, 301 Broad Street, Photograph by Susan Besser, 2016

The architect's mastery of this design is manifested in the use of the Syrian arch and combination of brick and cut stone. The two-story sanctuary is in the form of a front gable and side tower configuration. The entrance to the sanctuary is on Dallas Avenue and has a deeply recessed arched door opening with a band of molding following the curve of the Syrian arch. A four-story tower with rounded buttress and pyramidal standing-seam metal roof dominates this religious edifice.

This building is the second Presbyterian church on this site. The first church began in 1847 and featured a clock in the steeple; the clock was installed in 1857 at a cost of $500 "for the convenience of the townspeople." With the completion of the newer church and in keeping with the tradition of maintaining the city clock, the expenditure of $925 for the Seth Thomas clock was approved by the city council in October of 1893. In December of 1893, the council approved a measure to place the clock in the tower if the dial was raised five feet to the prescribed height of sixty feet. The church agreed to this condition, with the building being dedicated June 3, 1894, along with the city clock, which prompts locals to say, "Selma runs on Presbyterian time."[17]

People's Bank & Trust Co. • 420 Broad Street
Constructed 1980

FIGURE 2-31, People's Bank & Trust Co., 420 Broad Street, Photograph by Susan Besser, 2002

The People's Bank & Trust building draws from the Selma French Colonial architectural heritage. It is a two-story, seven-bay brick free-standing commercial building with a flat roof and a stepped parapet. A two-story gallery with cast-iron frieze supports and a balustrade enriches the façade of the building. Two entries of single doors with glazing and transom are centrally located on the façade. The exuberant pediment draws on Water Avenue architecture and reflects the Italianate influences seen on Main

---

17. Alston Fitts III, *Historic Churches of Selma Prior to 1925* (City of Selma, 2006), 11.

Streets in the nineteenth century. Over scaled fluted eave brackets with finials enhance the triangular pediment and the corners of the buildings.

Trailways Bus Station • 434 Broad Street
Constructed circa 1940

The Greyhound Lines had grown steadily in the 1920s and 1930s, and the Interstate Commerce Commission encouraged the founding of independent transportation companies. Burlington Transportation, which started in 1929, formed the basis of National Trailways Bus System in 1936 and was made up of independent motor-coach owners. During the Civil Rights Movement participants in the movement came to Selma by the Trailways system.

FIGURE 2-32, Trailways Bus Station, 434 Broad Street, Photograph by Susan Besser, 2002

The Trailways Bus depot is a one-story, brick, flat-roof building reflecting the horizontality of the Modernist movement. The primary entry is a recessed single door with a metal canopy attached above the recess. A planter is to the south and is an extension of the entry bay. A bank of four fixed glass windows is behind the planter and to the south. A porte cochère is to the north and is supported by metal posts. Two-over-two double-hung metal windows are on the north elevation. Coping finishes the roofline.

440 Broad Street • *Constructed 1926*

FIGURE 2-33, 440 Broad Street, Photograph by Susan Besser, 2002

The original owner, John Fuller, a local dentist, constructed this graceful dwelling circa 1926. This elegant Renaissance Revival building is a two-story, three-bay brick with hipped roof of tile. Corinthian columns support a two-story curved portico with pilasters at the juncture of the porch and façade. A balustrade of turned balusters embellishes the portico. Brick steps fan outward and lead to the single door entry with glazing and cut-glass sidelights and transom. To the north and south of the entry are single windows with cut-glass transoms. Stone lintels surmount the windows and entry. Second-story windows are one-over-one configuration. Typical of the style is the wide overhanging eave. Stone quoins embellish the corners, and the shaped dormer is enriched with arched louvered vent and windows.

Temple Mishkan Israel • 503 Broad Street
Constructed 1900 • Sully & Stone Co., Limited, Architect
Thompson & Company, Contractor

Families such as Plattenburg, Loeb, Maas, Leva, Gusdorf, Eliasberg, Adler, Tepper, and Rosenberg occupied Broad Street. The Jewish population of Selma emigrated upriver from the port city of Mobile. Known for their expertise in the retail businesses, many of them began as peddlers in the 1830s, having migrated from Europe to the West Indies during the Inquisition. A second wave of immigration took place in the 1840s, primarily from Germany, motivated by the economic situation and a desire to avoid a military draft. In the late 1880s a third wave of immigration brought Jewish settlers from Eastern Europe. These settlers entered through Northeast ports and then migrated to the South and established small businesses, which thrived and prospered. The late nineteenth and early twentieth centuries in Old Town Historic District saw the genesis of businesses such as Tepper's, Kayser's, Lilienthal's, Liepold's, Rothchild's, Meyer and Elkan, Fink's Jewelry, Klotzman Furniture, M. Leva, and Eliasberg's.[18] These businesses continued throughout the World War II era. Solomon Kohn, who emigrated from Germany in 1859, was a local businessman and city treasurer who helped to found the city infirmary and was a director of the Hotel Albert as well as a trustee of the Mishkan Israel congregation.[19] Alston Fitts in *Historic Churches of Selma Prior to 1925* notes the prominent role the Jewish community played in Selma with having three Jewish mayors—Simon Mass, Marcus J. Meyer, and Louis Benish.[20]

In 1867 people began meeting at the home of Joseph Meyer, establishing the Reform Congregation, which continued to meet in members' homes. Beginning in 1876, an Episcopal church was used for the services, and in 1879 the interior was refurbished by Andrew J. Mullen, contractor,

---

18. Jerry Siegel, "History of Selma Jewry," undated manuscript.

19. Walter M. Jackson, *The Story of Selma* (Birmingham: Birmingham Printing Company, 1954), 357.

20. Fitts, *Historic Churches of Selma Prior to 1925*, 17.

and M. J. Miller, architect. It was described as having "carved panels, rich altars, breathtaking frescoes, brilliant chandeliers, carpets of finest texture, and all that will or can make a temple charming."[21] In 1892 they acquired a site used temporarily for a school. In June of 1899, the congregation broke ground, completing the temple in February of 1900.

FIGURE 2-34, Temple Mishkan Israel, 503 Broad Street, Photograph by Susan Besser, 2002

Acknowledged for their outreach, the Jewish community was instrumental in helping to fund the League of United Charities, whose mission was to provide health care for the lower-income and economically disadvantaged people of Selma. Solomon Kohn, city treasurer, and Dr. A. W. Cawthon organized fundraising for two hospitals, Dallas Avenue Charity for African Americans and Selma Infirmary for whites.[22]

Built in close proximity to the Jewish residential neighborhood, Temple Mishkan Israel is attributed to architect Thomas Sully, who presented the

---

21. "Dedication Services of the Synagogue," *Selma Times*, June 8, 1879, 3.
22. Alston Fitts, "Built on Faith," *Spanish Moss*, Winter 2011.

plans in January of 1899.[23] It resonates with the hallmarks of the Romanesque style with Syrian arches on brick piers within the arcaded entry. The Temple is built in the rotunda plan. This two-story edifice has two-story bell towers with slate pyramidal roofs to the north and south. The blind arcaded second story of the tower is broken by a stone course. One-over-one stained-glass double-hung windows with stone lintel and stone sill course enhance the towers. The arcaded entry porch has Syrian arches on brick piers with stone corbeled trim while a cast-iron balustrade adds an unexpected regional architectural accent. A stained-glass window in the Star of David design dominates the gable end of the Broad Street façade. This element appears on the north and south gables as well. An octagonal rotunda with slate roof and triple stained-glass windows pierces the roof.

Jackson Manor • 515 Broad Street
Constructed 1890

FIGURE 2-35, Jackson Manor, 515 Broad Street, Photograph by Susan Besser, 2002

---

23. "Notice to Contractors," *Selma Times-Journal*, April 28, 1899, 4; *Selma Times-Journal*, January 14, 1899, 4.

Jackson Manor is a handsome one-and-one-half-story dwelling indicative of the Queen Anne Free Classic style with a hipped roof with multiple cross gables and shingled corner turret to the south with one-over-one windows and conical roof. The inset bowed porch exhibits paneled detailing in the gable end and has paired Doric columns on wood piers connected by lathe-turned balusters. The gable front bay to the north has cutaway bays and flat-sawn vergeboard enriched with paterae and imbricated shingles in the gable end. One of the early residents, Mathile Wolf, was married to Monroe Gusdorf in a quiet ceremony performed by Rabbi J. H. Kaplan in the bride's home in 1908.[24]

Paul M. Grist YMCA • 532 Broad Street
Constructed 1925; remodeled 1986 • *William Welton, Architect*

FIGURE 2-36, Paul M. Grist YMCA, 532 Broad Street, Postcard Collection of Susan Besser

In 1925 this was a state-of-the-art physical fitness center with an indoor swimming pool and gymnasium and was built at a cost of $150,000.[25]

---

24. "Stag Dinner," *Selma Times-Journal*, October 7, 1908, 5.
25. "Architect to Be Chosen for Y," *Selma Times-Journal*, October 31, 1923, 10.

H. C. Armstrong, who was president of the YMCA, oversaw the construction of this building, which was originally a Spanish Colonial Revival design by William Welton of Birmingham, as noted in the *Manufacturers Record* of June 28, 1923. Interior detailing included a beautiful cut stone fireplace of the period. The three-story, seven-bay-façade, brick-veneer building originally had a stucco exterior that was covered in 1986. A partial portico with decorative metal screening was part of the 1986 remodeling.

Paul M. Grist moved to Selma from Atlanta in 1919, taking on the role of physical director of the Selma YMCA and significantly increased membership by visiting schools and stressing the importance of regular exercise. Grist assumed the leadership over the entire YMCA program in 1934, holding that position for thirty years.[26] Initially, this location of the YMCA was segregated. With the help of Rev. Frederick Douglas Reese, it was quietly integrated in 1970.[27]

706 Broad Street • *Constructed circa 1850*

FIGURE 2-37, 706 Broad Street, Photograph by Bill Tomey

Formerly known as the Seigel Gallery, this one-story stucco Creole cottage with Greek Revival influences is typical of this style with four-pane,

---

26. Alston Fitts III, *Selma: A Bicentennial History* (Birmingham: University of Alabama Press, 2017), 187.

27. Fitts, *Selma: A Bicentennial History*, 282.

full-height casement windows surmounted by window crowns. Squared Doric columns with a plinth and base support the full-width porch. Mary Morgan Keipp (1875–1961) resided here in the 1940s. Trained as a nurse-anesthetist, Keipp worked at King Hospital but exhibited her creative side as an amateur photographer and is highly regarded for her photographs of rural American life. From 1899 to 1904 her photographs of African American residents of Selma were exhibited in New York, London, Philadelphia, Pittsburgh, and Washington, D.C. Her work was shown along with that of imminent photographers such as Edward Steichen, Alfred Stieglitz, and Thomas Eakins. An assemblage of her work is at the Old Depot Museum. In 1990, quite by accident, Jean Martin, director of the museum, found the negatives in a paper bag in a filing cabinet. The Birmingham Public Library

FIGURE 2-38, *Grapevine Swing*, Photograph by Mary Morgan Keipp, Old Depot Museum Archives

created large-format negatives in order to archive the originals.[28] Keipp's work is significant for how it portrays African Americans and her appreciation of their traditional culture.[29] One of her most famous works, *Grapevine Swing*, has two platinum prints that survive, one residing at the Old Depot Museum and the other in the Smithsonian American Art Museum, Washington, D.C.

Lauderdale Street

Standard Oil Station/Miller Chevron
30 Lauderdale Street • *Constructed 1924*

FIGURE 2-39, Standard Oil Station/Miller Chevron, 30 Lauderdale Street, Photograph by Susan Besser, 2002

Formerly a Standard Oil Station, the stucco structure retains the porte cochère and the historic multilight entries with transoms and casement windows of the 1920s era. Standard Oil Stations throughout the United States were often designed in a domestic architecture style in order to project the feeling of a "mom & pop" venture. Service stations during this time

---

28. Frances Osborn Robb, *Shot in Alabama: A History of Photography, 1839-1941* (Tuscaloosa: University of Alabama Press, 2016), 163.

29. Robb, *Shot in Alabama*, 175.

paid special attention to cleanliness. In their 1935 manual Standard Oil of California noted, "If there's any place about a station that can lose customers in a hurry, it's an untidy rest room." Unlike today's self-serve gas operation, the attendants would pump your gas, clean your windshield, check the oil and wiper blades, and put air in the tires. Before conversion to Speir Land Company it was known as Miller Chevron, owned by Fred Miller.

Dallas County Courthouse, NRHP 1975 • 105 Lauderdale Street
Constructed circa 1910, circa 1925, circa 1958
W. Chamberlain & Co., Architect
Frank Lockwood, Architect, addition, 1925
Warren, Knight & Davis, Architect, 1958 renovations

FIGURE 2-40, Dallas County Courthouse, 105 Lauderdale Street, Photograph by Susan Besser, 2002

The Dallas County Courthouse is a key building in the Civil Rights Movement as it is where African Americans were refused entry to register to vote in January of 1965. Built circa 1910, it was originally a Neoclassical building. W. Chamberlain & Co. architects of Knoxville, Tennessee, were architects of the building and designed numerous courthouses through the southeast, such as Franklin County Courthouse, Georgia, and Pulaski County Courthouse, Virginia. W. Chamberlain & Co. designed primarily in the Neoclassical architectural style. The annex/addition was designed by Frank Lockwood in 1925 and was built at a cost of $50,000.[30]

FIGURE 2-41, Dallas County Courthouse, 105 Lauderdale Street, c. 1910, Postcard Collection of Susan Besser

During the 1910 construction of the courthouse the clock tower caught fire. That same tower in 1957 collapsed and necessitated the reworking of the façade. Starting in 1958 a synthetic marble was added to the exterior creating a more modernistic feel, bringing the style of the courthouse into the Mid-Century Modern era. The remodeling of the exterior was in a sense a harbinger of change as the courthouse was a place of demonstrations by African Americans and shows of power by local law enforcement from 1960 to 1965 as African Americans attempted to register to vote.

---

30. "Adopt Lockwood Plan for Addition to Courthouse," *Selma Times-Journal*, August 4, 1925, 8.

St. Paul's Episcopal Church, NRHP 1975
210 Lauderdale Street • *Constructed 1875*
Richard M. Upjohn, Architect
Frank Lockwood, Architect, addition; McIntosh
and Yonge Construction Company

FIGURE 2-42, St. Paul's Episcopal Church, 210 Lauderdale Street, Photograph by Susan Besser, 2016

St. Paul's Episcopal Church was organized in 1838 and consecrated in 1843 with the original building, located at Alabama Avenue and Lauderdale Street, destroyed during the Battle of Selma. A second church was built on that site and served the congregation until the more permanent structure was built. The cornerstone was laid in 1871 and the building was completed in 1875. St. Paul's Episcopal Church was designed by the renowned architectural firm of R. and R. M. Upjohn and is in the Decorated Style rather than the Perpendicular Style of Gothic Revival. The style is influenced by traditional English parish churches and features a tower rather than a spire. Constructed of 12-inch-thick outer wall and 8-inch-thick inner wall with 4-inch ventilation between these walls, it reflected the sophisticated technological knowledge of the firm and acted to naturally cool the building.

The bricks were handmade on site. Granite sills, steps, and buttress caps came from Stone Mountain, Georgia, at a cost of $3,500. The church is in the cruciform plan and incorporates a large rose window of stained glass into the gable front. Double-leaf Tudor arched doors provide entry into the sanctuary. An archivolt surmounts the entry. Two narrow Tudor stained-glass windows flank the entry. A four-story tower with crenellation dominates the façade. The tower is entered through double-leaf arched doors. The second and third stories of the tower have slit windows and are defined by a stone belt course. The fourth story of the bell tower has louvered vents with tracery detail on all sides. The crenellated parapet is embellished with finials at the corners.

The interior of the sanctuary has a dramatic hammer-beam ceiling and features an Italian mosaic altar and reredos by Lamb Company of New York. The Hardee family donated the stained-glass window above the altar that depicts scenes from the life of St. Paul, with the window frame echoing the detailing of the trefoil and fleur-de-lis of the woodwork. Tiffany windows were added to the sanctuary in the late 1800s and are attributed to Clara Weaver Parrish. The windows are dedicated to the memory of Mrs. Parrish's parents and husband.

The cloister and parish hall were designed by Frank Lockwood and added in 1924. According to the *Selma Times-Journal* the building would be pure Gothic in style and faced with old brick, which came from Cahaba[31] and other sources, "to correspond with the soft hues of weather-beaten brick of St. Paul's."[32] Clara Weaver Parrish was commissioned to design the stained-glass window of the parish hall. It illustrates the wedding feast at Cana and features Christ in the center with the bride and groom to his right wearing period clothing of the 1920s and is dedicated to Mary Indiana Jones.

---

31. "Elect Vestry and Delegates at St. Paul's," *Selma Times-Journal,* January 12, 1925, 6.

32. "Selma Builders Get Contract," *Selma Times-Journal,* May 21, 1924, 1.

First Baptist Church • 218 Lauderdale Street
Constructed circa 1904 • Wilson & Edwards, Architect
Dougherty & Gardner, Architect, addition 1923

FIGURE 2-43, First Baptist Church, 218 Lauderdale Street, Photograph by Susan Besser, 2015

The congregation of First Baptist Church was organized on May 29, 1842, pastored by Rev. Solon Lindsey. First Baptist Church, with entrances on Lauderdale and Dallas, is fashioned in the grand Chateauesque style of the High Victorian era. Dominated by a four-story tower with a conical roof flaring to bellcast eaves, the rough-cut stone edifice is indicative of this style. The first, second, and third stories of the tower have lancet arch windows. Tracery enriches the belt courses between the stories. Gargoyles project from the belt course between the third and fourth stories. The front gabled parapeted entrance has three sets of double-leaf Tudor arched doors surmounted by ogee arches each capped with a boss creating a handsome entry for Lauderdale Street. Stained-glass windows in the Tiffany style by Clara Parrish embellish the end of the entrances. Built in the Akron plan, First Baptist Church is replete with copper-capped towers, spires, and pinnacles enriched with crockets.

FIGURE 2-44, First Baptist Church Annex, 218 Lauderdale Street, Photograph by Susan Besser, 2002

The first building for the First Baptist Church was constructed in 1850 at the corner of Church Street and Alabama Avenue. According to Alston Fitts the church was able to have services after the Battle of Selma, the only church to do so. The church was involved in serving African American young people, providing schooling in the basement in 1866, and has continued its mission to serve greater Selma, fostering numerous churches including First Baptist Church on MLK, Jr. Street.[33]

---

33. Fitts, *Historic Churches of Selma Prior to 1925*, 2.

Gamble House • 219 Lauderdale Street
Constructed circa 1875

FIGURE 2-45, Gamble House, 219 Lauderdale Street, Photograph by Susan Besser, 2002

Gamble House is an L-shaped plan in the Italianate style and is a two-story, five-bay brick structure with low-pitched hipped roof of standing-seam metal. Foliated-patterned cast-iron posts support a full-width hipped roof entry porch. The entrance features a four-panel door to the south that is surmounted by a segmental arched transom. The fenestration is composed of segmental-arched windows of two-over-two configuration. Relieving arches cap each window and door. The denticulated cornices of the porch and second story are enriched with single-eave brackets at each porch support and paired-eave brackets on the second story.

325 Lauderdale Street • *Daugherty & Gardner Architects, Architect*
Constructed 1964

In addressing the need for a building to accommodate the growth of First Baptist Church, Dr. P. B. Moss, chairman of the building committee,

FIGURE 2-46, 325 Lauderdale Street, Photograph by Susan Besser, 2002

"smilingly" said, "the problem facing the Baptist church has resolved itself into this: We must either build an addition large enough to take care of the growing congregation which is flocking to the church under Dr. Tucker's ministry, or we must get another preacher, who will attract a smaller crowd, so we can accommodate them in the present chuch [sic] building."[34]

The Education Building of Selma First Baptist Church is located diagonally across from the church and resonates with the Gothic influences of the church. This is a three-story, free-standing rectangular building of cut stone, and it has seven bays and a flat roof with a parapet of openwork quatrefoils. It features a symmetrical, basket-handle compound-arch entry with three doors. The façade has seven bays each with paired casement/awning windows with metal trim except for the central bay. Within the central bay above the doors are four casement/awning windows with metal trim on the second and third stories. The decorative spandrels of the second story and third story have two ribs terminating in a cinquefoil design.

---

34. "Either Erect $75,000 Sunday School Plant Extension or Get Preacher Who Won't Draw Such Big Crowds," *Selma Times-Journal*, April 25, 1923, 5.

Decorative tracery embellishes the area within the spandrels of the first-story windows and the spandrels above the third-story windows. The Education Building is an excellent example of how the architects addressed the context of the building in relationship to the late nineteenth-century ecclesiastical building.

400 Lauderdale Street • *Constructed 1903*
Charles H. Hopson, Architect

FIGURE 2-47, 400 Lauderdale Street, Photograph by Susan Besser, 2002

This Neoclassical, two-and-one-half-story, three-bay dwelling has a T-plan form and scored stucco exterior and was designed by Charles H. Hopson, architect, as noted in the *Selma Times* in 1903. The wraparound porch to the north of the façade has paired Doric columns resting on stone pedestals. Other elements indicative of this style are the modillion cornice, the bull's eye window in the gable end, and the distinctive entry of double-leaf wood doors with leaded glass sidelights and transom. Esteemed Selma resident Aimee Nelson DuBose, one of the five original members of the Selma Suffrage Association, resided here in the early 1900s. Her husband, Dr. Francis Goodwin DuBose, established the DuBose Sanitarium in 1904, which unfortunately burned in 1910. At that time, he requested the establishment of a hospital in what is now presently the Vaughan-Smitherman Building.[35]

Hobbs House • 401 Lauderdale Street
Constructed circa 1825

FIGURE 2-48, Hobbs House, 401 Lauderdale Street, Photograph by Susan Besser, 2002

Hobbs House is considered to be the oldest dwelling in Selma. A. H. Conoly purchased the property from the Selma Town and Land Company and built the house circa 1825. The Voeglins assumed ownership in 1840, selling it in 1867 to Mary and Emile Gilman. In 1872 John Hinton purchased the property for $3,350 and held ownership until 1891, when it passed into the Burns family, who maintained ownership of the property for over ninety years. Ross and Julia Hobbs purchased it and restored it.

One of the few Federal-influenced houses in Selma, the Hobbs House is a one-story L-shaped plan dwelling with three bays and side gable roof of standing-seam metal. A full-width porch with six square columns leads to a single-leaf wood door with glazing and transom. Casement windows feature a jib door below, which would have provided cool breezes during the hot summers. A rear addition connects to the original kitchen.

---

35. *Selma Times*, September 11, 1903, 5.

Burns-Bell House • 412 Lauderdale Street
Constructed 1847

FIGURE 2-49, Burns-Bell House, 412 Lauderdale Street, HABS, Library of Congress

The Burns-Bell House was photographed as part of the HABS project and is an Italianate two-story dwelling that displays a full-height triangular pedimented portico with bracketed cornice supported by square columns. Surmounting the entry is a hooded balconet above an arched vertical-panel wood door with sidelights, broken transom, and pediment. Bay windows feature flat-cut balustrades. The second-story windows are hooded with scroll-sawn trim. The interior features an unsupported, wide-stepped spiral staircase.

413 Lauderdale Street • *Constructed 1876*

The lot for this fine Italianate dwelling was purchased from Emile Gilman by Major Franklin Fisher Wise in 1872. Local historians date the building of the dwelling between 1872 and 1876. On January 1, 1876, Margaret A. Saffold sold the house to Franklin A. Wise. Three years later in 1879 Emeline A. Wise purchased the house for $2,800 and lived there until she passed away in 1921. Her heirs sold the house to James W. Craig.

FIGURE 2-50, 413 Lauderdale Street, Photograph by Susan Besser, 2002

This symmetrical dwelling is a two-story, three-bay central passage with weatherboard exterior and hipped roof with center gable of pressed metal shingles. The entry is a single-leaf door with sidelights and broken transom. Elements such as the entry porch with paired chamfered columns with flat-cut balustrade and bracketed cornice are typical of the Italianate style. Angled bays have a concave mansard roof with paired-eave brackets.

418 Lauderdale Street • *Constructed 1842; remodeled circa 1890*

FIGURE 2-51, 418 Lauderdale Street, Photograph by Susan Besser, 2002

This dwelling, originally constructed in 1842, was modified in the 1890s to this prominent Queen Anne, two-story, three-bay dwelling featuring a decorative gable with imbricated shingles alternating with fish scale, square, and sawtooth patterns. Typical Queen Anne details such as the cutaway bay and wraparound-turreted porch with spindlework frieze, lathe-turned columns, scroll-sawn porch brackets, and balustrade are evident. A detailed entry with wood door has handsome stained glass with stained-glass transom. The window on the first level of the entry is adorned with beautiful stained glass. Louis Benish, who began his career as a clerk at Meyer, became part owner of Benish and Meyer, a cigar and tobacco retailer. Benish was the mayor of Selma from 1915 to 1920. His wife, Belle, was a music teacher. The Benish family occupied the dwelling from the early part of the twentieth century through the 1930s.

430 Lauderdale Street • *Constructed circa 1935*
Charles Henry Hopson, Architect

FIGURE 2-52, 430 Lauderdale Street, Photograph by Susan Besser, 2002

This 1930s-era Tudor Revival is a two-story, painted-brick, five-bay façade. Its most notable feature is the "tower entrance" with a single door entry with a bracketed hood. The north bay has Tudor arched lentils above the multi-pane casement windows. In the *Selma Times-Journal* of August 1935, it is noted that Mrs. Joe Rosenberg conferred with Charles Henry Hopson on a new dwelling. At the time Mr. Hopson resided in Atlanta but returned to Selma for the consultation. The *Times-Journal* observed that the design is "strongly reminiscent of French provincial type."[36]

The cost of the dwelling was $15,000, and it is noteworthy that Mrs. Rosenberg was the first woman in Alabama to have an FHA loan. FHA loans originated in 1934 as a means to provide longer-term mortgages and smaller down payments on homes. Before this a buyer was required to make a 30 to 50 percent down payment in order to secure the loan with a repayment period of five to ten years.

Lucien Burns House • 436 Lauderdale Street
Constructed circa 1879–1890

FIGURE 2-53, Lucien Burns House, 436 Lauderdale Street, Photograph by Susan Besser, 2022

---

36. "First Woman in State to Secure FHA Loan Builds Residence Here," *Selma Times-Journal*, August 18, 1935, 6.

This property was part of a land grant from President Monroe to George Phillips and William Rufus King in November 1823. Fannie and Elisha Jackson purchased the property on February 25, 1879, from the Commercial Bank of Selma and constructed the dwelling between 1879 and 1890. Minnie Powell Burns and William W. Burns purchased the house for $4,600 and it remained in their family for over eighty years. Sadly, Minnie died, leaving William and three sons, Lucien, William, and Charles. Minnie's mother stepped in to help raise the boys. Lucien, mayor of Selma for seventeen years, bought out the other heirs and resided there until 1957. His widow, Anna, resided here until 1972. Exhibiting elements of the Italianate era, this two-story, four-bay façade has the original full-width porch with arch supports resting on Doric columns, a nod to the Neoclassic era. The gracious single-leaf entry with glazing is flanked by sidelights and surmounted by a transom. Full-height four-over-four windows flanked by shutters complete the fenestration. Eave brackets embellish the cornice.

Ware-Baker-Jones House/Grace Hall • 506 Lauderdale Street
Constructed 1857 • Thomas Helm Lee, Architect

FIGURE 2-54, Ware-Baker-Jones House/Grace Hall, 506 Lauderdale Street, Photograph by Susan Besser, 2002

The Ware-Baker-Jones House has an illustrious history. Henry H. Ware built Grace Hall in 1857. Clara and Madison Jackson Williams, editor and founder of the *Selma Morning Times*, assumed ownership of the house in 1864. Williams served during the Civil War in the Confederate Army and as mayor of Selma. Historians purport that Wilson's Raiders occupied the house during the Battle of Selma, thus ensuring it would not be destroyed. The house functioned as a boarding house operated by Grace Baker Evans from 1878 to 1930. The arrival of Craig Air Force base necessitated the alteration of the building to apartments during World War II. The Dillons purchased Grace Hall in 1981, returning it to its original configuration.

The Ware-Baker-Jones House is a superb example of the Italianate style and is believed to have been built by builder/designer Thomas Helm Lee. This two-story, three-bay central passage dwelling with one-story lateral wings exhibits the high style of this period with elements such as the Palladian window flanked by sidelights, angled bay windows, and balustrade surmounting the entry porch and bay windows. The primary entry with a wood door, sidelights, and a broken transom are embellished with stained glass. Two-story servants' quarters are visible to the north of the dwelling.

601 Lauderdale Street • *Constructed 1875*

FIGURE 2-55, 601 Lauderdale Street, Photograph by Susan Besser, 2021

This handsome Italianate dwelling built circa 1875 with hipped roof of pressed metal shingles has many elements indicative of the style such as the concave mansard roof of the entry porch, a harbinger of the Second Empire style, chamfered support columns, carved incised frieze, paired-eave brackets with dentil molding at the eaves, and single and double segmental arch double-hung windows. Note the angled bay of segmental arch windows with paired brackets and a mansard roof. During the late nineteenth century Mrs. J. H. Marion had a dressmaking shop in the dwelling.[37] In the 1910s, cotton buyer Frederick J. Johnstone made his residence here.

Pitts-Ellwanger-Weerts House • 619 Lauderdale Street
Constructed 1904

FIGURE 2-56, Pitts-Ellwanger-Weerts House, 619 Lauderdale Street, Photograph by Susan Besser, 2015

The Pitts-Ellwanger-Weerts House is Queen Anne Free Classic as exhibited by an outstanding octagonal-roofed turreted porch embellished with a wide band of trim. The Queen Anne Free Classic was essentially an

---

37. "To the Ladies," *Selma Times-Journal*, September 18, 1896, 4.

asymmetrical plan with applied details recalling the classical elements of the Classical and Greek Revival periods of the nineteenth century. Other elements indicative of the Free Classic variation are the denticulated cornice that enriches the porch and second story and Doric columns supporting the porch and pilasters along the corners of the second story. Other notable elements are the wood door with sidelights and transom as well as the elliptical oculus enriching the front gable. Pilasters embellish corners of the second story. The second story windows to the north have diamond-pane leaded-glass windows.

The house was built by Selma attorney Alexander Pitts and his wife, Juliet Pitts. The Pitts family lived in the house until Alexander's death. Walter Ellwanger, a Lutheran pastor, purchased the house in 1945, residing there with his wife, Jessie, until the early 1970s. Dr. Ellwanger was the administrator of the Lutheran churches and schools during this time. He served as president of Concordia College, an historic Black Lutheran college. During the 1950s the house functioned as a house church for both African Americans and whites. Rosa Young, an African American who was a founder of Alabama Lutheran Academy (later known as Concordia College) and promoted schools in rural Alabama, resided here. So too did Jonathan Daniels, a Civil Rights martyr. The Ellwangers' son, Joseph W. Ellwanger Jr., led the only white Civil Rights march in Selma in 1965 while pastor at St. Paul's Lutheran Church in Birmingham.

In 2000 the Weerts purchased the dwelling, restoring the once-enclosed octagonal porch to its present splendor. It is interesting to note the leaded-glass windows in the front entryway are in the shape of fish, an early Christian symbol first used during the Early Christian era.

Weaver House, The Castle • 625 Lauderdale Street
Constructed 1882 • Michael J. Miller, Architect

Designed by Englishman Michael J. Miller, the Weaver House is a magnificent Gothic Revival dwelling with Romanesque influences built by William Weaver in 1882. Located on the former Weaver's Grove property, Weaver House has the distinction of having brick for the dwelling fired in a kiln on the property and walnut wainscoting and mantels and woodwork fashioned from trees in the grove. According to the *Selma Times-Journal*, a Mr. Rigdon, an Englishman, was responsible for the carpentry.[38] The house is patterned from a castle on the Rhine. The brick two-and-one-half-story, multigable, three-bay dwelling has a standing-seam metal roof. The shed roof porch is supported by cast-iron clustered columns surmounted by bracketing and connected by a flattened arch and semicircular arches. The entry bay has double-leaf doors with Tudor arch. The second story of the central bay has three lancet arch double-hung sash windows. An arcaded corbel table and dentil band enrich the cornice of the central bay.

FIGURE 2-57, Weaver House, The Castle, 625 Lauderdale Street, Photograph by Susan Besser, 2016

---

38. "An Elegant Mansion," *Selma Times-Journal*, September 14, 1882, 4.

The projecting north bay has an angled bay with lancet arch and cast-iron window grates in a grape pattern. A copper hood with concave mansard roof and metal frieze and brackets graces the second story. Embellishing the gable end are a stepped corbel table and eave brackets along the cornice.

William and Lucia Weaver acknowledged the artistic talent of their daughter, Clara. In the 1880s Clara was sent to study at the Art Students League of New York and Paris where she studied under Carro Rosse and Raphael Coil. She married William Peck Parrish of Selma in 1889. They had two daughters, who tragically died at an early age. Clara gravitated to stained-glass design and became a designer for Louis Comfort Tiffany. Her commissions included the windows for New York's St. Michael's Church in 1895, First Baptist Church of Selma, and St. Paul's Episcopal Church in Selma. As part of her legacy she created the Weaver-Parrish Memorial Trust Fund to aid poor African Americans of Selma, which is overseen by St. Paul's Church. Her sister, Rose Pettus Weaver, became a sculptor and carved wood in the Beaux-Arts style, including the staircase at the Weaver house.

Church Street

Vaughan-Plant-Patterson House • 209 Church Street
Constructed circa 1891–1895

Constructed between 1891 and 1895 by P. T. Vaughan, the Vaughan-Plant-Patterson House is a unique Queen Anne of the Free Classic subtype. The Nat Waller family and Jacob Tepper, owner of Tepper's on Broad Street, were former occupants. William Henry Plant, merchant and banker, purchased the dwelling in 1913. Renovations were made on the dwelling by Mary Ann Morthland Patterson, granddaughter of Plant, between 1980 and 1981 and included converting the original kitchen to a family room. This singular one-and-one-half-story, steeply pitched hipped-roof Queen Anne exhibits many elements of the Free Classic subtype. The angled bay to the south has a front gable embellished with scroll-sawn vergeboard with drop pendants, a multilight window, and imbricated shingles.

FIGURE 2-58, Vaughan-Plant-Patterson House, 209 Church Street, Photograph by Susan Besser, 2002

Most noteworthy is the turreted dormer with dentil course that has inset wood panels, multilight windows, and imbricated shingles. The triangular pedimented porch embellished with paneling creates another layer of detail with the classic colonettes that rest on decorative wood pedestals connected by a bowed balustrade.

Church Street United Methodist Church • 214 Church Street
Constructed 1901, alterations 1949 and 1989
J. W. Golucke & Co., Architects

James Wingfield Golucke was an architect who specialized in courthouses and churches and was based in Atlanta, Georgia. On his own he designed fifteen courthouses in Georgia. In February of 1901 during the time of construction of Church Street United Methodist, he published a "Notice to Those Contemplating Building" with this remarkable statement: "will guarantee to give you a better design for less money than any architect in the South."

FIGURE 2-59, Church Street United Methodist Church, 214 Church Street, Photograph by Susan Besser, 2016

Church Street United Methodist Church is built in the Romanesque manner, has a front gable with side tower, and is in the Akron Plan. Built in 1901 the Church Street façade is dominated by a four-story bell tower with a conical copper roof. The first story of the tower features a turret form with a band of stained-glass windows and a rock-faced stone lintel and stone sill. Two stained-glass windows with rock-faced stone lintels and stone sill comprise the second story of the tower. The third story of the tower has a two-part window of diamond panes with a stone archivolt. Narrow slit windows flank the central window. A projecting stone course defines the fourth story of the bell tower. The arcaded fourth story with cushion capitals and stone voussoirs enriches the tower. At the cornice is foliated banding. Arches of rock-faced voussoirs springing from clustered colonettes on rock-faced stone piers dominate the gabled recessed entry into the sanctuary. A large round window with rock-faced voussoirs and keystones is centered within the gable end and flanked by blind slits embellished with rock-faced arches. Courses of rock-faced stone enrich the gable end and incorporate paired arches. A two-story turret is to the south and consists of bands of stained-glass windows with rock-faced stone lintels and sills. An annex was added in 1949 with an addition in 1989. This is the only church that occupies the plot assigned by the Selma Town and Land Company for the major church denominations.

Voeglin-Barker-Smitherman House • 308 Church Street
Constructed 1840 • Thomas Helm Lee, Architect

FIGURE 2-60, Voeglin-Barker-Smitherman House, 308 Church Street, Photograph by Susan Besser, 2002

The Voeglin-Barker-Smitherman House was built by Frederich Voeglin and designed by Thomas Helm Lee. Once part of the Dubose estate, Miss Lucille Edwina Dubose deeded the property to relatives who attended three different churches, Methodist, Episcopalian, and Presbyterian, with the stipulation that the property was not to be sold to "the Baptists." The two-story, five-bay Greek Revival with Italianate influences has a weatherboard exterior and low-pitched hipped roof of standing-seam metal. Eave brackets follow the roofline. The full-width, full-height porch is supported by four square columns.

DuBose Cottage • 309 Church Street
Constructed circa 1895

FIGURE 2-61, DuBose Cottage, 309 Church Street, Photograph by Susan Besser, 2002

The Queen Anne influence is evident in this turreted porch that extends from a hipped-roof porch with lathe-turned columns, spindlework frieze, and balustrades. Queen Anne windows that are large clear panes bounded by multilight stained glass add another distinctive feature to the one-and-one-half-story dwelling. The handsome entry has double doors of large etched glass bounded with multi-panes over an incised carved wood panel. The original owners were James and Alice DuBose. Mack Strong, Manager at Tissier Hardware, and his wife, Houston, lived in this dwelling in the 1920s.

Churchview, Lamar-Henry House • 327 Church Street
Constructed 1893

FIGURE 2-62, Churchview, 327 Church Street,
Photograph by Susan Besser, 2002

Built by brick manufacturer Ernest Lamar in 1893, Churchview is a two-and-one-half-story Queen Anne dominated by a wraparound porch. Originally the house had a turret, which was removed during a renovation early in the twentieth century. The distinctive urn-shaped columns with Ionic capitals were added by the present owners, Ted Henry and his wife, De'be. The irregular plan displays an angled projected bay and a polygonal projection and is typical of high-style Queen Anne houses. A second-story balcony has lathe-turned posts and balustrade. The balcony entry is a glass-over-wood door surmounted by a transom. The cornice is embellished with eave brackets with a pendant drop and alternates with modillions. A rope design belt course creates a division between the first and second stories. The triangular pedimented dormer contains triple windows with stained-glass multilights surrounding a clear pane over one pane.

Lanford-Portis House • 331 Church Street
Constructed 1900

FIGURE 2-63, Lanford-Portis House, 331 Church Street, Photograph by Susan Besser, 2002

Actress Jessica Lange resided in this dwelling while filming *Blue Sky*, a movie that earned her an Academy Award for best actress. This dwelling first appeared on the Sanborn map of 1903. Reason H. Lanford was the original owner of this house. The house changed ownership numerous times over the next thirty years. Miss Richard Rivers Portis and Miss Janie Pruitt purchased the house in 1932 and lived there for fifty years, offering it as a boarding house for schoolteachers. Bill and Penny Jasper were owners from 1988 until 1994, when it was purchased by Aubrey and Sandra Smith. This Queen Anne, two-story frame has six bays with a hipped roof of pressed tin sheet metal and a front gabled bay. A defining characteristic of the Queen Anne is the cutaway bay with incised corner brackets featured on the front gable. The vergeboard in the front gable is incised. A one-story wraparound porch with lathe-turned columns and balusters and spindlework frieze is in keeping with the period.

Williams House • 406 Church Street
Constructed circa 1890

FIGURE 2-64, Williams House, 406 Church Street, Photograph by Susan Besser, 2002

Prominent African American businessman Fred D. Williams, who operated Fred's Flowers, an institution in Selma since the 1970s, resided here for much of his time in Selma. Exhibiting the Folk Victorian style, the one-story, four-bay gable front and wing form with a weatherboard exterior and pressed metal gable roof with brick foundation has two interior brick chimneys. Note the louvered operable shutters with a paterae detail. The inset entry porch has a flat roof with pressed metal shingles, is enriched with eave brackets, and is upheld by cast-iron decorative supports.

411 Church Street • *Constructed circa 1905*

Complimenting the artfully landscaped yard surrounded by a cast-iron fence is an elegant example of Colonial Revival domestic architecture. Influenced by the Centennial celebration of 1876, Americans looked to the classical styles such as the Neoclassical and Greek Revival for inspiration. The welcoming entrance to this wraparound porch features a

FIGURE 2-65, 411 Church Street, Photograph by Susan Besser, 2002

triangular pediment supported by Ionic columns. Note the rounded bay and an angled bay with one-over-one windows flanking the entry and the paneled wainscoting of the façade. A triangular pedimented dormer with pent roof enclosing the gable has a louvered vent. Paired modillions embellish the cornice at the second story and the dormer. A ballroom is located on the third floor.

Caroline and Charles Marshall purchased this property from Carrie Tarver and W. W. Steward in 1899. When Mrs. Marshall died in 1927 the property fell to the heirs who subsequently sold it to Mary Marshall Coffee and Richard Freeman Coffee. Mrs. Coffee's family owned the livery stable C. L. Marshall and Sons.

Bushleigh • 423 Church Street
Constructed 1906

Bushleigh was constructed as a wedding gift to Hattie Lamar by her father, Ernest, in 1905 on her marriage to P. T. Shanks. This two-and-one-half-story Queen Anne brick with three bays and hipped roof with cross gables exemplifies the high style of its period. Dominated by a one-story wraparound porch supported by fluted Ionic columns, the dwelling

FIGURE 2-66, Bushleigh, 423 Church Street,
Photograph by Susan Besser, 2015

illustrates the classic influences of Queen Anne. The entry doors of arched glass lights over wood are surmounted by a transom of diamond-pane glass and flanked by sidelights. To the west of the entry is a tripartite window with engaged columns surmounted by an elliptical fanlight with brick lintel with keystone. This same element is seen above the entry with an added element of an arched, dressed-stone keystone lintel. Notable elements of the Queen Anne are the dormer composed of a large pane of glass surrounded by multilights, two chimney clusters with chimney pots, and front gables enhanced with imbricated shingles. A distinctly classical element are the dressed stone quoins at each corner. Polygonal bays are on the north and south elevation.

Kingston House • 432 Church Street
Constructed 1867

Cotton planter Samuel P. Steele had Kingston House built in the Italianate style two years after the Civil War in 1867. Steele later sold the house to Confederate Captain Joseph Forney Johnston. Johnston was an attorney who had studied at Jacksonville, Alabama, and in 1866 had moved to Selma, where he practiced law for seventeen years. In 1884 he moved to Birmingham, where he was president of the Alabama State Bank and first president of the Sloss Iron and Steel Co. He served as governor of Alabama for two terms and then in the U.S. Senate, succeeding Senator Pettus in 1907 and serving until his death in 1913. Dr. Goldsby King, who in 1896 sponsored the first private hospital in Selma (bearing his name), also resided here.

FIGURE 2-67, Kingston House, 432 Church Street, Photograph by Susan Besser, 2002

Kingston House is a three-bay, two-story Italianate central passage form with low-pitched hipped roof of standing-seam metal with bracketed cornice. The central bay has a four-panel single door with five-light sidelights and broken transom. The entry porch has a scroll-sawn spandrel and chamfered columns and is surmounted by a cast-iron balconet manufactured at the local foundry. The entry displays an etched ruby-glass window and hipped-roof entry porch with four square columns. Angled bays on either side of the central entry enhance the symmetrical balance of the façade and have bracketed window hoods on the first story and bracketed cornices on the second story.

513 Church Street • *Constructed circa 1900*

FIGURE 2-68, 513 Church Street, Photograph by Susan Besser, 2002

The Queen Anne style was very prevalent in Selma, attesting to the fact that the late nineteenth century was a prosperous time. These styles emphasized verticality and wall surfaces rich in detail. This two-and-one-half-story, three-bay Queen Anne dwelling with hipped roof is a textbook example of the Spindlework subtype. The south bay is two stories with cutaway bay windows and gable end with spindlework bargeboard. The central bay has an inset entry porch with spindlework frieze and balustrade and lathe-turned columns. Note the decorative dormer with a gable roof featuring a sunburst design in the gable end. The north bay three-story tower is set at an angle and has a pyramidal roof. Scroll-sawn brackets embellish the cornice of the house and tower.

Lt. John Tillman Melvin resided here before enlisting in the Navy during World War I. Lt. Melvin, an Annapolis graduate and the son of Bishop Melvin, was the first commissioned naval officer to die at the beginning of U.S. involvement in World War I when his ship, the *U.S.S. Alcedo*, was hit with a torpedo by a German submarine on November 5, 1917.

602 Church Street • *Constructed 1885*

FIGURE 2-69, 602 Church Street, Photograph by Susan Besser, 2002

A wraparound porch with chamfered columns and balustrade of lathe-turned balusters graces the façade of this Italianate six-bay, two-story dwelling with a low-pitched hipped roof of standing-seam metal. To the north is an angled bay with two-over-two arched double-hung sash windows and a hipped roof with brackets at the cornice. Paired four-over-four windows on the second story surmount the bay. Directly above the wraparound porch is a balcony with chamfered columns and balustrade. In the 1893 Sanborn map the dwelling appears as a duplex, and it retains the two entrances. Fenestration beneath the porch shows a four-over-four double-hung sash.

Rutledge House • 619 Church Street
Constructed circa 1840

Rutledge House can be traced to the land grant from President Monroe to George Phillips and Williams Rufus King in November of 1823. The house originally sat on two lots, numbers 47 and 48 of what was Parkman's "Tremont Tract." Sarah McKee purchased the property from Mr. and Mrs. B. J. Duncan. This house, which was moved from Cahawba, was placed

FIGURE 2-70, Rutledge House, 619 Church Street, Photograph by Susan Besser, 2002

on the center of the two lots. Before building Ashford on the adjacent lot, Emma Mary Lanford Lee, wife of Julian H. Smith, had the house moved to its present location. Rutledge House is a five-bay, one-story raised cottage central passage form with weatherboard exterior with a side gable roof with cross gable. Eave brackets embellish the cornice while Doric columns grace the full-width porch and support a standing-seam shed roof and wide detailed frieze. Notable interior features are the Greek Revival elements such as "shouldered" door and window trim and wide, heart-pine floors.

Ashford • 627 Church Street
Constructed 1903

City engineer Julian Smith, who served on the state highway commission, built this stately two-and-one-half-story, Neoclassical dwelling. The house was sold in the 1960s and had numerous owners before the Delps purchased the house in 1982. The house was named after the Delps' daughter, Ashley. The central passage form has a grand two-story rounded portico

FIGURE 2-71, Ashford, 627 Church Street,
Photograph by Susan Besser, 2002

with colossal Corinthian columns centered between a wraparound porch supported by paired fluted Ionic columns. The double-door entry with glazing and sidelights surmounted by an elliptical fanlight is flanked by Chicago windows with elliptical fanlights. A wide frieze along the cornice is restrained but elegant, and dressed stone quoins enrich corners of the façade. The balconet with lathe-turned balustrade leads to double doors with sidelights and a leaded-glass fanlight. A porte cochère to the right harkens to the horse-and-buggy days.

Tremont Street

Woolsey-King-Craig House • 413 Tremont Street
Constructed 1880 • Michael J. Miller, Architect

The lot was purchased by Lucinda C. Swift Woolsey, wife of Benjamin Minthorne Woolsey, on January 15, 1880, from Gertrude J. Jones for $2,750. The house was designed by Michael J. Miller, an Englishman, who moved his practice to Florida and did significant work there including El

FIGURE 2-72, Woolsey-King-Craig House, 413 Tremont Street, Photograph by Susan Besser, 2002

Pasaje, also known as the Cherokee Club, a Renaissance Revival building in Tampa.[39] William Swift Woolsey inherited the property upon Mrs. Woolsey's death. The property became rental property after Woolsey's wife died. Joey Dillon restored the house.

The Woolsey-King-Craig House is a two-story Italianate that features many of the defining elements of that period—segmental arched windows flanked by arched louvered shutters and a modillion course along the cornice. Dominating the façade is a pyramidal roofed tower with flared eaves. Note the inset entry porch with Doric columns surmounted by a balustrade.

---

39. *Selma Times*, March 4, 1880.

Kelso Cottage • 509 Tremont Street
Constructed 1866

FIGURE 2-73, Kelso Cottage, 509 Tremont Street, Photograph by Susan Besser, 2015

In 1866 Selma cotton factor and banker H. A. Stollenwerck built Kelso Cottage, an Italianate one-story raised cottage with a full-width porch embellished with scroll-sawn stair rail, balustrade, and porch supports. Eave brackets are detailed with drop pendants. The kitchen wing is a late nineteenth-century addition and includes a breezeway that has been enclosed. This stylistic variation of the Louisiana raised cottage offered nineteenth-century Selmians a respite from the summer heat with increased ventilation, high ceilings, generous porch, and full-length windows. M. J. Williams, a former mayor of Selma, owned the property for a time, as did Mr. and Mrs. Bob Ed Morrow, who purchased the property from Miss Alice Carothers. A guest cottage to the rear was originally quarters for live-in domestic workers. A smokehouse of the late 1860s is also associated with the property.

Strother House • 510 Tremont Street
Constructed 1903

FIGURE 2-74, Strother House, 510 Tremont Street, Photograph by Susan Besser, 2002

The Strother House is a brick two-and-one-half-story, three-bay Queen Anne and was built by Harry Martin Smith, owner of a local brick company. Smith utilized solid brick, making the walls over one foot thick. The exuberance of the period is displayed in the wraparound double-tiered porch with onion dome roof surmounted by a finial. Dwellings of the late Queen Anne period exhibit classic influences, as is evidenced by the Doric columns of the porch. High-style Queen Anne houses tended to abandon the rectilinear forms of Federal and Greek Revival. The Strother House exhibits this in the rounded bay to the east and polygonal bay to the west. A guest house also of the Queen Anne period is located on the property. In the 1940s the house was subdivided into apartments. Claude and Bettie Strother renovated the house in 1985, returning it to a single dwelling.

Tremont High School • 517 Tremont Street
Constructed 1913 • William T. Warren, Architect

FIGURE 2-75, Tremont High School, 517 Tremont Street, Photograph by Susan Besser, 2002

Birmingham architect William T. Warren received an engineering degree from Alabama Polytechnic (Auburn University) in 1897 and a degree in architecture from Columbia University in 1902. After his graduation from Columbia, he joined the New York firm of McKim, Mead & White and stayed until 1906. His design for Tremont High School, a Neoclassical two-story brick structure, features a shaped parapet wall and raised basement. A dramatic inset entry of double-leaf wood-panel doors with diamond-pane transom is flanked by Doric columns and surmounted by an entablature and prominent classical broken pediment with dental course. An interesting detail is the carved stone relief work of an opened book with diploma on the center of the façade. Tremont has the distinction of being the first public high school for whites in Selma and was integrated in the mid-1960s.

Meriwether House • 609 Tremont Street
Constructed circa 1880

FIGURE 2-76, Meriwether House, 609 Tremont Street, Photograph by Susan Besser, 2002

Meriwether House, a Colonial Revival two-and-a-half-story dwelling, was built in the 1880s by Dr. Thomas Pickens Gary, who moved to Selma before 1877. Dr. Gary was in the wholesale grocery and cotton business under the name Gary and Raymond, in operation until 1888. Visitors enter the house through double-leaf wood doors with leaded-glass sidelights surmounted by a broken transom of leaded glass. Note the wraparound porch with polygonal bay supported by Ionic columns. A hallmark of the style is the Palladian window located here in the dormer, which is also detailed with imbricated shingles and a dentil course along the cornice and cornice return.

618 Tremont Street • Constructed circa 1880

FIGURE 2-77, 618 Tremont Street, Photograph by Susan Besser, 2002

This L-shaped one-story dwelling has elements of the Italianate such as the arched windows with hood molds, arched porch supports, and squared bay. A vergeboard, flat cut balustrade, decorative frieze along the porch, brackets, and drop pendants are typical of Folk Victorian detailing. The handsome entry displays double-leaf doors with raised panels, multi-pane sidelights, and an elliptical fanlight.

Mabry-Jones House • 629 Tremont Street
Constructed circa 1830

Dr. A. G. Mabry built this dwelling, which evolved from a Federal style to the Greek Revival style. Mabry was a leader in the establishment of a state mental hospital and raising awareness of mental illness.[40] Mabry's stepdaughter married Captain Catesby ap R. Jones, the Confederate naval officer who was in charge of the foundry. Captain Jones contributed to the design of the ironclad *C.S.S. Virginia*, or *C.S.S. Merrimac* as she was also

---

40. Robert Gamble, *The Alabama Catalog: Historic American Buildings Survey: A Guide to the Early Architecture of the State* (University of Alabama Press, 1987), 222.

known. Captain Jones commanded the *Merrimac* in its famous Civil War naval battle with the *U.S.S. Monitor*. After the war, Captain Jones returned to Selma and became a manufacturer of cast-iron stairways and decorative ironwork. The dwelling remains in the Jones family.

FIGURE 2-78, Mabry-Jones House, 629 Tremont Street, Library of Congress

The Historic American Building Survey (HABS), which began as a New Deal initiative in 1933, recorded the Mabry-Jones House. It is a two-story, five-bay brick dwelling, portions of which can be traced to the Federal period. In 1850 the Greek Revival temple tetrastyle portico with fluted Doric columns was added. The primary entry has a four-panel single door with sidelights and broken transom. The second-level balcony is enriched with a geometric patterned cast-iron balustrade. The shed roof porch to the south of the façade has cast-iron porch supports.

630 Tremont Street • *Constructed circa 1880*

FIGURE 2-79, 630 Tremont Street, Photograph by Susan Besser, 2002

This Italianate L-plan form features double-leaf wood-paneled doors with sidelights and an elliptical fanlight. Note the projecting bay surmounted by a bracketed hood featuring arched windows, a defining element of the Italianate. In the 1910s Frank and Nell Bates resided here. Mr. Bates was a traveling salesman.

Converse-Jackson House • 700 Tremont Street
Constructed 1955

FIGURE 2-80, Converse-Jackson House, 700 Tremont Street, Photograph by Susan Besser, 2002

Converse House is a one-story Colonial Revival with six-over-nine windows topped with keystone lentils. The entry porch is detailed with a dentil course and supported by Ionic columns. The house that originally occupied this lot was owned by Confederate Colonel N. H. R. Dawson and his wife. Col. Dawson was the U.S. commissioner of education under President Cleveland. His third wife, Elodie B. Todd, was half-sister of Mary Todd Lincoln, the wife of President Abraham Lincoln. Note the ornately carved doors, sidelights, and transom that were incorporated into the house from the Dawson house. The Converses were descendants of Captain Catesby ap R. Jones.

FIGURE 2-81, Doors from Historic Dawson House, HABS, Library of Congress

703 Tremont Street • *Constructed circa 1845*

FIGURE 2-82, 703 Tremont Street, Photograph by Susan Besser, 2002

Located at the corner of Tremont and McLeod is a two-story Italianate with full-height arched windows flanked with the original arched operable louvered shutters. Note the eave brackets embellished with drop pendants along the cornice of the second story and porch. A full-width porch supported by chamfered columns and embellished with lathe-turned balustrade leads to a handsome arched double-leaf wood door. Local historians believe this dwelling was the original governor's mansion in Cahawba.

Wilkinson-Lovelady House • 709 Tremont Street
Constructed 1912

Mary Quitman Waller Wilkinson obtained the lot in 1908 from A. L. McLeod and his wife, Bessie Hails McLeod, and Joseph Edgar Wilkinson, Wilkinson's husband. Mr. Wilkinson and Mr. McLeod were prominent Selma attorneys. Elizabeth W. Lollar, daughter of the Wilkinsons, occupied the house with her husband, Colonel William H. Lollar, until his death in 1987, when it was sold to Ed and Wanda Bass. Dayton and Dorothy Lovelady purchased the house in 1990 and continued the restoration process that began with the Bass family.

FIGURE 2-83, Wilkinson-Lovelady House, 709 Tremont Street, Photograph by Susan Besser, 2002

The Wilkinson-Lovelady House is a distinctive two-story painted-brick Neoclassical with Italian Renaissance influences such as the tiled roof with wide overhanging eaves. Graceful stone steps lead to the elegant, rounded two-story portico that features soaring Ionic fluted columns resting on square stone bases. The welcoming entry is composed of a single leaded-glass door with leaded-glass sidelights and leaded-glass transom. The second-story balcony with wood balustrade is supported by the Ionic columns. Note details such as the denticulated portico, stone lintels, and stone string course.

John Tyler Morgan House, NRHP 1972 • 719 Tremont Street
Constructed circa 1859

Known as the John Tyler Morgan House after a former Confederate general and prominent U.S. senator from 1877 to 1907, the residence was purchased in 1865 from Thomas Wetmore, the original owner. Wetmore was the Confederate provost marshal of Selma. John Tyler Morgan was originally from Tennessee, moving to Alabama in 1824 with his family.

FIGURE 2-84, John Tyler Morgan House, 719 Tremont Street, HABS, Library of Congress

He did not attend college but at the age of twenty passed the Bar exam and practiced law with his brother-in-law William Parish Chilton. As senator, Morgan was influential in promoting the Panama Canal. He was very vocal regarding the treatment of seals in the Bering Sea because he felt they would become extinct. J. Graham Melvin, vice-president of the Selma National Bank, resided here during the 1930s.

The Greek Revival dwelling has a triangular pedimented entry porch that projects from the two-story porch supported by square columns. The projecting angled entry displays double-leaf four-panel doors with sidelights and transom flanked by pilasters and full-height angled six-over-nine windows with cornice lentils. The second-story entrance also has double-leaf doors with sidelights and transoms, with a window configuration of six-over-six, and features a diamond-patterned cast-iron balcony. The HABS project documented the house in 1934.

801 Tremont Street • *Construction circa 1890*

FIGURE 2-85, 801 Tremont Street, Photograph by Susan Besser, 2002

This charming Queen Anne L-shaped cottage is notable for the wraparound porch with elaborate spindlework trim within the frieze, lathe-turned columns, and eave brackets featuring pendant drops. One of the key elements of Queen Anne is the cutaway bay incorporated into the front gable of the L-shape and enhanced with corner brackets. The double-leaf entry features stained-glass panels and stained-glass transom and is flanked by paneled stiles.

809 Tremont Street • *Constructed circa 1875*

FIGURE 2-86, 809 Tremont Street, Photograph by Susan Besser, 2002

This singular Italianate two-story, five-bay frame façade exhibits superb details such as bracketed hoods over the two-over-two windows, bracketed capitals above the chamfered porch columns of the attached inset porch, and the typical eave brackets of the Italianate style. Note the through-cornice shaped parapet.

Furniss Avenue

507 Furniss Avenue • *Constructed circa 1907*

FIGURE 2-87, 507 Furniss Avenue, Photograph by Susan Besser, 2002

This Colonial Revival building is a one-story, five-bay central passage form with weatherboard exterior, hipped roof, and brick foundation. Stone steps lead to the elegant porch, which has a rounded entrance portico and is supported by eight Doric columns. The balustrade of turned balusters follows the roofline of the porch. Typical of this era is the entrance, which features a wood door with glazing surrounded by sidelights and broken transom. Windows are two-over-two double-hung wood sash, surmounted by cornice lintels and flanked by louvered shutters. The decorative front gable dormer has a Palladian window. A garage of the period is associated with the property.

Portis Welch, a local cotton merchant, built this house in 1906 on property that was part of Fairoaks, now Henderson House. Edgar L. Ratliff and his wife, Christine, purchased the house in 1934. They remained in the house until 1941, when it was sold to Cecil and Louise Morgan. The Morgans lived in the house for over fifty years. In 1996 the house became part of the Henderson House/Fairoaks complex.

608 Furniss Avenue • *Constructed circa 1840*

This Colonial Revival one-story stucco house composed of load-bearing brick has a side gable roof. Note the double cross gables. A broken transom surmounts a single wood-panel door flanked by sidelights. The gable ends are enclosed by a pent roof and embellished by variegated shingles and louvered vent. Doric columns support the front inset porch and side porch. It is believed it was built by the Saffold Family and dates to the mid-nineteenth century. The Saffold Family was one of the early families in Selma. Their plantation house, Belvoir, which is still extant, is located in Pleasant Hill. The Furniss Avenue house appears on the 1887 perspective map of Selma.

FIGURE 2-88, 608 Furniss Avenue, Photograph by Bill Tomey, 2024

Judge Benjamin Franklin Saffold, a Civil War veteran, was born in 1826 and was an Alabama judge, mayor of Selma, and state senator. His son, Lt. Ray P. Saffold Sr., served in World War I. He was one of the eighteen Dallas County natives who are buried in the Suresnes American Cemetery in France.

Mabry Street

Roselyn • 25 Mabry Street
Constructed circa 1945

FIGURE 2-89, Roselyn, 25 Mabry Street, Photograph by Susan Besser, 2002

Roselyn characterizes the type of apartment building constructed after World War II and is a Colonial Revival two-story, seven-bay brick veneer apartment complex with a hipped roof and centered gable. The symmetrical façade has a centrally located six-panel door flanked by pilasters surmounted with an entablature and a wrought-iron balconet. An arched sash window is located above the entry and has radiating voussoirs with keystones. Six-over-six double-hung windows are to the north and south on the first and second stories. Integral porches with wrought-iron balustrades are to the north and south. Entries to the porches are to the east and west. Triangular pedimented dormers with louvered vents flank the centered gable.

Old Dallas Male and Female Academy • 114 Mabry Street
Constructed circa 1844

FIGURE 2-90, Old Dallas Male and Female Academy, 114 Mabry Street, Photograph by Susan Besser, 2002

The school had its genesis with the Ladies Educational Society of Selma and was chartered by the General Assembly of the State in 1839. William Johnson donated the lot to the society. The Masonic fraternity used the second story, and the school used the first floor until such time as the school outgrew the space. As the student population continued to grow a separate building for girls was constructed at the corner of Selma and Church. Professor L. B. Johnson and his wife, Harriet, were the instructors. In 1851 Professor and Mrs. Johnson were asked to start a school in Camden, Alabama. In their absence the Rev. A. R. Holcomb operated the school; however, the enrollment declined and thus income decreased. The trustees were forced to sell the building to Col. P. J. Weaver. In 1853 the Johnsons returned to Selma, but Professor Johnson contracted yellow fever and died. The institution continued until 1864 under the tutelage of Mrs. Johnson, operating the institution as the Dallas Female Academy.

Dr. Mallory Reeves and his brother, attorney Archie Reeves, gave the former Dallas Male and Female Academy to the Selma-Dallas County Preservation Society. Randy Malone purchased the building from the Society in the late 1990s and restored it to the original Federal style. He donated it to the Selma-Dallas County Preservation Society in 1999. Non-contributing porches were removed, as was the skim coat of plaster. In the process of the restoration, it was discovered the entry faced Alabama Avenue. Doors on the Mabry Street entrance were originally windows. This two-story Federal has a central passage form, four bays, and a single-leaf entry door with sidelights and transom. Note the sixteen-over-twelve pane windows indicative of the Federal era. The gable front entry porch has square Doric-style columns.

117 Mabry Street • *Constructed circa 1924*
John W. McKeil, Architect

FIGURE 2-91, 117 Mabry Street, Photograph by Susan Besser, 2021

This Colonial Revival, designed by John W. McKeil, is a one-story four-bay with stucco exterior. The entry porch with flat roof has paired fluted Doric columns leading to a paneled wood door entrance with multi-pane lights surmounted by a transom. Wide overhanging eaves display exposed rafters.

321 Mabry Street • *Constructed circa 1868; second story added 1886*

FIGURE 2-92, 321 Mabry Street, Photograph by Susan Besser, 2002

Samuel Freeman Hobbs, a prominent local jeweler, conveyed this lot to his brother, Edward Henry Hobbs. In 1868 Edward had a cottage built on the property. He and his wife had four children. Shortly after the birth of the fourth child, Edward Hobbs Jr., his wife died. S. F. Hobbs and his wife, Frances John Hobbs, adopted Edward. The house was enlarged in 1886, adding a second story. Mrs. Hobbs, who had been childless, at the age of forty-four had a son, Samuel Francis Hobbs, who became a U.S. congressman. Samuel Freeman Hobbs died in 1889, and two years later Edward Henry Hobbs married Frances. This Queen Anne two-story, four-bay dwelling has an inset porch with a hipped roof supported by square columns set on brick piers, which suggests the porch was remodeled circa 1910 to reflect Craftsman influences. Typical of this era are the single wood door with glazing and a segmental arched transomed entrance. The west bay has a gable front with clipped gable detail. The first story has paired, two-over-two segmental arched windows. The gable end is embellished with a multi-pane window with spindlework detail.

Phillips-Hobbs-Joyce House • 329 Mabry Street
Constructed 1837

FIGURE 2-93, Phillips-Hobbs-Joyce House, 329 Mabry Street, Photograph by Frances Benjamin Johnston, Library of Congress, 1939

The Phillips-Hobbs-Joyce House was built in 1837 by Dr. William S. Phillips, son of one of the founders of the Selma Land Company. Originally, Dr. Phillips's office was in the rear along with a detached kitchen that was later connected to the house. Samuel Freeman Hobbs, a native of Maine, purchased the house from an advertisement in the newspaper and later moved to Selma; soon after, he married Frances John. Frances Hobbs is associated with one of the town's many Civil War legends: she saved the jewels from the family's jewelry store by sewing them into her large petticoat. When Union soldiers ordered them to open the business safe, they found only inexpensive pieces. The soldiers never discovered the hiding place for the precious stones. The couple's only child, U.S. Congressman Samuel Francis Hobbs, and his wife, Sarah Ellen Green Hobbs, inherited the house and lived there until the 1950s. The house was inherited by Rosa

Miller Hobbs Joyce in 1956, and she and her husband, John Joyce, raised five children in the house, ultimately selling the house in 2005 to Mr. and Mrs. William Gamble.

This Greek Revival one-story, five-bay dwelling with hipped roof of standing-seam metal has an entry porch with stairs to either side leading to a four-panel door with sidelights and transom surmounted by an entablature. Four square columns with a hipped roof porch form a handsome porch. Six-over-six windows with louvered shutters are to the east and west of the entry. A lateral side gabled wing is to the rear and has a flat-roof porch supported by square columns and a roof of standing-seam metal.

330 Mabry Street • *Constructed circa 1873*

FIGURE 2-94, 330 Mabry Street, Photograph by Susan Besser, 2002

George Waller built this dwelling in 1873, but it is known locally as Miss Ruth May's house, for a beloved Selma teacher who resided there for many years. In 1973 John and Marienne Thomas purchased the house, which needed repairs and updating, and brought it back to its former glory. Subsequent owners have been Herbert Shuptrine and the Glenn Browns, who made additional improvements. This one-story, three-bay gable front and wing Italianate cottage has an inset porch with bracketed chamfered columns and flat-cut balustrade. Note the denticulated cornice of the angled bay window to the south and the use of segmental arched windows. A single-leaf door with segmental arch transom defines the entry.

403 Mabry Street • *Constructed circa 1893*

FIGURE 2-95, 403 Mabry Street, Photograph by Susan Besser, 2002

In 1893, Walter Roland Jordan built this house on land that had been in the family since 1837. The property passed to his son, Augustus Fletcher Jordan, who subsequently conveyed the property to Elizabeth Fairfax Lassiter in 1940. The property passed through several owners before it was purchased and restored by Ray and Judi Eggert. This Queen Anne one-story, four-bay cottage has a wraparound porch with a spindlework frieze, spindlework balustrade, and lathe-turned columns that enhances the façade and leads to a single wood door with glazing and transom surrounded by panel stiles. The west bay has a front gable and cutaway bays with corner brackets. A two-over-two window is in the gable front and the northwest cutaway bay. The gable ends are embellished with imbricated shingles, a vergeboard, and a louvered vent.

409 Mabry Street • *Constructed circa 1890*

FIGURE 2-96, 409 Mabry Street, Photograph by Susan Besser, 2002

This Queen Anne one-story, four-bay cottage has a hipped roof with cross gables. An inset porch with a spindlework frieze, flat-cut balustrade, and lathe-turned columns enhances the façade and leads to a single wood door with glazing and transom surrounded by panel stiles. The west bay has a front gable and cutaway bays with corner brackets. The gable end is enriched with imbricated shingles, a vergeboard, and a louvered vent.

Swift-Gamble House • 410 Mabry Street
Constructed circa 1850

FIGURE 2-97, Swift-Gamble House, 410 Mabry Street, Photograph by Bill Tomey, 2024

The Swift-Gamble House is a one-story, five-bay Greek Revival with a hipped roof with cross gable that pierces the roof and is embellished with imbricated shingles, circa 1890. Flush board exterior defines the entry and multi-panel French doors. A single-door entry with glazing and sidelights is surmounted by a transom. The full-width integral porch with square Doric columns is indicative of the Greek Revival period. Druggist George Swift and his wife resided here in the 1910s and 1920s.

415 Mabry Street • *Constructed circa 1890*

FIGURE 2-98, 415 Mabry Street, Photograph by Susan Besser, 2022

This Queen Anne one-story, five-bay dwelling has a hipped roof with cross gable of pressed metal shingles. A wraparound porch with a spindle-work frieze, turned balusters, and lathe-turned bracketed columns leads to a single wood door with glazing and transom surrounded by paneled stiles. The cross-gable end is enriched with fish-scale shingles and paired multi-pane windows with arched louvered vent.

423 Mabry Street • *Constructed circa 1893*

Benie G. Callen purchased the lot for this house from Walter Roland Jordan and Kate Menla Wood Jordan in 1893, building the house circa 1893–1894. In February of 1918 it was sold to Helen N. Grayson, who in turn sold it to local grocer Henry Herman Schiel. The Schiel family retained the property until the 1970s. Mr. and Mrs. Lloyd Park purchased the property in the 1980s and began a restoration process. The Anthony Sanfilippo family and Mark Singletary continued this process. Aaron Lerner purchased the house from the Singletarys.

FIGURE 2-99, 423 Mabry Street, Photograph by Susan Besser, 2002

A charming white picket fence leads to this Queen Anne one-story, four-bay dwelling that has a hipped roof with cross gables of pressed metal shingles. A full-width porch with a spindlework frieze, flat-cut balustrade, and lathe-turned columns enhances the façade and leads to a single wood door with glazing and transom surrounded by panel stiles. The west bay has a front gable and cutaway bays with spindlework brackets. The gable end is enriched with imbricated shingles and a vergeboard.

430 Mabry Street • *Constructed circa 1854*

FIGURE 2-100, 430 Mabry Street, Photograph by Susan Besser, 2002

This unique one-story, four-bay Italianate has stucco over load-bearing brick exterior and retains the original chimney pots. A broken segmental arched transom surmounts a single-door entry with arched panels and three-pane sidelights. Double-hung camber windows to the south of the entry are four-over-four pane and are flanked by operable louvered shutters. A dentil course follows along the cornice of the inset porch enhanced with bracket capitals on lathe-turned columns resting on paneled wood bases. The front gable has two camber windows and is embellished with masonry detailing topped with large eave brackets and dentil molding along the cornice.

431 Mabry Street
Constructed circa 1875; addition circa 1890–1910; kitchen and breakfast room addition/conversion 1980

This house was built originally as a front-gabled side-hall plan with two rooms on the first story and two rooms on the second story. The rooms to the north are original. Circa 1890–1910 four rooms were added to the south. In 1980 the back porch was enclosed and converted to a kitchen.

The original kitchen was connected and converted into a breakfast room. The lot was originally twice the size. Eugene Robbins sold half the lot to his brother in 1885. That portion of the lot is associated with the former Dunn Nursing Home. In 1889 Eugene Robbins sold the house and lot to Gertrude Jones. Ms. Jones was the daughter of Dr. Mabry and widow of Captain Catesby ap Roger Jones. T. J. Rowell and Louis Rowell, mayor of Selma in the 1920s, purchased the house in 1900. The Rowells' heirs conveyed the house to Sonny and Betty Edwards in 1976. In 1993, Mike and Lori Hungerpiller purchased the house from the Edwardses.

FIGURE 2-101, 431 Mabry Street, Photograph by Susan Besser, 2002

This two-story, five-bay dwelling has a front gable roof of standing-seam metal. Paneled square columns support a full-width porch with hipped roof. A triangular pedimented entry portico leads to the single-wood-door entry. The incised carved wood door with glazing is surmounted by a segmental arched transom. To the east and west are two-over-two segmental arched windows. A single door with two-pane segmental arched transom creates an entry to the gable-roofed balcony with a solid weatherboard balustrade and paneled square columns.

500 Mabry Street • *Constructed circa 1860; porch addition circa 1925*

FIGURE 2-102, 500 Mabry Street, Photograph by Susan Besser, 2002

Built circa 1860, this one-story, three-bay, hipped roof cross-gabled dwelling with flush board façade retains the original entry—a handsome single-panel wood door with glazing surrounded by four-pane sidelights, six-pane transom, and shouldered door surround indicative of the Greek Revival. The dwelling gives a nod to the Queen Anne period with the imbricated shingles in the gable end. Circa 1925 a full-width Craftsman porch was added with tapered paneled columns resting on brick piers and a solid brick balustrade with decorative brickwork. Rufus Hogg, conductor of the Southern Railway, and his wife, Geneva, resided here in the 1910s.

King Memorial Hospital/Dunn Nursing Home • 515 Mabry Street
Constructed circa 1884; addition 1932
Frank Lockwood, Architect, addition

Dr. Goldsby King sponsored the Goldsby King Hospital, the first private hospital in Selma, in 1896. Dr. King received his training at the Medical College of Charleston and Johns Hopkins Hospital. Starting from a Queen Anne dwelling, King made additions to the house in the Neoclassical style. It is noted in the *Selma Times-Journal* that Frank Lockwood completed plans for the addition in 1932 that were valued at $60,000.[41] The institution was designated King Memorial Hospital on King's death and maintained operations as a hospital until 1953. Also known subsequently as Dunn Nursing Home, it is associated with the Civil Rights Movement. Charles Dunn fired Annie Lee Cooper and Elnora Collins for attempting to register to vote. Dunn tried to prevent Elnora Collins from getting a new position, with the end result of the entire staff of Dunn Nursing Home resigning in protest. Amelia Boynton stepped in to help the nurses by asking for a sewing machine from the SNCC organization so the women could sew as a way to make up for the lost income.[42]

FIGURE 2-103, King Memorial Hospital/Dunn Nursing Home, 515 Mabry Street, Photograph by Susan Besser, 2002

The building is a two-story, yellow-brick edifice of irregular shape built in the Neoclassical style. A monumental triangular pedimented two-story portico with denticulated cornice, wide entablature, and fluted Doric

---

41. "Local Hospital Plans Addition," *Selma Times-Journal*, September 20, 1932.

42. West et al., "Civil Rights Movement in Selma," 36.

columns projects a handsome entrance. Double plate-glass doors with transom, circa 1950, provide the primary entry. Windows are jalousie five-light configuration and double-hung one-over-one configuration. The façade is enriched with a glazed terra-cotta lintel course and belt course on the first and second stories. A one-story porch with turreted extension is to the north. To the rear are elements of the Queen Anne house that served as the original building.

520 Mabry Street • *Constructed circa 1890; porch alterations circa 1930*

FIGURE 2-104, 520 Mabry Street, Photograph by Susan Besser, 2002

Built circa 1890, this one-story Queen Anne five-bay has a hipped roof with cross gables covered with pressed metal shingles. Alterations to the original wraparound porch, circa 1930, were made to add additional interior space to the east portion of the porch and to reflect a variation of the Craftsman style. Doric columns on brick piers support the full-width porch with entry portico. A single wood door with glazing, beveled and leaded-glass sidelights, and beveled and leaded-glass broken transom provide the handsome entry.

530 Mabry Street • *Constructed circa 1875; porch alterations circa 1920*

FIGURE 2-105, 530 Mabry Street, Photograph by Susan Besser, 2002

A wraparound porch supported by Ionic fluted columns on rock-faced concrete block piers dominates the façade of this one-and-one-half-story Colonial Revival built circa 1875. Modifications such as the concrete block piers, circa 1920, gave the traditional Colonial Revival an Arts and Crafts appearance.

620 Mabry Street • *Constructed circa 1895*

This handsome two-and-one-half-story Queen Anne–style dwelling was built by Georgiana Baker Howard and Isaac Baker Howard, the lot having been purchased in January of 1891 from the heirs of Dr. Albert G. Mabry. Their daughter Mary Howard Raiford inherited the house. Mrs. Raiford and her husband, Frazier Titus Raiford, owned and published *The Selma Times-Journal* for a number of years. After Frazier's death in 1936, Mary oversaw the publishing of the *Journal* for another twenty-three years. Mary was one of the original members of the Selma Suffragette Association.

FIGURE 2-106, 620 Mabry Street, Photograph by Susan Besser, 2002

The Queen Anne influence is evidenced in the spindlework detailing the balustrade and frieze of the inset entry porch as well as the lathe-turned columns with bracket capitals. A modillion course follows the cornice and eave brackets embellish the frieze. Unique to this Queen Anne are the bull's eye panels in the gable end of the entry porch. On the south side of the dwelling is a tiered porch featuring spindlework detail in the balustrade and frieze.

Gillis House • 623 Mabry Street
Constructed circa 1850

Gillis House is a one-story central-passage Greek Revival with Italianate porch. Flanked by full-height operable louvered shutters, the double-hung windows have six-over-six windows with jib doors. The ornamental flat-cut balustrade and porch supports embellish the shed roof porch.

Selma artist Crawford Gillis resided here and took art lessons from Minnie Kent Fowlkes. He studied in New York at the National Academy of Design and became familiar with the work of the Mexican Muralist

FIGURE 2-107, Gillis House, 623 Mabry Street, Photograph by Frances Benjamin Johnston, Library of Congress

movement, which was based on Socialist ideals. His paintings can be categorized as those of the social realist who depicts subjects in a realist manner.[43] The Gillis House was moved to its present location in 1985 from Washington Street.[44]

628 Mabry Street • *Constructed circa 1900*

This dwelling at 628 Mabry was built between 1898 and 1903 and was owned by the Mabry family, for whom the street is named. The one-story Folk Victorian has a hipped roof with cross gable and retains the original pressed metal shingles. Typical of the style is the imbrication in the gable end. Chamfered columns support the primary porch and secondary porch, both of which have flat-cut balustrades. G. Crawford Phillips, a

---

43. "Gillis, Crawford (1914–2000)," The Johnson Collection, https://thejohnsoncollection.org/crawford-gillis/.

44. "Historic Gillis House Finally Moved to Mabry Street Site," *Selma Times-Journal*, October 16, 1985, 12.

FIGURE 2-108, 628 Mabry Street, Photograph by Susan Besser, 2021

Dallas County tax collector, and his wife, Florence, resided here in the 1910s and 1920s.

704 Mabry Street • *Constructed 1916*

FIGURE 2-109, 704 Mabry Street, Photograph by Susan Besser, 2002

This home in the Prairie style, associated with the early houses of Frank Lloyd Wright, is one of the true American house types. This is an excellent example of the style and is solid brick, three layers thick. Built in the Foursquare form, it is two-and-one-half stories with a full-width porch supported by brick columns that are embellished with bracket capitals. The wide overhanging eaves and porch would make this an ideal house form to combat the heat of the Deep South. Note the bracket capitals at the cornice and the porte cochère to the north. Dr. James S. Chisolm bought the property in 1912 and completed the dwelling in 1916. In the 1940s, the Chisolm family added the porte cochère and a side deck and exterior stairs to create an apartment. The house remained with the Chisolm family until 1992.

Atkins-Ratcliffe-Gray House • 710 Mabry Street
Constructed circa 1916; alterations 1950s

FIGURE 2-110, Atkins-Ratcliffe-Gray House, 710 Mabry Street, Photograph by Susan Besser, 2014

This unique two-story, brick, hipped-roof dwelling has a full-width shed porch with brick arches that lead to two sets of French doors. A. J.

Martin Atkins had the house built, and it remained in the Atkins family until it was sold as part of the estate of Mrs. Carrie W. Atkins. The original house was a one-story frame house and was renovated to its present-day configuration in the late 1950s. The second owner, Jeff Ratcliffe, was a local druggist with Pilcher-McBride Drug Co.

Sturdivant Hall, NRHP 1972 • 713 Mabry Street
Constructed 1852–1856 • Thomas Helm Lee, Architect

FIGURE 2-111, Sturdivant Hall, 713 Mabry Street, Photograph by Bill Tomey, 2024

Sturdivant Hall is of the Greek Revival style and was designed by Kentucky native architect Thomas Helm Lee, a master builder and son of Miller Lee of Buckingham County, Virginia, brother of Lighthorse Harry Lee. Thomas Helm Lee was the owner of an early Selma lumberyard. He married Mary Janes Blanks of Cahawba in 1839 and died in 1857 and is buried in Old Live Oak Cemetery. Also credited to him is the circa 1857 Church Street Methodist Church, no longer extant.

The original owners of Sturdivant Hall were the Edward T. Watts family, who built the house at a cost of $69,000. It is believed to have survived the Civil War due to the fact that the half-sister of Mary Todd Lincoln lived nearby in White Force Cottage.[45] Watts sold the property to John McGee Parkman in 1864. Parkman was president of the First National Bank of Selma and was arrested during Reconstruction as the bank was involved in speculating in cotton futures. Parkman was taken to Cahawba Federal Prison, leaving his young wife and two children. His friends planned a daring escape; they would rescue him and transport him by boat. Unfortunately, he died during the escape, either from a possible gunshot wound or by drowning in the Alabama River.

FIGURE 2-112, Sturdivant Hall, Interior, Photograph by Carol Highsmith, Library of Congress, 2010

Emile Gillman, a Selma merchant, purchased the house in 1867 for $12,500, and it remained in the Gillman family until 1957. At that time, it was sold to the City of Selma and Dallas County for $75,000. The estate of Robert Daniel Sturdivant provided $50,000 of the amount and the

---

45. Jennifer Hale, *Historic Plantations of Alabama's Black Belt* (Charleston, SC: History Press, 2009), 86.

building was named in his honor. The Sturdivant Museum Association maintains the collections of valuable antiques and Native American artifacts bequeathed to the City of Selma by Sturdivant.

Sturdivant Hall is considered to be one of the finest examples of antebellum architecture in the State of Alabama. A monumental hexastyle portico of Corinthian columns on stone bases dominates the façade and leads to double-leaf four-panel doors flanked by Doric columns with sidelights and surmounted by a broken six-pane transom. The capital is a simplified version of the Greek Corinthian noted as the Tower of the Winds order as it has a row of acanthus leaves below a row of palm leaves and a square abacus. The denticulated cornice is surmounted by a commanding cymatium. Full-height louvered shutters flank double-hung windows over jib doors. A distinctive hipped-roof belvedere is enriched with eave brackets and paired windows. A wrought-iron balustrade embellishes the balcony accessible from the four-panel wood door flanked by Doric columns with sidelights and surmounted by a broken transom. Thomas Lee brought craftsmen from Italy to execute the plaster and marble designs of the interior. The ironwork was produced at the local Selma Foundry.[46]

FIGURE 2-113, Sturdivant Hall, Slave Quarters, Photograph by Susan Besser, 2022

---

46. Hale, *Historic Plantations of Alabama's Black Belt*, 85.

Accessory buildings dating to the antebellum period are extant and include a kitchen with slave quarters on the second floor, smoke house, carriage house, and overseer's office.

The kitchen is a two-story brick building with a standing-seam hip roof and dentil molding along the eave line. Three sets of double doors lead to the kitchen. The second-story fenestration is composed of three double-hung sash windows of six-over-six configuration flanked by operable shutters. The smokehouse is a two-story brick building with hip roof of standing-seam metal and has three sets of doors, each serving a different function—smokehouse, root cellar, and storage. The carriage house is a frame one-story building with a side gable roof and two sets of carriage doors. The overseer's office has brick steps that lead to a single-leaf wood door with transom above. A shallow hip roof bracketed overdoor shelters the entrance. Brick-relieving arches surmount the door and windows of six-over-six configuration.

Fitts Cottage • 715 Mabry Street
Constructed circa 1840

FIGURE 2-114, Fitts Cottage, 715 Mabry Street, Photograph by Susan Besser, 2002

Fitts Cottage was used as a pharmacy and physician's office and was originally located on a plantation near Uniontown. It is a one-story front gable Greek Revival with flush board façade and weatherboard on the north, south, and west elevations. The simple cornice is embellished with dentil molding. A door with two vertical panels creates the entrance. Four Doric square columns stand symmetrically along the original full-width wood porch with Doric pilasters at each corner of the façade.

802 Mabry Street • *Constructed circa 1890*

FIGURE 2-115, 802 Mabry Street, Photograph by Susan Besser, 2002

The hipped roof with cross-gable form is typical of the Queen Anne style. Note the stained-glass transom in the cutaway bay as well as the vergeboard and imbricated shingles of the gable ends of this Spindlework subtype. The wraparound porch displays spindlework frieze and balustrade and bracket capitals on lathe-turned porch supports. A single-leaf door of stained glass with transom is surrounded by paneled stiles.

White Force Cottage • 811 Mabry Street
Constructed 1859

C. S. and Martha Todd White built this Italianate cottage. Martha Todd White was a Confederate supporter and also the half-sister of Mary

FIGURE 2-116, White Force Cottage, 811 Mabry Street, Photograph by Susan Besser, 2002

Todd Lincoln. White achieved notoriety from the Northern press when she used her position to get supplies and medicine behind enemy lines. In 1869, Dr. Charles F. Force, son of historian Peter Force, purchased the house. After his death his wife, Mary Matthews Force, became one of the first postmistresses of Selma. She and their daughter, Mary Force, resided here until their deaths. White Force Cottage is an exquisite one-story, five-bay Italianate with hipped roof with center gable. Operable louvered shutters flank the six-over-six windows. Eave brackets with drop pendants follow the cornice line and are indicative of the Italianate period. An arched frieze and squared Doric columns support the full-width porch. The four-panel wood door is flanked with sidelights and broken transom.

814 Mabry Street • *Constructed circa 1890*

The Queen Anne style assumed many forms, this dwelling being of the Free Classic owing to the wraparound porch supported by Ionic columns and Ionic pilaster at the corner. Note the sunburst design above the entry portico and entrance comprised of double-leaf doors with leaded glass,

FIGURE 2-117, 814 Mabry Street, Photograph by Susan Besser, 2002

sidelights, and transom. A second entrance is to the south. The one-over-one jib windows would have offered a respite from the summer heat. Mr. and Mrs. Roger ap C. Jones resided here in the 1920s. Mr. Jones was President of Mabry Security Company.

901 Mabry Street • *Constructed circa 1900*

FIGURE 2-118, 901 Mabry Street, Photograph by Susan Besser, 2015

This grand two-and-one-half-story Queen Anne Spindlework residence features a wood-paneled entry with sidelights and transom, attached inset porch with spindlework frieze, and turned balusters supported with turned columns. The second story is embellished with balconet with turned balusters and spindlework frieze. Gable ends with fish-scale shingles and spindlework vergeboard define the essence of the style.

Blake-Gantt House • 911 Mabry Street
Constructed circa 1856–1861

FIGURE 2-119, Blake-Gantt House, 911 Mabry Street, Photograph by Frances Benjamin Johnston, Library of Congress

Samuel R. Blake, a Selma lawyer and state senator, built Blake-Gantt House before the onset of the Civil War. The ladies of Selma prepared bandages for Confederate soldiers in the dwelling. Local historians purport the house was pierced by a cannonball during the Battle of Selma, but no one was injured. In 1948 Mr. and Mrs. L. S. Gantt bought the house. The Gantts owned the house for fifty years and Ruth Gantt ran a private school in a separate structure. The one-story Italianate vernacular side gable with center gable solid-brick residence has camber windows with segmental arched lintels flanked by louvered shutters. The entry porch has a cast-iron balustrade and cast-iron porch supports.

J. L. Chestnut Boulevard

Gantt School • J. L. Chestnut Boulevard

FIGURE 2-120, Gantt School, J. L. Chestnut Boulevard, Photograph by Susan Besser, 2002

Associated with the Blake-Gantt House on Mabry, this building served as a private kindergarten led by Ruth Gantt in the 1950s. The exterior has been modified by enclosing the front entrance and the cupola that would have housed the school bell.

Union Street

4 Union Street • *Constructed circa 1900; alteration to columns circa 1925*

A fine example of the Queen Anne period, this brick-veneer dwelling with hipped roof with double cross gables is distinctive for its engaging

FIGURE 2-121, 4 Union Street, Photograph by Susan Besser, 2002

handling of brick recesses enframing the two-over-two windows. Stone steps lead to the full-width hipped-roof porch of standing-seam metal with triangular-pedimented entry portico. The spindlework frieze and bracketed lathe-turned columns set on brick piers, circa 1925, illustrate the ornamental quality of that period. Double-leaf single-light doors with transom create the entrance. A triangular dormer with six-light window pierces the roof of pressed metal shingles. Note the triangular pedimented dormer.

Central Masonic Institute, Joseph T. Smitherman Historic Building, NRHP 1975
109 Union Street • *Constructed 1847*

The Joseph T. Smitherman Historic Building is a Greek Revival three-story, seven-bay brick building. It is dominated by a monumental porch supported by Ionic columns with wrought-iron balustrades on the second and third stories. The building embodies the symmetry of the Greek Revival movement. Each of the three entries is composed of a four-panel wood door flanked by three-light sidelights and a six-light transom. Windows are six-over-six configuration with a stone lintel. Brick belt courses define the second and third stories. A wide band of trim follows the cornice.

FIGURE 2-122, Central Masonic Institute, Joseph T. Smitherman Historic Building, 109 Union Street, Photograph by Susan Besser, 2002

Known originally as the Central Masonic Institute, Joseph T. Smitherman Historic Building was constructed as a school for orphans by the Selma Fraternal Lodge No. 27 of the Free and Accepted Masons for $15,000. The building served as a Confederate hospital during the Civil War. After the Civil War, the hospital served as the Freedman's Bureau Hospital. It later served as the Dallas County Courthouse until the completion of the courthouse at Alabama Avenue and Lauderdale Street. From 1904 to 1908 it served as the location for the Selma Military Institute, shown on the 1907 Sanborn map as the Presbyterian High School with Military Barracks. In 1908 the property was purchased by trustees of Henry W. Vaughan's estate and served as Vaughan Memorial Hospital until 1960. It remained unoccupied for several years until it was purchased by the City of Selma, who renovated and reopened the facility in 1971 as the Historic and Civic Building. In 1979 the building was named after Mayor Joseph T. Smitherman, who originally opposed and then accepted the Civil Rights Movement in Selma and is an historic house museum furnished with period antiques. The building directly behind was designated as the Nurses' Home during the time this building functioned as a hospital. The gardens contain columns from the Hotel Albert, no longer extant, which was located on the site of the present Selma City Hall.

Nunnelee House • 322 Union Street
Constructed 1895

FIGURE 2-123, Nunnelee House, 322 Union Street, Photograph by Susan Besser, 2021

Records for this property date to 1895 when the lot was sold by Burtred G. Bacey to James Howell Nunnelee. Nunnelee deeded the property to his wife, Emma Leonard Williams Nunnelee, in 1896. James Nunnelee was the editor and publisher of the *Selma Morning Times* during the period 1892–1907. He also oversaw the editing and publishing of the Tuscaloosa *Gazette*, 1878–1888, Anniston's *Evening Times*, 1888–1892, Tuscaloosa's *News & Times Gazette*, in 1915, and the *Montgomery Times*. The Nunnelees held the property until 1907 when it was conveyed to Mrs. Helen Kayser. Note the unique decorative dormer, which features two roof types, conical and gable. The finial-topped turreted wraparound porch has lathe-turned columns and bracket capitals. Paneled stiles surround the paneled wood entry, which features etched glazing in the door and transom above.

Jordan House • 329 Union Street
Constructed 1869

Note the impeccable detailing in this two-story Italianate at 329 Union Street. The Gus Jordan family were the original owners of the house, and it remained in the Jordan family until 1978.

FIGURE 2-124, Jordan House, 329 Union Street, Photograph by Susan Besser, 2002

The original inset porch displays a flat-cut balustrade, chamfered columns, bracket capitals, and dentil course. The three-panel camber arch double-leaf wood entry has etched glass within the top panel. The window configuration incorporates segmental-arched and full-arched windows. A denticulated cornice is enriched with paired brackets. The angled bay to the south has a concave mansard roof surmounted by a balustrade and is embellished with dentil molding and paired eave brackets.

Atkins-Duncan House • 415 Union Street
Constructed 1918

FIGURE 2-125, Atkins-Duncan House, 415 Union Street, Photograph by Susan Besser, 2002

The Atkins-Duncan House was built for Mr. and Mrs. W. T. Atkins and is a two-story, three-bay symmetrical Tudor Revival side gable with double cross gables. The exterior is horizontal tongue and groove on the first story with stucco with decorative half-timbering on the second story. The front gabled entry porch has complex detailing with vents, finials with drop pendants, and decorative brackets and exposed rafters. The handsome entry features a single wood door with stained- and clear-glass sidelights and broken transom. A bank of casement windows surmounted by transoms is to the north and south. Metal casement windows of eight panes each are to the north and south on the second story. Note the center windows of diamond-pane leaded glass. Decorative trussing enriches the gable ends while a finial with pendant is at the apex of the gables.

Robbins-Moseley House • 431 Union Street
Constructed 1864

FIGURE 2-126, Robbins-Moseley House, 431 Union Street, Photograph by Susan Besser, 2002

The original owner of the Robbins-Moseley House was John Robbins. Dr. and Mrs. Samuel O. Moseley Sr. purchased the dwelling in 1938. The Moseleys' granddaughter, Margaret Moseley Utsey, assumed ownership in 1987. The two-story brick Italianate-style house with stucco exterior has a hipped roof of standing-seam metal. Decorative eave brackets with drop pendants enrich the cornice of the porch and second story. First-story full-length double-hung windows have a six-over-nine pane configuration and are flanked by full-length louvered shutters. Note the wraparound porch with slender cast-iron columns rather than the typical chamfered columns. Mr. Robbins was the owner of Dallas Iron Works, where the columns were produced. It stands to reason that Robbins would incorporate products from his industry. The original kitchen is attached to the dwelling by a breezeway and has been restored to the 1860s era. A playhouse is associated with the property.

503 Union Street • *Constructed circa 1940*
Paul Friday, Contractor

FIGURE 2-127, 503 Union Street, Photograph by Susan Besser, 2002

Located at the corner of Union Street and Abbott Avenue is this one-story, four-bay brick Colonial Revival with a side gable roof that was built in the late 1940s by master builder Paul Friday for Mr. and Mrs. Bill Agee. According to Mr. Friday, "only the best materials" were used to construct this charming brick cottage. The recessed paneled entry is enriched with Doric pilasters surmounted by an entablature and leads to a six-panel wood door. The elegance of the interior is enhanced by Mr. Friday's use of double-crown moldings on nine-foot ceilings. The floor plan includes generous closets and a triple garage, an unexpected luxury for that time period.

506 Union Street • *Constructed 1870*

This house has elements of the Greek Revival such as the full-width porch with Doric columns, the entry surrounded by sidelights and transom,

FIGURE 2-128, 506 Union Street, Photograph by Susan Besser, 2002

and six-over-six-pane windows with jib doors. However, there are elements of Italianate as well, noticeable in the bracketed cornice along the porch and first story.

511 Union Street • *Constructed circa 1900*

FIGURE 2-129, 511 Union Street, Photograph by Susan Besser, 2002

The triangular pedimented entry porch supported by Doric columns and enhanced with a cornice return dominates this one-story side gable Colonial Revival. Note the engaged columns at the façade. The two-over-two windows are surmounted by wood lintels and flanked by louvered shutters.

Henderson House/Fairoaks, Kings-Siddons-Welch House
607 Union Street • *Constructed circa 1853*

Henderson House, formerly known as the King-Siddons-Welch House, is a handsome Greek Revival two-story with a monumental two-story porch supported by Doric columns and a balustrade on the second story. Four-panel doors with four-light sidelights and broken transom provide entries to the first and second stories. A wide band of trim enriches the cornice, and pilasters define the corners of the building. A lantern surmounts the hipped roof. Windows are six-over-six double-hung and are flanked by louvered shutters. Four brick interior chimneys pierce the roof.

Fairoaks was built in 1853 for slave owner William B. King, nephew of Vice President William Rufus King, and was named Fairoaks for the numerous trees on the property. This dwelling represents the high level of craftsmanship by the African Americans of that era who would have assisted in the construction of the house. In the aftermath of the Civil War Battle of Selma, Union troops occupied the house and used it as a hospital for Union soldiers. At that time, the Judge Franklin Siddons family resided on the property and was allowed to occupy two upstairs rooms. In 1887 William Pressley Welch purchased the place from the Siddons and it remained in his family for almost one hundred years. In 1980 the house was in a poor state of repair and the City of Selma acquired it as part of a downtown stabilization program. The Alabama Historical Commission provided U.S. Department of Interior funds that aided in restoration. Circle "S" Industries, Inc., led by Larry Striplin Jr., purchased the property in April 1981 and restored the house. On March 12, 1982, the mansion was officially dedicated Henderson House in honor of Striplin's mother, Ethel Henderson Striplin, a longtime Selma resident. In 1971 he had brought Disco Aluminum Products to Selma, which had resulted in an influx to the

174 A Field Guide to Selma's Architectural Legacy

FIGURE 2-130, Henderson House/Fairoaks, Kings-Siddons-Welch House, 607 Union Street, HABS, Library of Congress

area. As a preservationist Striplin had formed Circle "S" Industries, which oversaw the rehabilitation not only of the house itself but also of Folk Victorian cottages on the site.

618, 622, 626, 632 Union Street • *Constructed circa 1910*

These cottages are part of what is known as Fairoaks Square and were due to be condemned by the City of Selma when Circle "S" Industries purchased the property in 1980 and oversaw the rehabilitation. The exteriors were restored to their original appearance and the interiors were rehabilitated to incorporate contemporary features. The project received a 1983 Honor Award from the National Trust for Historic Preservation. The one-story gable front and wing dwellings that occupy this block are indicative of the Queen Anne Spindlework subtype as illustrated by the flat-cut frieze, turned balusters, and corner brackets with drop pendants embellishing the

FIGURE 2-131, Streetscape of Fairoaks Square, Photograph by Bill Tomey, 2024

inset porch. The front gable has cutaway bays with corner brackets and gable end enriched with vergeboard and variegated shingles.

Abbott Street

811 Abbott Street • *Constructed circa 1890*

FIGURE 2-132, 811 Abbott Street, Photograph by Susan Besser, 2002

This circa 1890 Queen Anne Spindlework has a unique polygonal bay with conical roof and attached spindlework entry porch. Note the wood door with etched glazing and transom. Typical of this style is the hipped roof with cross gables of standing-seam metal. The front gable has a clipped roof, imbricated shingles, and cutaway bays.

Lapsley Street

203 Lapsley Street • *Constructed circa 1925*

FIGURE 2-133, 203 Lapsley Street, Photograph by Susan Besser, 2002

Illustrating the mastery of the Arts and Craft style is the dwelling at 203 Lapsley Street. A two-and-one-half-story three-bay with weatherboard exterior, the dwelling embodies the Arts and Crafts movement with its low-pitched rooflines of the front gable and triangular knee braces. Brackets enrich the columns. Stucco columns with battered sides begin at ground level and support a shed-roof full-width porch with a front gabled entry and shed-roofed porte cochère. A solid balustrade typifies this style. Concrete steps faced with tile lead to the double-leaf doors of wood with glazing surmounted by a transom. Band molding defines the gable end. Phil Bloom, district superintendent of PanAm Petroleum, resided here in the 1920s. Rabbi Abraham Shinedling lived here in the 1940s.

Haralson-Stewart-Rogers-Sublet-Carmichael House
213 Lapsley Street • *Constructed circa 1869*

FIGURE 2-134, Haralson-Stewart-Rogers-Sublet-Carmichael House, 213 Lapsley Street, Photograph by Susan Besser, 2002

The dwelling was built in 1869 by Hugh A. Haralson and then sold to Enos R. Stewart, an agent with the Selma streetcar line. J. H. Rogers purchased the dwelling in 1901, remodeling it in 1903. A real-estate group purchased the dwelling in 1940, making renovations to the rear of the home and ultimately selling it to Nelson and Pearl Sublet in 1945. In 1976 Martha Carmichael purchased the dwelling and managed an antique business known as "The House Next Door" for many years. The exquisite one-story, four-bay Italianate is an L-shaped plan with roof of pressed metal shingles. The front gable has a squared bay with a six-pane fixed-glass window surmounted by a stained-glass transom. Inset panels surround the fixed windows. The mansard roof of the bay has a bracketed cornice, as does the gable end of the bay and porch. The inset entry porch is richly detailed with lacy scroll-sawn spandrels, chamfered columns with brackets, and a flat-cut balustrade. Double-leaf doors of cut glass with cut-glass transom and sidelights form the entry.

Chapman House • 219 Lapsley Street
Constructed circa 1900

FIGURE 2-135, Chapman House, 219 Lapsley Street, Photograph by Susan Besser, 2002

John and Katherine Chapman were the original owners of this circa-1900 dwelling. Mrs. Chapman, writing under the pen name of Katherine Hope, was the author of numerous works such as *Letters on Life in the South, Chautauqua Chats, The Quilt That Built a Battleship, Love's Way in Dixie,* and *The Alabama Girl.* Mrs. Chapman studied at Shorter College and Lake Chautauqua, New York.

A group of ladies of Selma—Nancy Gantt, Judy Oxford, Gloria Sims, and Anita Bryant of recording artistry fame—purchased the house in the 1980s and renovated it for use as a dress shop. In 1993 Kimberly Duncan assumed ownership and began renovations to return it to a private dwelling. The Breedloves continued the renovation process after they bought the house. This stately Queen Anne of two-and-one-half stories and three bays displays the complex rooflines of the period. The hipped roof with cross gables of pressed metal shingles is pierced with a turret. The turret has fixed-glass windows on three sides and a polygonal roof with bellcast eaves. A wraparound porch follows the lines of the north polygonal bay and leads to a double-leaf entry of wood doors with fixed glass and a transom. Illustrating the Queen Anne Free Classic subtype are the paired columns set on piers.

Hardee House • 307 Lapsley Street
Constructed circa 1885

FIGURE 2-136, Hardee House, 307 Lapsley Street, Photograph by Susan Besser, 2016

Hardee House was the home of General William Joseph Hardee, author of *Infantry, Rifle, Tactics*, commonly called *Hardee's Tactics*, which was widely used during the Civil War. He was a graduate of the United States Military Academy in 1838 and served in the Seminole Wars and

Mexican-American War. He moved up quickly through the ranks at the beginning of the Civil War and was nicknamed "Old Reliable" due to his competence in handling difficult situations.

The dwelling is a two-and one-half-story, four-bay dwelling of the Queen Anne period. Double-leaf arched doors with glazing surmounted by transom provide the entry. Doric columns support a wraparound porch with gable front entry porch. The second story has an integral balcony with an arched opening set on columns. Within the cross gable and dormer are decorative Palladian-style vents. The gable end is embellished with variegated shingles.

Roy-Moore House • 309 Lapsley Street
Constructed circa 1860; second story added 1882
Michael J. Miller, Architect, second story

FIGURE 2-137, Roy-Moore House, 309 Lapsley Street, Photograph by Susan Besser, 2016

The Roy-Moore House is of the Italianate style and is a two-story, three-bay house with a one-story lateral wing. The entry porch is supported by bracketed columns and is enriched with a dentil course along the cornice. The handsome entry has double-leaf doors with arched single lights and is surmounted by a transom. Windows are two-over-two configuration and are full height on the first story and retain the original louvered operable shutters necessary to provide protection from the summer heat. The second-story cornice is embellished with eave brackets with drop pendants. The second-story windows are surmounted by cornice lintels. The Roy-Moore House was occupied by General Hardee's daughter, Mrs. T. B. Roy. Her husband, Col. T. B. Roy, is listed as hiring architect M. J. Miller to create a second story to the residence in 1882. M. J. Miller partnered with Francis J. Kennard to design and build the Belleview Biltmore in Clearwater, Florida, a National Register property. Additionally, he made renovations to the Edwards Opera House in Selma in the 1880s, which is no longer extant.

319 Lapsley Street • *Constructed 1928*
William T. Warren, Architect

FIGURE 2-138, 319 Lapsley Street, Photograph by Susan Besser, 2002

The Selma Times-Journal announced that Mr. and Mrs. Harry Maring would move into their "handsome brand-new brick home" in September of 1928.[47] This distinctive two-story, four-bay Tudor Revival exemplifies the storybook quality of the era and is an L-plan form with the entrance perpendicular to the street. The front gabled entry bay is located in the juncture of the L-plan and features a paneled wood door with semicircular transom surrounded by limestone quoins. Above the entry is an arched window with a wrought-iron balconet. Windows are ten-light metal casement. A one-story angled bay faces Lapsley Street. The brick mortar has been applied to form skintled joints, a technique that requires special skills in a mason.

321 Lapsley Street • *Constructed circa 1900*

FIGURE 2-139, 321 Lapsley Street, Photograph by Susan Besser, 2002

This two-story, three-bay multi-dwelling of Colonial Revival influences has a brick exterior and hipped roof with cross gables of pressed metal

---

47. "Moving Time Here for Many Selmians," *Selma-Times Journal*, September 23, 1928, 8.

shingles. The double-leaf entry has single-light doors and transom. Window configuration is one-over-one with an arched wood lintel with relieving arch of brick. On the second story are paired six-light casement windows with an arched wood lintel with brick relieving arch. The flat-roof entry porch is supported by Ionic columns and set on brick piers.

Brownstone Manor • 330 Lapsley Street
Constructed 1904

Brownstone Manor is known as the "mirrored house" as it was designed so the chandeliers were centered between the windows and doors to optimize the light at night. It is an elegant Neoclassical two-and-one-half-story three bay with hipped roof and cement-block exterior, which gives the appearance of stone. The Corinthian columns soar from the original full-length porch to the detailed frieze. The double-leaf door entry with glazing is surrounded by cut-glass transom and sidelights surmounted by stone arches with keystone. The symmetrical façade is composed of elliptical, arched,

FIGURE 2-140, Brownstone Manor, 330 Lapsley Street, Photograph by Bill Tomey, 2024

tripartite double-hung one-over-one pane windows surmounted by stone arches with keystone. A modillion course follows the roofline. The balcony of the second story is enriched with a turned balustrade and the decorative dormer has a triangular pedimented roof with Palladian window.

Built in 1904 by J. B. Ellis, who owned an investment firm in Selma, and purchased by the Hoopers, the residents of this beautiful dwelling were very active in the community during the World War I era. Eleanor Gray Hooper, or "Nellie," was the head of the Women's Division of the Alabama Council of Defense and took on the task of promoting the conservative use of consumer goods. Her husband, Lloyd McKee Hooper, became the head of the Alabama Council of Defense.

The grandeur of this house is evident, and it would have been an ideal location for the lavish parties of the 1920s, so it should be no surprise that F. Scott and Zelda Fitzgerald were guests of the next owner, Lamar Hooper. The house suffered fire damage to the third story in 1983 but has been artfully restored. The house has three resident ghosts and has been documented by paranormal teams.

403 Lapsley Street • *Constructed circa 1900*

FIGURE 2-141, 403 Lapsley Street, Photograph by Susan Besser, 2002

Located at the corner of Lapsley Street and Parkman Avenue is this Colonial Revival one-and one-half-story, four-bay dwelling with weatherboard exterior. Ten Doric columns support a wraparound porch and lead to an impressive entrance of an eighteen-light beveled-glass door with sidelights and broken transom. Note the angled bay to the north.

William Benjamin Craig, who studied law at Cumberland University in Lebanon, Tennessee, and served in the U.S. House of Representatives from 1907 to 1911, resided here in the 1920s.

423 Lapsley Street • *Constructed circa 1913*

FIGURE 2-142, 423 Lapsley Street, Photograph by Susan Besser, 2002

Built circa 1913, this Spanish Eclectic–style two-story stucco multi-dwelling has a foundation of rock-faced molded concrete block and a hipped roof with cross gable of pressed tin. A wraparound Moorish arcaded porch dominates the façade. Note the angled bays and flat sawn balustrade that surmounts the arcaded porch. Spanish Eclectic was rare in Selma; however, local architect Charles Henry Hopson designed his own dwelling reflecting the style at 22 View Street.

Smith-Quarles House • 439 Lapsley Street
Constructed circa 1859

FIGURE 2-143, Smith-Quarles House, 439 Lapsley Street, Photograph by Susan Besser, 2002

Built by Colonel Washington McMurray Smith, this dwelling is a two-story brick Greek Revival with Italianate influences. The monumental porch is supported by fluted Doric columns on a square base. The fenestration is composed of a four-panel wood door with sidelights and transom and six-over-six windows with stone lintels. Eave brackets with drop pendants of the Italianate era enrich the pediment of the portico and cornice of the wide overhanging eaves. During the antebellum era monumental houses such as this would have been constructed by the labor of those enslaved by the owner. The level of craftsmanship of the African Americans contributes to the fine quality of the dwelling.

According to local historians, Susan Park Smith purchased the lot for $1,000 from John Mitchell in April of 1859. Her husband was a banker, lawyer, and founder of Selma and Dallas County and was president of the Selma Bank. Mrs. Smith is said to have hidden the gold from the Selma Bank in one of the columns of the front porch. Following the Battle of Selma, Union soldiers occupied the lower story of the house. The Smith family lived upstairs during this time. The Union Army did not find the hiding place, and the gold was retrieved afterwards. Ellen Smith, daughter of Col. and Mrs. Smith, married Colonel Hillary A. Herbert, a member of congress and secretary of the Navy under President Grover Cleveland. The house continues to be occupied by the Quarles family.

Haisten House • 500 Lapsley Street
Constructed circa 1905

FIGURE 2-144, Haisten House, 500 Lapsley Street, Photograph by Susan Besser, 2002

William J. Rountree sold this property to F. W. Stephens in 1904 for $1,275. According to local historians, a dwelling was built between 1904 and 1906. Cliff and Vera Haisten bought the house in the 1930s. This one-story, three-bay Queen Anne with beaded weatherboard has a wraparound porch supported by classic columns. Note the intricate gable end enclosed by pent roof and enriched with denticulated raking cornice, imbricated shingles, and the window flanked by louvered vents. A dentil course follows the cornice line, along gable and wraparound porch.

508 Lapsley Street • *Constructed circa 1900*

FIGURE 2-145, 508 Lapsley Street, Photograph by Susan Besser, 2002

This one-story, three-bay Colonial Revival is notable for the classic columns that support the original wraparound porch with engaged columns at the façade. The gable end contains a variation of the Palladian form with a two-over-two window topped with a semicircular louvered vent and flanked by one-over-one windows.

517 Lapsley Street • *Constructed circa 1890*

FIGURE 2-146, 517 Lapsley Street, Photograph by Susan Besser, 2002

This richly detailed one-story, three-bay Queen Anne has all the elements of the Spindlework style. Note the spindlework vergeboards with drop pendants and corner brackets at the cutaway bays and paired two-over-one windows within a field of diagonal beadboard. The inset porch with scroll-sawn balustrade has a delicate frieze with bracket capitals enriched with drop pendants on lathe-turned columns.

Carlisle-Cawthon House • 605 Lapsley Street
Constructed circa 1875; rebuilt 1910
Chambers, McKeil & Co., Architects, 1910 rebuilding

FIGURE 2-147, Carlisle-Cawthon House, 605 Lapsley Street, Photograph by Susan Besser, 2002

According to local historians this two-story, four-bay elegant Queen Anne with paneled exterior was built by cotton factor Edward Kenworthy Carlisle Jr. His father, Edward Kenworthy Carlisle Sr., built Kenworthy Hall in Marion, Alabama, an Italianate villa designed by Richard Upjohn. After Edward Sr. passed, his wife, Lucinda, divided her time between Kenworthy Hall and the Carlisle House here in Selma. Florence Carlisle Vaughan, daughter of Edward Carlisle Jr., and her husband, Graham Grey

Vaughan, conveyed a one-half interest in the property to Florence's sister, Lucy Carlisle Cawthon, on July 29, 1898. Lucy Carlisle Cawthon's husband, Orville, managed a wholesale drug company, Cawthon and Coleman. Lucy Cawthon Weil, Lucy and Orville's daughter, inherited the property in the 1930s. The Lucy Cawthon Weil Scholarship from the school of pharmacy in Auburn honors Mrs. Weil. According to the *Tradesman* of 1910 the house was destroyed by fire and rebuilt in 1910 with Chambers, McKeil & Company overseeing the project.[48]

The wraparound porch with Corinthian columns follows the circular bay to the north. The impressive entrance is comprised of a double-leaf door with glazing of cut glass with transom surmounted by elaborate entablature and surrounded by paneled stiles. A second-story porch supported by Corinthian columns displays a balustrade wrapped with fish-scale shingles. Full-length louvered shutters flank full-length windows on the first story. Swag detail can be found in the tympanum of the triangular pedimented entry portico.

There is a carriage house associated with the property according to Sanborn maps from 1907 and 1913. It is now designated as 616 Pettus Avenue.

610 Lapsley Street • *Constructed circa 1900*

FIGURE 2-148, 610 Lapsley Street, Photograph by Susan Besser, 2002

---

48. *The Tradesman*, 1910, 56.

This charming one-story, raised-cottage, three-bay Folk Victorian has a hipped roof and drop siding exterior. The full-width integral porch has a flat-cut balustrade, lathe-turned columns, and spindlework frieze and leads to a paneled wood door with glazing as entrance. The pressed-tin-covered roof has a wide overhang with exposed rafters. A decorative hipped-roof dormer has a single-pane window.

614 Lapsley Street • Constructed 1915
John W. McKeil, Architect

FIGURE 2-149, 614 Lapsley Street, Photograph by Susan Besser, 2002

Raised cottages were very popular in Selma. This one-story, raised-cottage, three-bay Folk Victorian has a hipped roof and drop siding exterior. Typical of these cottages was a full-width integral porch. Note the flat-cut balustrade, lathe-turned columns, and arched lattice frieze. A wide overhang displays exposed rafters on the pressed-tin-shingle roof. A decorative single-pane window in the hipped roof dormer surmounts the roof.

620 Lapsley Street • *Constructed circa 1912*
John W. McKeil, Architect

FIGURE 2-150, 620 Lapsley Street, Photograph by Susan Besser, 2002

A charming picket fence leads to the raised cottage at 620 Lapsley Street, which has a bracketed cornice and gable-roof decorative dormer with arched niche detail. The house is generously illuminated with multi-paned casement windows and multi-paned entry door with multi-paned sidelights. The full-width porch with Doric columns gives respite from the hot Alabama summers. In the periodical *The Tradesman* of 1912, it is noted that W. P. Welch Jr. had John W. McKeil prepare plans for this residence to be built for $2,500.[49]

Byrd Learning Center, Byrd Elementary School
621 Lapsley Street • *Constructed circa 1919*
William Warren, Warren & Knight, Architect

Built on the former site of Judge William Byrd's dwelling, Byrd Learning Center is a one-story brick building that exhibits elements of the Beaux

---

49. *The Tradesman*, 1912, 1.

FIGURE 2-151, Byrd Learning Center, Byrd Elementary School, 621 Lapsley Street, Photograph by Susan Besser, 2015

Arts with the triple-arcaded loggia leading to double-leaf doors with transom all surmounted by a fanlight. To either side of the loggia are stone niches embellished with a swag-and-urn detail. Banks of five one-over-one windows are to the north and south of the entrance. The L-shaped building is connected by hyphens to one-story gable roof additions and has a stone-capped parapet. A blind window surmounted by a fanlight and accentuated by corbels is centered on the façade of north and south portions as well as the additions. Judge Byrd was a prominent attorney in Dallas County and a member of the state supreme court. According to an article in *The Selma Times-Journal* the school was built at a cost of $34,149 and was "the handsomest school building erected in Selma and is admired by all as a structure of convenience and beauty."[50]

---

50. "Final Inspection for Byrd School," *Selma Times-Journal*, March 20, 1919, 6.

628 Lapsley Street • *Constructed 1931*

FIGURE 2-152, 628 Lapsley Street, Photograph by Susan Besser, 2018

This one-story, triple-gable brick Tudor Revival dwelling with exterior front chimney features an arched entry with the original arch paneled door with octagonal window. Note the arched multi-paned window in the gable roof dormer. The arched detailing is carried through with the brickwork of the multi-paned casement windows to the south and a multi-paned arched window to the north.

700 Lapsley Street • *Constructed circa 1922*

FIGURE 2-153, 700 Lapsley Street, Photograph by Susan Besser, 2015

The popularity of Tudor Revival grew out of America's fascination with English architecture and the advancement of masonry veneering methods to give the appearance of the English prototypes.[51] This stucco one-story has a half-timbered front and side gable. Multi-paned casement windows with transoms create the focal point of the façade. Entry porch and side porch have flattened arches, typical of the Tudor Revival, and were a prominent element of Gothic Revival, which is a precursor to the period.

704 Lapsley Street • *Constructed 1924*

FIGURE 2-154, 704 Lapsley Street, Photograph by Susan Besser, 2015

This classic symmetrical, two-story, stucco side-gable dwelling creates a stately presence on Lapsley Street. The form references the nineteenth-century I-houses and has end chimneys, typical of the South, and nine-over-one windows. A simple flat-roof entry porch is supported by classic columns and leads to a paneled door, transom, and sidelights. This was the residence of Henry Lee Smith and his wife, Kitty. Mr. Smith was part

---

51. Virginia McAlester and Lee McAlester, *A Field Guide to American Houses* (New York: Alfred A. Knopf, 2015), 455.

owner in Creagh and Smith, a dealer for Hood tires and inner tubes for automobiles.

Old Live Oak Cemetery

One of the treasures of Selma is the Old Live Oak Cemetery or the West Selma Cemetery, which was established in the 1830s. The entrance to the cemetery is through cut-stone pillars off Dallas Avenue. According to John Hardy the cemetery suffered from a lack of "systematic regulation" with the result that the initial land belonging to West Selma Cemetery was laid out sporadically. Additional land was purchased in 1877 to accommodate a more commodious space and allow for allées.[52] In April of 1878, the purchase was completed and the cemetery was designated Old Live Oak Cemetery.[53] The live oaks which dominate the landscape of the cemetery are attributed to a resolution that came before the City Council on December 4, 1879, to furnish eighty live oak trees and eighty magnolia grand to beautify the cemetery. Colonel N. H. R. Dawson is credited for the placement of the trees. The Confederate Monument was built by stonecutter Pat Murphy of the Montgomery and Sons Marble Yard, formerly on Broad Street, and is in the likeness of Charlie Davidson, a member of the Selma Guards.[54] This section was set aside as a green space for the purposes of ornamentation.[55] The stone fence around the original portion that defines the boundaries of Old Live Oak Cemetery was built in the fall of 1906.[56] Buried here are the following: William Rufus King, 1786–1853, vice president of the United States 1853; John Tyler Morgan, 1824–1907, U.S. senator, Brig. Gen. C.S.A.; Edmund Winston Pettus, 1821–1907,

---

52. Hardy, *Selma: Her Institutions and Her Men*, 151.

53. Jackson, *The Story of Selma*, 306.

54. C. C. Grayson, *Yesterday and Today: Memories of Selma and Its People* (New Orleans: Pelican Press, 1948), 13.

55. Jackson, *The Story of Selma*, 310-311.

56. Jackson, *The Story of Selma*, 444.

U.S. senator, Brig. Gen. C.S.A.; Nathaniel H. R. Dawson, 1829–1902, U.S. Commissioner of Education; William J. Hardee, 1815–1873, Lt. Gen. C.S.A., author *Hardee's Tactics*; Catesby ap Roger Jones, 1821–1877, Commander, C.S.N., commanded *Virginia* (*Merrimac*) in battle with *Monitor* 1862; Benjamin S. Turner, 1825–1894, first African American member of the U.S. House of Representatives; and Robert W. Barnwell, 1849–1902, Episcopal bishop of Alabama.

FIGURE 2-155, Old Live Oak Cemetery, Photograph by Susan Besser, 2002

A pigeoneer is located in the center of the cemetery and was built in 1870. The frame building has a weatherboard exterior with side gable with cross gables of standing-seam metal. Chamfered columns with bracketed capitals support the hipped-roof veranda. The gable ends have imbricated shingles.

FIGURE 2-156, Pigeoneer, Old Live Oak Cemetery, Photograph by Susan Besser, 2002

The monument for Elodie Todd Dawson (1844–1881) was carved in Italy. Colonel N. H. R. Dawson was disappointed with how the sculptor had portrayed her hair and sent the monument back to Italy to be reworked. Mrs. Dawson was a sister-in-law of Abraham Lincoln. Her husband was a Confederate colonel and went on to become U.S. commissioner of education.

Drury Fair Jones, son of Richard Starkey and Martha Jones, died in 1878 at the age of 22. This burial vault has a canopy with four simplified Corinthian columns supporting a hipped roof. The frieze of the canopy has flat arches. An angel holding a tablet inscribed with

FIGURE 2-157, Elodie Todd Dawson Monument, Old Live Oak Cemetery, Photograph by Susan Besser, 2002

Drury Fair Jones's name stands watch over the vault. The flat arches are detailed with a bead-and-reel element. There is a cresting along the ridgeline and a cross crowns the monument.

FIGURE 2-158, Drury Fair Jones Monument, Old Live Oak Cemetery, Photograph by Susan Besser, 2022

William Rufus King (1786-1853) was a founder of Selma, Alabama, U.S. senator, and vice president of the United States. He was a founding father of Selma and is credited with the naming of Selma. As a senator from Alabama, King worked tirelessly to bridge the tensions over "slavery and sectionalism."

FIGURE 2-159, Rufus King Monument, Old Live Oak Cemetery, Photograph by Susan Besser, 2002

FIGURE 2-160, Benjamin Sterling Turner Obelisk, Old Live Oak Cemetery, Photograph by Dr. Carroll Van West, NRHP 2013

Benjamin S. Turner is noted for his leadership in the nineteenth century when he became the first African American elected member of the U.S. House of Representatives in 1870. He introduced legislation that would have given amnesty to Confederate leaders. His bill did not pass but a subsequent bill was enacted in 1872.[57]

Pettus Street

213 Pettus Street • *Constructed circa 1905*

FIGURE 2-161, 213 Pettus Street, Photograph by Susan Besser, 2002

The shotgun house originated in New Orleans with the Haitian population—formerly enslaved people of West African descent who migrated to New Orleans—and this house type is believed to reflect the architecture of their homeland. Typically, the house had a living room at the front with one or two bedrooms with a kitchen at the back of the house. Originally, there were four houses here, all owned by Sophia Kingston, an educator of

---

57. Fitts, *Selma: A Bicentennial History*, 110.

African Americans, who also owned the adjacent house at 319 Selma Avenue, which is no longer extant. These one-story, frame, two-bay, shotgun houses were in Old Town Historic District, an anomaly for this section of town. Remaining are this house and one at 211 Pettus Street. Kingston was the principal of Knox Academy. She was a pioneer in education, and East End School was renamed Sophia P. Kingston School in her honor.

Dallas Avenue

Kayser-Turner-Searcy House • 500 Dallas Avenue
Constructed 1917

FIGURE 2-162, Kayser-Turner-Searcy House, 500 Dallas Avenue, Photograph by Susan Besser, 2016

The Turner House is an outstanding example of the Italian Renaissance Revival. The original owner of the dwelling was Isadore Kayser, who owned Kayser's Department Store. This two-story, three-bay brick-veneer dwelling has a low-pitched hipped roof covered by ceramic tiles. The shed-roof entry porch is supported by massive square piers. Leading to the double-leaf

French doors of twelve lights each is a front gable roof supported by Doric columns and corbeled brackets and an arched brick opening supported by brick piers. Other details on the Dallas Avenue façade include a Palladian window with an arched trellis supported by brackets. On the Lapsley Street side is a second entrance with a louvered weather door surmounted by a cartouche with swag. The interior retains period wainscoting, an inglenook influenced by the Arts and Crafts era, and an elevator, original to the house. A garage of the period is associated with the property. W. M. Turner, president of the Turner Motor Company located at the corner of Lapsley Street and Dallas Avenue, and his family were the second owners of this residence.

Gregory-Thrash House • 509 Dallas Avenue
Constructed 1885

FIGURE 2-163, Gregory-Thrash House, 509 Dallas Avenue, Photograph by Susan Besser, 2002

Built by Edward G. Gregory, part owner of Gregory and Coe Lumber Co., in the late 1880s, Edward and his wife, Margaret, lived in the dwelling until their deaths. The house was sold to Bertha Dublon Liepold in 1894. Her daughter Jeanette married Samuel A. Sommers Sr., and the house remained in the Liepold-Sommers family until Roy and Sheilah Thrash, who did extensive renovations, acquired the house in 1986. The Gregory-Thrash House is a two-story, three-bay L-shaped Italianate with a low-pitched hipped roof of standing-seam metal embellished by a one-story wraparound porch with a mansard roof. Chamfered columns with richly detailed bases and bracketed capitals stand regally along the façade. The classic elegance of the style is enhanced by the paneled wood door with cut-glass sidelights and transom. Full-height windows with cornice lintels grace the first story. The façade of the first story is clad with flush board, while weatherboard siding covers the second story and remaining elevations. Windows of the second story have segmental arches. Slightly arched window crowns surmount the windows. The eaves are embellished with a modillioned cornice and paired brackets. A gazebo and guest house are located on the property.

519 Dallas Avenue • *Constructed circa 1890*

FIGURE 2-164, 519 Dallas Avenue, Photograph by Susan Besser, 2002

The lot for this home was purchased from Bertha Liepold by Moses Siegel in 1888. Moses and his wife, Mamie, built the home circa 1890. The home remained in the Siegel family until 1994 when it was sold to Mr. and Mrs. David Massey III. The handsome leaded-glass door with sidelights and transoms provides a gracious entrance to the four-bay, two-story hipped roof with cross-gabled Queen Anne. Details such as the two-story turret with polygonal roof covered with pressed metal shingles and two-story porch supported by Doric columns are indicative of the period. A balustrade surmounts the angled bay. Fish-scale shingles enrich the façade below the second-story windows and gable ends of the cross gables.

Perkins-Baker House • 520 Dallas Avenue
Constructed circa 1861

FIGURE 2-165, Perkins-Baker House, 520 Dallas Avenue,
Photograph by Susan Besser, 2002

This stately two-story Italianate displays segmental arched hood molds surmounting segmental arched windows, a bracketed cornice, and wrap-around porch with tapered columns set on a square base. The entry is composed of a double door with segmental arched transom and entablature with paneled stiles. A polygonal bay is to the west.

Baker House • 600 Dallas Avenue
Constructed circa 1860

FIGURE 2-166, Baker House, 600 Dallas Avenue, Photograph by Susan Besser, 2002

The Baker House was built by George Baker, a mining engineer and founder of the first cottonseed mill in Selma, and is said to have features that are copied from his ancestral home in Philadelphia. Baker brought craftsmen from Philadelphia to ensure that the details were done correctly. It is a one-story, five-bay handsome Italianate with a hipped roof of standing-seam metal. A wraparound porch with hipped roof of standing-seam metal has square paneled columns with capitals and a frieze embellished with dentil mold. Contributing to the graceful quality of the Baker House are the double-leaf arched panel doors and segmental arched transomed entrance. Full-height four-over-four windows are covered with louvered shutters. Paired-eave brackets enrich the porch cornice and single-eave brackets enrich the eave cornice. A pyramidal roofed cupola, saved when fire destroyed the second floor, is enhanced with a balustrade.

The house was the site of a skirmish during the Battle of Selma. Reportedly, a wounded Union soldier hid behind the staircase and died there. Paranormal activity in the dwelling has been reported numerous times.

The Reverend Edward W. Gamble, pastor of St. Paul's Episcopal Church, resided here from the 1930s until his death in 1958. Gamble was an ardent supporter of an African American community center and a strong proponent of Prohibition legislation.

Bloch House • 601 Dallas Avenue
Constructed 1926 • William T. Warren, Architect

FIGURE 2-167, Bloch House, 601 Dallas Avenue, Photograph by Susan Besser, 2002

Formerly owned by Maurice Bloch, who was president of the league overseeing the Cloverleafs, an early Selma baseball team that ran from 1928 to 2003, the house boasts a gable-front portico with arched entry supported by Doric columns. Brick columns on a full-width stoop create an impressive entrance to this asymmetrical brick two-story dwelling of Tudor Revival influences with a Colonial Revival portico. The paneled-wood entry with five-light transom is enriched with a cast-stone surround incorporating an arched entablature and quoins. Paired casement windows and multi-pane double-hung windows surmounted by transoms illuminate this dwelling.

607 Dallas Avenue • *Constructed circa 1880*

FIGURE 2-168, 607 Dallas Avenue, Photograph by Susan Besser, 2018

Kitti Elizabeth Windham, director of the Striplin Performing Arts Centre, formerly the Walton Theater, was once the owner of this charming house. Under Ms. Windham's leadership the Centre achieved status as a center for drama, arts, and theatre. Ms. Windham could be heard on the local radio station WHBB, which broadcast her "Miss Kitty" show. She began her radio career in Key West as the first female disc jockey.

Stone steps lead to this one-story, five-bay L-shaped dwelling of Italianate and Greek Revival influences. The dwelling has flush board exterior on the façade. The shed-roof inset entry porch is supported by square fluted columns and is enriched by a dentil band at the cornice and brackets above each column. The distinctive wood entry has double arched paned windows, elongated curvilinear sidelights, and a broken transom with an elongated curvilinear light.

615 Dallas Avenue • *Constructed circa 1890*

FIGURE 2-169, 615 Dallas Avenue, Photograph by Susan Besser, 2002

Joseph Hampshire built this dwelling between June of 1874 and May of 1890. Minnie Lee Esler inherited the property from Hampshire, a business partner of her father. A brick sidewalk and steps lead to this one-story, three-bay raised cottage of Italianate influences. The central entry has a four-panel wood door with three-pane sidelights and decorative inset panel, and the entry porch has a low-pitched gable roof with wide band of trim and is supported by cast-iron foliated columns. Double-hung windows have a decorative inset panel below and are flanked by shutters. Eave brackets enrich the cornice.

618 Dallas Avenue • *Constructed circa 1872*

FIGURE 2-170, 618 Dallas Avenue, Photograph by Susan Besser, 2002

The dwelling was built circa 1871–1872 by George and Marcy Beach. A. D. Bloch, who owned Selma Furniture Company, lived here for several years. Restoration of the dwelling was done by two families, the Herbert Shuptrines and Paul James. It is a stately two-story three-bay of the late Italianate period with a hipped roof of standing-seam metal. The richly detailed arcaded full-width one-story porch has a mansard roof surmounted by cresting. Note the bracketed modillion course along the porch and second story. Double-leaf arched doors have arched lights and floriated panels and a molded surround.

Hooker-McEachern House • 619 Dallas Avenue
Constructed circa 1840, 1870

The Hooker-McEachern House is a brick two-story, five-bay dwelling and illustrates how a house from an earlier period such as this Federal central

FIGURE 2-171, Hooker-McEachern House, 619 Dallas Avenue, Photograph by Susan Besser, 2002

passage house was updated to reflect the current architectural trends. In this case a handsome Italianate porch with bracketed chamfered columns, flat-cut balustrade, and mansard roof of standing-seam metal dominates the façade and was added circa 1870. Cresting, an Italianate detail, surmounts the roofline of the mansard roof porch. The entry has a four-panel wood door with sidelights and transom. Above the transom is a slight arched wood lintel with a brick relieving arch. Full-height windows on the first story contribute to the grandeur of the dwelling. This was home to Hattie Hooker Wilkins, the first woman Alabama legislator, serving 1913–1924, who was a graduate of Normal College in Nashville, Tennessee, and a pioneer suffragist in Alabama and founding member of the Alabama Equal Suffrage Association. In 1997 she was elected to the Alabama Women's Hall of Fame.

625 Dallas Avenue • *Constructed 1913*

FIGURE 2-172, 625 Dallas Avenue, Photograph by Susan Besser, 2023

James and Eloise Fowlkes built this charming one-story Craftsman bungalow in 1913. Mrs. Fowlkes resided there after her husband's death in 1922 until her passing in 1976. Ed and Jan Leicht purchased the house in June of 1988. A wood-rail balustrade and paired Doric columns on brick piers offer a Southern vernacular variation to the Craftsman style of this handsome wraparound porch with a single-door entrance with glazing, sidelights, and broken transom. Atypical for the Craftsman is the hipped roof, which is covered with pressed metal shingles. Note the decorative hipped dormer.

Bloch-James House • 631 Dallas Avenue
Constructed 1872

The Bloch-James House is a two-story Italianate L-plan with segmental arched double-hung full-height windows. Doric columns on a solid brick balustrade support the shed-roof porch. A segmental arched leaded-glass transom surmounts the entry of double-leaf doors with glazing and leaded-glass sidelights. A square bay to the east has paired segmental arched

FIGURE 2-173, Bloch-James House, 631 Dallas Avenue, Photograph by Susan Besser, 2002

double-hung windows with eave brackets and modillion course along the cornice. Mary Amelia John Watson, daughter of Dr. J. R. John, resided here in the 1920s and was one of the five founding members of the Selma Suffragette Association.

710 Dallas Avenue
Constructed circa 1890; porch alterations circa 1980

FIGURE 2-174, 710 Dallas Avenue, Photograph by Susan Besser, 2002

This Italianate two-story three-bay with one-story wing retains much of historic detail. The camber windows of two-over-four and two-over-two configuration are of this period. Notable is the single-door entry with double arched glazing and camber transom. The porch has been altered to ground level and brick steps lead to the entry. Original columns have been replaced; however, the bracketed capitals and scroll-sawn frieze are intact.

Calloway House • 721 Dallas Avenue
Constructed circa 1884

FIGURE 2-175, Calloway House, 721 Dallas Avenue, Photograph by Susan Besser, 2002

Calloway House was built in 1884 for $2,500. The owner had stored her savings in a cigar box that remained unharmed when the original house was destroyed by fire. This Queen Anne two-story, five-bay façade with hipped roof with cross gables has a wraparound porch with classic columns on paneled bases, turreted bay with fish-scale shingles on the first story, and drop siding on the second story. A portion of the wraparound porch was enclosed with a bank of casement windows circa 1930. Note the paneled detailing in the tympanum of the enclosed porch.

Reese-Hain-Nixon House • 722 Dallas Avenue
Constructed circa 1900; alterations 1903
Charles H. Hopson, Architect, alterations

FIGURE 2-176, Reese-Hain-Nixon House, 722 Dallas Avenue, Photograph by Susan Besser, 2002

The Reese-Hain-Nixon House is a fine example of the classical influences of the Renaissance Revival style and is noted to have had extensive alterations overseen by architect Charles H. Hopson.[58] This two-story, five-bay dwelling has a scored stucco exterior and hipped roof of clay tiles. Paired Ionic columns support a one-story, flat-roof entry porch that is surmounted by a wrought-iron balustrade. The central porch leads to the double-leaf entry surrounded by cut-glass sidelights and transom. Windows are one-over-one double-hung sash. A bow in front to the west lends an elegant element to the façade. The central bay of the second story is front gabled with cornice returns enriched by corbels. Adding to the stateliness of the dwelling are the second-story Palladian window with a heavy entablature

---

58. *Selma Times*, September 11, 1903, 5.

and a bull's eye window, both exhibiting glazing that gives a nod to high-style Federal dwellings.

Walker-Plant House • 725 Dallas Avenue
Constructed 1915 • Frank Lockwood, Architect

FIGURE 2-177, Walker-Plant House, 725 Dallas Avenue, Photograph by Susan Besser, 2002

T. Merriott W. Walker built this house for his wife, Mamie Stubbs Walker. In 1951 the Plant family acquired it. This central passage form is an elegant brick two-story Colonial Revival with Georgian influence. The entry porch is supported by Ionic columns and is enriched with dentil course and elaborate swag of garland ribbons along frieze. Casement windows surmounted by elliptical fanlights are to the east and west of the façade. Ribbed arched lintels with keystone cap the fanlights. The bow in front of the second story is embellished with Doric pilasters. A wide frieze band and modillion course follow the cornice line. Note the segmental arched belvedere, which has a double-hung window flanked by louvered vents to give the appearance of shutters.

729 Dallas Avenue • *Constructed 1904*

FIGURE 2-178, 729 Dallas Avenue, Photograph by Susan Besser, 2002

The founder of Central City Laundry, Frank Wise, was once owner of this house. His wife, Juliette, was an historian and witnessed the burning of Selma in April of 1865. This brick two-story Neoclassical with modified four-square form has a wraparound porch and distinctive octagonal columns. The arched entry leads to a wood door with full glazing and leaded-glass sidelights surmounted by an arched leaded-glass transom. Note the triangular pedimented parapet with stone coping. Pressed metal quoins enhance the corners of the façade.

Koenigstahl-Williamson-Luker House • 730 Dallas Avenue
Constructed circa 1884 • Attributed to Michael J. Miller, Architect

Built in 1884, this grand Shingle Style with Queen Anne influences epitomizes the elegance and grace of the period. Jean Martin described it best in September of 1979 in *The Selma Times-Journal*, "The house was born a lady in the year 1884. As modish as Queen Anne for whom its style was named, it was frilled and furbelowed in true Victorian manner . . .

dressed for callers with its shingled gables, conical roofed veranda and Grecian frieze running full circumference under the overhanging eaves."[59] The architect for this sublime dwelling was M. J. Miller, who partnered with Francis J. Kennard to design the Biltmore Belleview, a Queen Anne and Shingle Style hotel in Belleair, Florida.

FIGURE 2-179, Koenigstahl-Williamson-Luker House, 730 Dallas Avenue, Photograph by Susan Besser, 2002

Levi Koenigstahl resided in the house from 1884 to 1979. Koenigstahl was a local businessman originally from Germany and owned a wholesale meat company. The Williamsons resided in the dwelling from 1979 until the 1990s. Robert and Edie Luker purchased the dwelling in 1997, restoring it to its former glory. The dwelling had been condemned by the City of Selma and was hidden by vegetation.

---

59. Jean Martin, "The House Was Born a Victorian Lady," *Selma Times-Journal*, September 23, 1979.

Constructed of two-and-one-half stories, the five-bay dwelling's exterior is of shingles and weatherboard, the multigabled roof with flared eaves has pressed metal shingles, and a handsome chimney with diagonal brickwork graces the façade. A hipped-roof wraparound porch and turreted projection is covered with pressed metal shingles and has a triangular pedimented entry portico. The portico is enriched with spindlework detail. The frieze and balustrade of the porch are in the spindlework manner as well. Double-leaf doors with glazing and transom provide the entry. To the west of the entry are a multi-pane-over-one window and a cutaway bay at the northwest corner. To the east are two multi-pane-over-one windows. The second story has double-leaf doors with glazing and a balconet with arched opening supported by colonnettes. Modillion courses enrich the porch cornice and second-story cornice. Foliate carving embellishes the frieze.

804 Dallas Avenue • *Constructed circa 1950*

FIGURE 2-180, 804 Dallas Avenue, Photograph by Susan Besser, 2002

This refined ranch is a one-story, six-bay, brick-exterior dwelling that reflects the influences of Selma architecture with the foliated cast-iron porch posts of the shed-roof porch and large window expanses of twelve-over-twelve windows.

807 Dallas Avenue • *Constructed circa 1925*

FIGURE 2-181, 807 Dallas Avenue, Photograph by Susan Besser, 2002

The entry porch of this handsome one-and-one-half-story Craftsman has square paneled columns on brick piers connected with a solid brick balustrade. The wood panel door with small single-pane glass is indicative of the Craftsman period, as are the exposed rafters, triangular knee brackets, and paired casement windows in the front gable.

St. Andrew's Hall • 1127 Dallas Avenue
Constructed circa 1881

St. Andrew's Hall, which functioned as a Catholic boys' boarding school, was formerly Cahawba Masonic Hall and was moved by the Jesuits in 1881. The Second Empire–influenced building is two-and-one-half-story stucco with cut-stone decorative elements and arched dormers. Note

FIGURE 2-182, St. Andrew's Hall, 1127 Dallas Avenue, Photograph by Susan Besser, 2002

the full-height Doric columns juxtaposed against a concave mansard roof, which is atypical of this style. The central pavilion of the façade is enriched with cut stone quoins. Details such as eave brackets, stone segmental arched hood mold, and stone lintels display the Second Empire influence.

McCleod Avenue

Miss Minnie Sue House • 622 McLeod Avenue
Constructed circa 1820, alterations 1910

FIGURE 2-183, Miss Minnie Sue House, 622 McLeod Avenue, Photograph by Susan Besser, 2002

The Miss Minnie Sue House, circa 1820, is a one-story central passage form with a side gable with center cross gable and retains the pressed tin shingles. Double-hung nine-over-nine windows are flanked by the original louvered shutters. The flat-cut porch supports and the balustrade of the porch were added circa 1910. According to local historians the house is fashioned from hand-hewn timbers and joined with wooden pegs and was moved from its location on Mabry Street within the same block in 1910. The Ensign family resided here for a number of years. The house was subdivided into two apartments during the depression and rented for $7.50 a month. Henry and Christine Vaughan restored the house, naming the dwelling for Miss Minnie Sue Neville, a friend of Mrs. Vaughan who owned an antique shop in Selma.

James Martin Calhoun Law Office
McLeod Avenue/Heritage Village • *Constructed 1833*

FIGURE 2-184, James Martin Calhoun Law Office, McLeod Avenue/Heritage Village, Photograph by Susan Besser, 2002

The James Martin Calhoun building, historically a law office, is a one-story, front gable Greek Revival with Doric columns supporting a full-width porch. The gable end's raking cornice and wide frieze are indicative of the Greek Revival period. Calhoun, a native of Vienna, South Carolina, married Susan Wilkinson Pickens, daughter of Andrew Pickens, governor of South Carolina, and moved to Selma. The office is a replica of the office of his uncle, John C. Calhoun, who was a member of the U.S. House of Representatives and Senate serving between 1831 and 1861. The office was donated to the city of Selma by Andrew Calhoun, grandson of James Calhoun.

McKinnon-Riggs Doctor's Office • McLeod Avenue/Heritage Village
Constructed circa 1850

FIGURE 2-185, McKinnon-Riggs Doctor's Office, McLeod Avenue/ Heritage Village, Photograph by Susan Besser, 2002

Of the antebellum period, this Greek Revival doctor's office has an impressive full-width porch supported by square Doric columns. The double-hung full-height windows and entry are surmounted by triangular pediments. A wide frieze band and pilasters at the corners of the porch are typical of this style. This building served as a lawyer's office for H. B. Boynton from 1852 to 1871. Dr. Kenneth McKinnon practiced medicine in this building beginning in 1871. From 1905 to 1945 Dr. S. W. Riggs used this building for his practice, and then Dr. William Staggers of Benton in the

1950s. Originally located in Pleasant Hill, the building was in disrepair and was threatened with demolition. The heirs of William B. Jones, who had acquired the building for $300 in 1946, donated it to the Selma-Dallas County Preservation Society and it was moved to this site in 1981.

Parkman Avenue

510 Parkman Avenue • *Constructed circa 1880*

FIGURE 2-186, 510 Parkman Avenue, Photograph by Susan Besser, 2002

A polygonal wraparound porch augments the circular portico of this handsome one-story beaded-weatherboard Queen Anne dwelling. Double-leaf doors with incised carving and glazing surmounted by a transom grace the entry. Cutaway bays to the west and pent roof enclosing the gable end enriched with variegated shingles are typical of the style.

613 Parkman Avenue • *Constructed circa 1890*

FIGURE 2-187, 613 Parkman Avenue, Photograph by Susan Besser, 2002

This handsome Queen Anne one-story, four-bay dwelling has a hipped roof with cross gables and a one-story wraparound turreted porch enriched with spindlework frieze and balustrade supported by lathe-turned columns. Paneled stiles enhance double doors with glazing and transom. The front gable bay to the west has cutaway bays with spindlework corner brackets and the gable end is enclosed with a pent roof and is enriched with imbricated shingles and a spindlework vergeboard. Additional details such as the cross gable with spindlework vergeboard piercing the roof and a pent roof enclosing the gable are typical of the era. The porte cochère is to the east and has a spindlework frieze with lathe-turned columns.

The original owner, Dr. W. W. Harper (1869–1941), a local physician, had strong credentials pursuing studies in medicine in Edinburgh, London, and Paris. Harper was a strong proponent of prohibition and offered a petition that had the backing of Selma physicians in support of making drinking illegal. He was commissioned a captain in the medical corps and served in France during World War I.

614 Parkman Avenue • *Constructed circa 1900*

FIGURE 2-188, 614 Parkman Avenue, Photograph by Susan Besser, 2016

This distinctive Queen Anne cottage has a robust concave cornice embellished with curved brackets. Ionic columns support the wraparound porch. Fish-scale shingles and a bull's eye window embellish the gable end of the portico, which is enclosed with a pent roof. A single wood door with arched windows and two-pane segmental arched transom defines the entry. To the north of the entry is a two-over-two segmental arched window. The Reverend Jacob H. Kaplan, Rabbi of Mishkan Temple, and his wife, Adele, resided here during his tenure in Selma before leaving for Terre Haute, Indiana. In a tribute published in the *Selma Times-Journal* shortly before Rabbi Kaplan moved to Indiana, he acknowledged his admiration for the city: "And that is why Selma is a great city. . . . Her sons and her daughters behold her beauty, and her spiritual strength, and her beautiful human life, and return to pay homage to her."[60]

---

60. "Tribute Paid to Lovely Selma," *Selma Times-Journal*, August 1, 1912, 3.

619 Parkman Avenue • *Constructed circa 1890*

FIGURE 2-189, 619 Parkman Avenue, Photograph by Susan Besser, 2002

This two-and-one-half-story, three-bay Folk Victorian has an inset porch with a standing-seam metal roof. The porch exhibits elements of the Queen Anne style such as the spindlework frieze, lathe-turned balustrade, and lathe-turned columns. Fenestration of the dwelling to the east and west exhibits paired one-over-one windows flanked by louvered shutters on the first and second stories. The double-leaf wood-door entry with glazing is surmounted by a transom. Cross gables are enriched with variegated shingles and enclosed with a pent roof.

715 Parkman Avenue • *Constructed circa 1940*

Built circa 1940, this one-and-one-half-story, front-gabled, three-bay Craftsman with an integral full-width porch has a cedar shingle exterior. Hallmarks of this style are evident such as the triangular knee braces and

FIGURE 2-190, 715 Parkman Avenue, Photograph by Susan Besser, 2002

exposed rafters. Battered ground-level piers support paneled dwarf columns of the integral porch, and a solid brick balustrade anchors the porch.

Parkman-Smitherman House • 721 Parkman Avenue
Constructed circa 1839

FIGURE 2-191, Parkman-Smitherman House, 721 Parkman Avenue, Photograph by Susan Besser, 2002

In 1858, John W. Lapsley conveyed this lot to Mrs. Ellen C. Lindsey with the proviso that she provide a home for the orphaned children of Rev. J. B. King. According to local historians, this house built by Elias Parkman before 1839 was moved from its original location to the lot. Mrs. Lindsey occupied the dwelling with the King children until June of 1879. The Young sisters purchased the house for $3,000 and operated Home High School here for nearly fifty years. The diplomas were hand drawn on sheepskin. In November of 1935, the executor of the last remaining sister conveyed the property to Isoline W. Robbins for $2,750. Mr. and Mrs. David D. Martin purchased the house from Mrs. Robbins. The Parkman-Smitherman House is a two-story, three-bay Greek Revival side hall plan with weatherboard exterior and hipped roof of standing-seam metal. The triangular pedimented entry porch has square columns and a simple balustrade and leads to a louvered weather door surrounded by four-light sidelights and a six-light transom. Windows are six-over-six double-hung wood sash. The original school is extant and associated with the property.

801 Parkman Avenue • *Constructed circa 1900*

FIGURE 2-192, 801 Parkman Avenue, Photograph by Susan Besser, 2002

This Colonial Revival, one-story, five-bay dwelling has an elegant arched entrance onto the circular wraparound porch supported by Doric columns and embellished with eave brackets under the cornice. The handsome single door with glazing has sidelights and transom.

809 Parkman Avenue • *Constructed circa 1915*

FIGURE 2-193, 809 Parkman Avenue, Photograph by Susan Besser, 2002

Projecting an air of elegance, this simple Queen Anne Free Classic features a wraparound porch with Doric columns, lathe-turned balustrade, and hipped roof with cross gable of pressed metal shingles. A delicate incised ornamentation graces the gable roof dormer. The entry is a single-leaf door with arched windows surmounted by a transom.

Washington Street

Baker School • 300 Washington Street
Constructed 1902 • H. D. Breeding, Architect

The Baker School is a fine example of the manner in which monochromatic brick of the Renaissance Revival period is emphasized with the semicircular arch of the window openings. The free-standing two-story building

FIGURE 2-194, Baker School, 300 Washington Street, Photograph by Bill Tomey, 2025

has an asymmetrical façade of five bays with a three-story bell tower to the south of the façade with segmental-arched windows and semicircular arched openings. A shaped parapet with stone coping and finial creates the focal point of the building. Baker School is built on a raised basement of corbelled brick to give the effect of rustication, a hallmark of the Renaissance Revival style. Built at a cost of $18,473.36,[61] it was noted in the *Selma Times* of February 23, 1902, that "while the committee considered a convenient and well-arranged school to be of prime importance, they were not unmindful of its appearance, and the picture of the house as drawn by the architect, with its tower, gray brick walls, and handsome ornamentation, is very attractive."[62]

---

61. "Baker School," *Selma Times*, October 19, 1902, 5.
62. "The New School Building," *Selma Times*, February 23, 1902, 3.

Queen of Peace Roman Catholic Church/Assumption Roman Catholic Church/St. Andrews Catholic Church
309 Washington Street • *Constructed 1869*
A. Von Fichert, Architect

FIGURE 2-195, Queen of Peace Roman Catholic Church/ Assumption Roman Catholic Church/St. Andrew Catholic Church, 309 Washington Street, Postcard Collection of Susan Besser

The Catholic presence was evidenced as early as 1855, when services were held in the second story of a building at 308 Broad Street, no longer extant. Rev. D. Gibbons came to lead the parishioners in 1863 and was succeeded by Rev. P. McMahon in 1865, and he served until 1867. Father John J. O'Leary was assigned to the church at that time and oversaw the construction of the present building. The cornerstone was laid by Reverend

Bishop Quinlan of Mobile on April 11, 1867, who was also there for the dedication on June 19, 1870. The Jesuit Fathers of New Orleans assumed leadership in 1880. Father O'Shannahan, of the Jesuit order, oversaw the building of St. Andrews Hall, which was a boarding school for Catholic boys. Queen of Peace Roman Catholic Church is constructed of rubble stone taken from the Confederate arsenal and is of the front gable form with a slate roof. Entry of the central bay has a flattened arch of wood. The fascia has quatrefoil trim. The second story has a basket-handle-arch window of three parts and is composed of two lancet arches and a center panel, all of stained glass. Two-story arch trim is enriched with carved wood trim that reflects the stone compound arch of its thirteenth-century predecessors. To either side of the two-story nave are one-story shed sections that are buttressed on either side. The fenestration of the church on the front and sides is of the lancet arch form.[63]

The School of Discovery • 400 Washington Street
Constructed circa 1925 • Frank Lockwood, Architect

FIGURE 2-196, Auditorium, School of Discovery, 400 Washington Street, Photograph by Susan Besser, 2002

---

63. Fitts, *Historic Churches of Selma Prior to 1925*, 5.

The School of Discovery, formerly Selma Junior High School, is a Neoclassical brick edifice of two stories and flat roof with a parapet. Engaged columns and keystone arches surround the entrances. Above the entrance are three nine-over-nine windows enframed in stone. Stone quoins define the corners. Above the drip course is a shaped parapet. The primary entrance is a double-leaf door with glazing surmounted by a blind arch. Pilasters and entablature surround the entrance. Banks of two and four double-hung nine-over-nine windows constitute the fenestration. To the south is the auditorium, which has a three-bay entrance of double-leaf doors with six lights with fanlights surmounted by a balustrade.

Fort W. W. Quarles Armory • 528 Washington Street
Constructed circa 1935

FIGURE 2-197, Fort W. W. Quarles Armory, 528 Washington Street, Postcard Collection of Susan Besser

The W. W. Quarles Armory is a one-story, Art Deco–influenced building with a two-story central block with a brick exterior and flat roof with parapet. The building is named for Col. W. W. Quarles, who commanded the third regiment of the Alabama State Troops in the 1890s. The setback façade is typical of New Deal buildings constructed during this era.

Concrete steps lead to an entry of two sets of plate-glass doors, circa 1950. The entry has a stepped façade typical of the era. Three octagonal openings are above the entry. A flat-roofed portico is attached to the side of the projecting bays.

534 Washington Street • *Constructed circa 1905*

FIGURE 2-198, 534 Washington Street, Photograph by Susan Besser, 2002

A four-panel door with sidelights and transom creates a handsome entry to this central passage, one-story, five-bay, Neoclassical cottage that has a hipped roof and flush horizontal board façade. Six-over-nine windows are full height. Columns of the integral porch are square and are enriched with a simple balustrade.

Wesley Plattenburg House, Dr. Kirkpatrick House, NRHP 1993
601 Washington Street • *Constructed circa 1842*

Wesley Plattenburg immigrated to Selma in 1829 from Maryland and was a merchant tailor. According to John Hardy's *Selma: Her Institutions and Her Men* he inherited an estate from a Mr. Wood, after which he "devoted

FIGURE 2-199, Wesley Plattenburg House, Dr. Kirkpatrick House, 601 Washington Street, HABS, Library of Congress

his entire attention to planting near the city."[64] The Federal Census Slaveholder Schedule shows that Plattenburg in 1850 owned eighty-seven slaves. Plattenburg served on the Alabama & Tennessee Railroad Company in 1850 and was a member of the City Council in the 1840s and a trustee of Dallas Academy. He is listed as petitioning for amnesty and pardon for $20,000 on August 19, 1865, for being a Confederate supporter. In his petition, he stated that he "honestly believed that the condition of the country was such that the South could have no safety except through a withdrawal from the Union." In 1866 the house was sold as a small parcel to Mrs. Emily C. Bayne. The Plattenburgs remained in Selma until they moved to Giles County, Tennessee. Plattenburg died in 1882 and is buried in Old Live Oak Cemetery. This property had several owners before its purchase by Dr. Samuel and Mary Kirkpatrick in 1904 for $4,500.

---

64. Hardy, *Selma: Her Institutions and Her Men*, 190.

FIGURE 2-200, Wesley Plattenburg House,
Drawing by Casey Tramel, November 2023

Listed on the National Register of Historic Places as of February 2, 1993, and photographed as part of the HABS survey in the 1930s, the Wesley Plattenburg House, built of stucco circa 1855, is a rare surviving example of the raised plantation form in the Dallas County area and has elements of the Greek Revival and Italianate. The house originally sat on 2,200 acres and can be recognized on the Battle of Selma map. The French Creole plantation house form emanates from the Louisiana area and served to protect the main living quarters during times of flooding. The fenestration reveals that the façade of the second story had a double-door entry and windows with wood lintels. The basement story has one entry and a window. A wraparound porch with a roof that is an extension of the standing-seam metal hipped roof is embellished with square columns and eave brackets at the cornice. The second-floor entry is accessed by an exterior stair as is typical of the raised plantation house.

Franklin Street

George D. Wilson Selma Community Center • 16 Franklin Street
Constructed circa 1935 • George Wilson, Architect

In the 1930s Jim Crow segregation necessitated a center where African American families could come to rest and take care of the children when they made the trip into Selma from the outlying areas of Dallas County. The location for the community center was chosen due to the close proximity of African American businesses, many of which were located in the now demolished three-story brick building at 21-25 Franklin Street. African American businesses in this building in 1930 included S. M. Boynton, county agricultural agent, who worked with farm communities to aid with crop selection and fertilizer usage; J. M. Powell, agent, Central City Relief Insurance Co.; Excelsior Club; Masonic Hall; S. T. Powell, photographer; Dr. C. S. Taylor; Ducies Café; and Benjamin Miller, barber. The Sullivan Building at the corner of Franklin Street and Alabama Avenue contained offices of Atlantic Life Insurance Co., Dr. D. C. Carter, Pilgrim Life

FIGURE 2-201, George D. Wilson Selma Community Center, 16 Franklin Street, Photograph by Susan Besser, 2016

Insurance Co., and Washington Benevolent Protective Association. Many businesses were located on Alabama Avenue including Crocheron & Lewis, undertakers, at 1220 Alabama Avenue; Annie M. Stone, restaurateur at 1205 Alabama Avenue; Moses Lovett, dry cleaners, 136 Washington Street; and Arthur Weaver, barber, at 1209 Alabama Avenue.

The George D. Wilson Selma Community Center is a yellow-brick two-story with a flat roof. The fenestration of the first-story façade consists of two recessed single-door entries and a one-over-one window in the center. The second-story fenestration comprises five one-over-one windows. The corners of the building project approximately two feet and have projecting brick courses forming quoins. Metal coping caps the top course of brick.

African American leaders Samuel W. Boynton, assistant county agent, and Charles J. Adams had long supported this project, but when Dr. E. W. Gamble of St. Paul's Episcopal Church came forward promoting the project it became a reality with the city donating the land and the WPA contributing $40,000 for the building.

FIGURE 2-202, *George Washington Carver Feeding the Masses*, Photograph by Susan Besser, 2015

Amelia Pitts Boynton observed: "It was once the pride of south-central Alabama, where all of the big bands like Duke Ellington, Earl Hines, Nat King Cole, Fats Domino, and others came to play for the black servicemen from Craig Air Force Base."[65] The importance of this building to the African American community is threefold—the primary function as a central meeting place for African American women and children during the Jim Crow era as well as music venue for well-known African American artists; a venue to display art by an African American commissioned during Roosevelt's New Deal artists program; and lastly, that it was the work of a local builder/contractor—George D. Wilson.

FIGURE 2-203, *Swing Low, Sweet Chariot*, Photograph by Susan Besser, 2015

Murals added circa 1937 were part of the WPA Federal Art Project and were done by noted African American artist Felix Benjamin Duncan Gaines. These were located on the first story and are now displayed at the Old Depot Museum. The murals are entitled *Swing Low, Sweet Chariot*

---

65. West et al., "Civil Rights Movement in Selma," 15.

and *George Washington Carver Feeding the Masses*.⁶⁶ Gaines was a graduate of Ohio State College, the Federal Schools of Art in Minneapolis, and the New York School of Design, the latter made possible by Cooper Green, president of Birmingham City Commission. Gaines was an art teacher at Parker High School in Birmingham and won the commission to paint the murals in a competition with over eight hundred artists. While in Selma during World War II he served as director of the Dallas County Colored Community Center, then known as the Negro USO Center.⁶⁷ He is noted for producing a "Psycho Beautograph," his own patent for a technique that utilizes pen and inks to create photo-lithographs. Gaines used it to make images of George Washington Carver. He toured throughout the South to promote these reproductions and sought to continue the work of Carver. In 1947 he presented one to Selma University. These photo-lithographs were also distributed to Selma public schools as a way to encourage African American young people to strive for higher education as a way to foster "racial tolerance and understanding." It was noted in the *Selma Times-Journal* that the distribution of these was approved by the superintendent of schools and civic and education leaders.⁶⁸ Gaines continued his work as an illustrator working for southern publications and created an art school to foster the talents of African American youth.⁶⁹

McDowell House • 302 Franklin Street
Constructed circa 1875

McDowell House is a Queen Anne two-story five-bay with one-story wraparound porch with turreted extension supported by lathe-turned columns. Note the spindlework and flat-cut balustrade and bracketed capitals

---

66. *Alabama Citizen*, August 9, 1947.

67. "Negro Artist Visits City for Art Program," *Anniston Star*, May 19, 1947, 16.

68. "Portraits of Carver Presented to Schools," *Selma Times-Journal*, July 11, 1947, 7.

69. "Southern Negro Artist Visits Heflin in Interest of Better Race Relations," *Cleburne News*, January 19, 1950, 2.

FIGURE 2-204, McDowell House, 302 Franklin Street, Photograph by Susan Besser, 2002

of the columns. The second-story balcony has a shed roof with lathe-turned columns, spindlework, and flat-cut balustrade.

Selma Avenue

313 Selma Avenue • *Constructed circa 1900*

FIGURE 2-205, 313 Selma Avenue, Photograph by Susan Besser, 2002

Unique to this one-story Queen Anne hipped-roof-with-cross-gables dwelling is the stucco exterior. The entry is a single incised carved wood door with glazing surmounted by a transom. A singular treatment to the door surround is the addition of panels that consist of double-paneled stiles with diagonal wood infill. The front gable end has an angled bay with concave mansard roof and trim that creates a scalloped effect over the two-over-two windows. The inset porch terminates in a pyramidal roof with bellcast eaves. Lathe-turned columns with bracketed capitals support the porch, enhanced with a spindlework frieze.

500 Selma Avenue • *Constructed circa 1920*

FIGURE 2-206, 500 Selma Avenue, Photograph by Susan Besser, 2002

This side-hall form of the Craftsman style is a two-story, two-bay, brick-veneer dwelling with low-pitched hipped roof of pressed metal shingles. Both the wood door entry with transom and windows have Tudor arched lintels with brick relieving arches. Massive brick piers with corbeling support the full-width hipped-roof porch. Decorative brackets enrich the columns. Wide overhanging eaves have exposed rafters.

506 Selma Avenue • *Constructed circa 1900*

FIGURE 2-207, 506 Selma Avenue, Photograph by Susan Besser, 2002

This distinctive one-and-one-half-story dwelling with wood shingle exterior has a side gable roof and a front gable entry porch with massive square piers. Influences of the Prairie movement are exhibited in the exposed rafters of the overhanging eaves and decorative brackets enriching the piers. The entry is composed of a wood door with nine lights and sidelights in the unique configuration of six lights with two lights above. The gable end of the entry porch is paneled, and square columns augment the brick piers of the porch. The casement window configuration is six lights with transoms. A shed-roof dormer with casement windows provides light to the second story.

511 Selma Avenue • *Constructed 1925*

Entered through a wrought-iron fence of the Victorian era on the property, which originally belonged to Albert Parrish, this Neoclassical one-and-one-half-story dwelling has a side gable roof with full-width porch supported by fluted Doric columns. Double-leaf fourteen-light doors with seven-light sidelights provide the entry. A large front-gabled dormer with

Palladian window is indicative of the Neoclassical influences. Note the interior brick chimneys with arched hoods.

FIGURE 2-208, 511 Selma Avenue, Photograph by Susan Besser, 2002

Dr. Clarence C. Elebash and his wife, Belzora, resided here in the 1920s. Belzora was the daughter of Albert Parrish. Margaret Elebash, daughter of Belzora and Clarence, married B. Frank Wilson in the dwelling in 1940. Wilson was vice president of the Peoples Bank and secretary of the Hotel Albert. The Wilsons resided here from the 1940s to the 1960s.

520 Selma Avenue • *Constructed 1908*

Built in the Queen Anne style, this one-story dwelling has a gable on hipped roof with flared eaves. The porch is supported by Doric columns set on a solid stucco balustrade. Double-leaf louvered weather doors with a stained-glass transom create an impressive entry. Note that the stained-glass artist incorporated the street address in the transom above the entry. Four two-over-two windows are within the porch and two windows are canted. Windows at the corner of the house are canted and have corner brackets supported by a Doric column.

FIGURE 2-209, 520 Selma Avenue, Photograph by Susan Besser, 2015

The house is referred to as "A Plastered House" and is a variation of design No. 599 from George Barber's *Art in Architecture*; it was built by the Eliasberg family. This particular design for the exterior is influenced by the "Japanese" aesthetic.[70] In a stroke of good fortune Herman Eliasberg, who had just purchased the house from Edward D. Eliasberg on July 20, 1909, sold the property to Eugene Robbins for $5,000 the very same day. In 1914 Robbins sold the house for $4,450 to William I. Smith, who was the superintendent of the Coca-Cola Bottling Company in Selma. The house was purchased by Bernard Adams Reynolds and his wife, Bertha Lee ("Bee") Reynolds, in the mid-1940s. Bernard Reynolds, who died in 1986, was the Dallas County coroner for six years and Dallas County probate judge for more than twenty years.

---

70. Michael D. Alcorn and Christopher R. Dimattei, *Architectural Ragtime: The Houses of Geo. F. Barber & Co.* (Alcorn/Dimattei, 2017), 403.

Milhous-Childers House • 601 Selma Avenue
Constructed circa 1858–1861; second-story addition circa 1902

According to local historians the dwelling began as a one-story brick stucco-veneer residence. The original owner of the dwelling was Samuel C. Tanner, who purchased the lot in 1858 from John D. Palmer of Brooklyn, New York, for the sum of $450. Tanner heirs sold what was still a one-story house and the property to Joseph L. Perkins in March of 1866 for $6,750. Philip Milhous purchased the property from Perkins's estate in 1887. Circa 1902 Milhous's widow, Harriot Martin Milhous, added the second story with her $2,500 inheritance. After her death the estate was divided between her children, Leonard Seawell Jones and Mrs. B. M. Miller Childers (née Hallie Milhous Jones). Mrs. Childers purchased her brother's share and renovated the house in the 1980s.

FIGURE 2-210, Milhous-Childers House, 601 Selma Avenue, Photograph by Susan Besser, 2018

Milhous-Childers House is a unique two-story three-bay with Queen Anne influences and has a hipped roof with cross gable covered with pressed metal shingles. Paired Doric columns support a wide fascia with decorative rectangular inset panels and second-story balcony with wrought-iron balustrade. The bowed front bay to the west has three one-over-one windows while the second story has two one-over-one windows with an exterior of imbricated shingles. The denticulated cornice of the front gable and wide band of trim enframes a gable end of imbricated shingles with louvered vent. A louvered weather door entry has diamond-pane sidelights and diamond-pane broken transom.

Hunter-Hamilton House • 602 Selma Avenue
Constructed circa 1895; alterations circa 1920

FIGURE 2-211, Hunter-Hamilton House, 602 Selma Avenue,
Photograph by Susan Besser, 2018

Originally constructed in 1895 as a winter home for Charles D. Hunter, the house suffered damage due to a fire in the attic in the 1920s. The roofline was reconfigured at the time and deteriorating porches were removed. This unique two-story frame dwelling with hipped roof of pressed metal shingles has an arched overdoor supported by square columns creating the entry porch. The façade is further enhanced with full-height pilasters that enframe a swag detail and multi-pane window in the second story above the entry. Double doors with glazing, arched transom, and paneled surround add to the Colonial Revival detailing. A polygonal bay is to the west.

McPhillips House • 610 Selma Avenue
Constructed circa 1892; alterations 1890

FIGURE 2-212. McPhillips House, 610 Selma Avenue, Photograph by Susan Besser, 2015

E. B. Ward was the original owner of what was once a one-story Italianate dwelling constructed in 1892. The dwelling appears on the Sanborn map in 1898 in its present configuration. The Colonial Revival two-story, three-bay dwelling's most commanding feature is the turret with a conical roof with a flared eave on the bay to the east, embellished with variegated shingles. A polygonal bay is to the west. The impressive entry porch is supported by triple Ionic fluted columns set on brick bases. Note the denticulated cornice along the rooflines of the porch and second story. A single door with full glazing, sidelights, and transom defines the entry. The interior retains much of its historic character, such as the original mantels, leaded- and stained-glass windows, and an impressive coffered ceiling and wainscoting in the dining room. A portion of the original Italianate dwelling eave brackets can be seen on the west elevation. Glenn and Tomeko McPhillips purchased the dwelling in 2002 and installed an energy-efficient geothermal system.

Middleton House • 613 Selma Avenue
Constructed circa 1860; addition circa 1920
Frank Lockwood, Architect, addition

This two-story, five-bay Greek Revival with hipped roof displays Italianate and Colonial Revival details. The original dwelling is a side hall plan. A two-story addition with flush board exterior is to the east. The entry portico and enclosed inset porch have a denticulated cornice and Colonial Revival–period Doric columns. These are not original to the structure but are historic to the evolution of the dwelling. Cornice lintels surmount windows. Eave brackets of the Italianate period enrich the eaves. Two sets of French doors on the first story are four-pane with louvered full-length shutters.

FIGURE 2-213, Middleton House, 613 Selma Avenue, Photograph by Susan Besser, 2002

The Middleton family were the original owners of the dwelling. Local historians believe the original brick portion of the dwelling came from Cahawba. In the 1920s the dwelling was renovated to its present configuration by the Paul Munro family with Frank Lockwood acting as the architect.

The Joe-Ann/Rosenberg Apartments • 620 Selma Avenue
Constructed circa 1925 • John W. McKeil, Architect

The Joe-Ann is an Italian Renaissance brick, two-story, three-bay multifamily dwelling in a U-shaped form. A concave mansard tile roof covers the integral porches, which are enriched with brackets at the cornice. Decorative inset tile at the center of the façade indicates the historical name. The second-story porches to both the east and west of the façade have an elliptical arched transom and ornamental railing. A fifteen-pane entry door with sidelights and transoms is surmounted by a decorative hood.

FIGURE 2-214, The Joe-Ann/Rosenberg Apartments, 620 Selma Avenue, Photograph by Susan Besser, 2022

In March of 1924 Mrs. Joe Rosenberg contracted with John W. McKeil to design the "most complete and convenient apartments to be found in the state."[71] Each apartment was to have seven rooms in addition to a kitchen

---

71. "Contract Is Let for Apartment," *Selma Times-Journal*, March 6, 1924, 1.

and bath and the apartments were to be separated by soundproof walls. Mrs. Rosenberg intended to live in one of the apartments and stated the other three were spoken for.

Parke House • 623 Selma Avenue
Constructed circa 1860; entry 1900

Dr. Clifford Daniel Parke purchased this property in 1859 from Nathaniel N. Allen. Construction began on the property shortly after he purchased it. Dr. Parke's mother-in-law, Mrs. John Swift, had the house completed as a belated wedding gift for her daughter, Lucinda. Dr. Parke practiced in Selma until his death in 1886. Carrie McCord Parke, wife of Julian B. Parke (Dr. Parke's son) was a founding member of the local suffrage move-ment and was the president of the Alabama Equal Suffrage Association. The house remained in the Parke family until 1982 when Dr. Michael Soppet purchased it. Circa 1900 the house was remodeled with a new exterior entry and interior additions in keeping with the Edwardian period.

FIGURE 2-215, Parke House, 623 Selma Avenue, Photograph by Frances Benjamin Johnston, HABS, Library of Congress

This handsome Greek Revival, five-bay, two-story hipped roof has flush board exterior at the center of the façade and weatherboard exterior on the other elevations. The monumental entry porch is composed of fluted Doric columns. The elaborate double-leaf, four-panel entry with beveled- and leaded-glass sidelights as well as beveled- and leaded-glass broken transom is topped with a denticulated cornice, circa 1900. On the second story, double horizontal inset-panel doors with four-pane sidelights open out onto a balconet with decorative wrought-iron balustrade. The Parke House was photographed for the HABS project in the 1930s by Frances Benjamin Johnston and recorded in the *Carnegie Survey of the Architecture of the South*.

Platt-Lewis-Gayle House • 626 Selma Avenue
Constructed circa 1849; addition 1880

FIGURE 2-216, Platt-Lewis-Gayle House, 626 Selma Avenue, Photograph by Susan Besser, 2015

According to local historians, Dr. Elias Parkman built this house circa 1849. William and Cornelia Platt acquired the property in 1854 and then subsequently deeded the property to Charles and Emily Lewis in 1856. In the aftermath of the Battle of Selma, Yankee soldiers planned to raid the house but were compelled to spare it when the Yankee lieutenant in charge realized Mr. Lewis was wearing a Mason Button. The lieutenant, also a Mason, saw the button and protected the house from looting by posting a guard at the home. The richly detailed Italianate two-story side-hall-plan dwelling has a wraparound porch supported by columns with bracketed capitals covered by a concave mansard roof. Double-leaf doors with beveled-glass sidelights surmounted by beveled-glass transom and embellished with engaged columns provide the entry. The denticulated cornices at the rooflines of the second story and porch are enriched with paired-eave brackets. Note the polygonal wing, circa 1880, which also has a denticulated cornice and paired-eave brackets.

707 Selma Avenue • Constructed circa 1910
Chambers, McKeil & Co., Architect • Paul Seale, Contractor

FIGURE 2-217, 707 Selma Avenue, Photograph by Susan Besser, 2002

The Sears House No. 52 from the 1908 catalog that was modified by Chambers, McKeil & Co. for Nathan Liepold is a two-story foursquare and has an exterior of stone-faced concrete block and stucco, hipped roof of pressed metal shingles, and concrete block foundation.[72] A full-width one-story porch with piers and solid balustrade of stone-faced concrete block leads to a handsome single glazed door entry with beveled- and leaded-glass sidelights and transom. A cutwork metal balustrade surmounts the porch roof. The window to the west of the entry is a fixed window of beveled and leaded glass. The window to the east is a diamond-pane-over-one configuration. Fenestration of the second-story windows is paired diamond-pane-over-one configuration to the east and west. A decorative dormer with hipped roof has two narrow diamond-pane windows. There are two interior concrete block chimneys.

713 Selma Avenue • *Constructed circa 1900*

FIGURE 2-218, 713 Selma Avenue, Photograph by Susan Besser, 2002

This two-and-one-half-story, three-bay front gable dwelling has a scored stucco exterior, gable roof of tile, and stone-faced concrete block foundation. A one-story partial flat-roof porch is supported by Ionic columns set on stone-faced concrete blocks and leads to a single glazed door with leaded sidelights and transom. A simple wood balustrade is between the piers and extends beyond the porch to the corner of the dwelling. To the west is a one-over-one double-hung wood sash window. To the east is a tripartite window consisting of a clear fixed window with leaded glass

---

72. *The Tradesman*, 1910, 56.

on either side. The second story has a unique triangular cantilevered bay window of leaded glass capped with a window hood and gable roof of tiles. To either side are one-over-one double-hung wood sash windows. In the gable end is a leaded-glass window enframed with an entablature and dwarf pilasters with a louvered vent on either side. James B. Ellis, president of the Union Ironworkers Company, resided here in the 1920s.

811 Selma Avenue • *Constructed circa 1890*

FIGURE 2-219, 811 Selma Avenue, Photograph by Susan Besser, 2002

This handsome one-story, three-bay Queen Anne cottage has a weatherboard exterior and hipped roof with cross gables. The west bay is front gabled with cutaway bays and has three two-over-two windows flanked by louvered shutters. Corner brackets with pendants enrich the cutaway bays. A pent roof encloses the gable end, and a louvered vent is in the gable end. Paneled stiles enhance a single wood door with glazing and transom. Paired two-over-two windows are to the east. A partial porch supported by Ionic columns gives a Classical influence to the façade.

Little Red School House • 812 Selma Avenue
Constructed circa 1860

Constructed in the Gothic Revival style, this one-story, brick L-plan with front and side gables of pressed metal shingles has scroll-sawn

FIGURE 2-220, Little Red School House, 812 Selma Avenue, Photograph by Susan Besser, 2015

vergeboards with pendants and finials embellishing the gable ends. Note the louvered vents in the gable ends, which feature a Gothic-inspired hood mold. A hipped-roof porch located on the east elevation provides a covered entry to the two separate entrances. Miss Mary Lavender, who resided there, was known as Selma's "Florence Nightingale," as evidenced by her daily visits to the Confederate Hospital after the Battle of Selma, most likely influenced by her father, Dr. C. H. Lavender. Miss Lavender was a primary teacher for the Christian Church, her father being one of the founding fathers. It is noted in her obituary that she built the first green house in Selma. The Little Red School House served as an auxiliary building for Dallas Academy for the primary grades beginning in the early 1920s.[73]

---

73. "Beloved Woman Taken by Death," *Selma Times-Journal*, February 16, 1929, 3.

Dallas Academy • 816 Selma Avenue
Constructed 1889; renovated 1978
Chisholm & Green, Architect • Andrew Jackson Mullen, Contractor
Tiller/Butner/Rosa Architects, renovation, 1978

Dallas Academy had its beginnings as the segregated white-only Dallas Male and Female Academy. The original building is located at 114 Mabry Street. As the student population grew a two-story frame building was constructed on Selma and Church with the land donated by William Johnson. The brick building on Mabry Street was designated for the male students and the building at Selma Avenue and Church Street for the female students. In 1868 Captain N. D. Cross took over leadership of the school, which received $8,000 from the Peabody Fund and funding from the city and state. Cross went to Boston to observe their school system and brought back a study that was incorporated into the new system. In 1869 the State

FIGURE 2-221, Dallas Academy, 816 Selma Avenue, Photograph by Susan Besser, 2002

Board of Education formed a separate school district in Selma with Dallas Academy under the purview of this district.[74]

The two-story frame building was lost to fire in 1887 and in 1889 a new building was designed by Chisolm and Green to serve all the students. Dallas Academy is a three-story brick side-gable building with three front-gabled wings separated by hyphens forming a distinctive "H" shape that would have provided maximum ventilation and daylighting for the classrooms. Renaissance Revival influences are evidenced at the basement level with arched openings of corbelled brick with keystone and stone label stops that encase double arched doors. Arched two-over-two windows with stone-stepped arches and stone lintels emphasize the third story. The gable ends of the wings have imbricated shingles and louvered vents flanking triangular pediment windows. A tower with an S-curve mansard roof and cupolas on the rear of the building gives a nod to the Queen Anne style.

Chisholm & Green, the architects for Dallas Academy, had established themselves as a firm just before designing the building. B. S. Chisholm was a graduate of Union College and Lonsdale Green a graduate of MIT. The design for the building was considered forward thinking for that time. According to Robert Gamble, Dallas Academy "mirrors the influence of the 'London School Board Style,' developed during the 1870s" by a group of British architects for public schools. Indicative of this movement is the ground-level play area, now enclosed, which originally would have the capability of being open to the outdoors. This flexible play area and H-shaped design to maximize daylight created an innovative environment for learning.[75]

---

74. Hardy, *Selma: Her Institutions and Her Men*, 145-146.

75. Robert Gamble, "Old Dallas Academy," *SAH Archipedia*, Society of Architectural Historians, https://sah-archipedia.org/buildings/AL-01-047-0087.

Selma Buick Company • 901 Selma Avenue
Constructed 1922 • John M. McKeil, Architect

Built at a cost of $30,000, this one-story brick free-standing commercial building has a corner entrance and display windows on a brick bulkhead. Located at the corner of Selma Avenue and Church Street the building occupied a prominent place in the business district. The parapet wall echoes the stepped quality of the Art Deco movement, which is early in the movement and is embellished with cut-stone coping. An awning shelters the display windows. An insignia with the letter "B" denotes the original function of the building as a Buick dealership—built at a time when automobiles became more affordable to the general public.

FIGURE 2-222, Selma Buick Company, 901 Selma Avenue, Photograph by Susan Besser, 2002

According to the *Selma Times-Journal* the "best building materials, from the sand, which underlies all the mass of concrete work, to the soft, gray-toned brick and hollow tile which makes the building most pleasing to the eye, are to be obtained right here in Selma."[76]

---

76. "Selma Buick's New Building Monument to Home Products Open to Public Monday at 4," *Selma Times-Journal*, January 29, 1922, 9.

Chamber of Commerce, Carnegie Library • 912 Selma Avenue
Constructed circa 1903 • Charles Henry Hopson, Architect

The Renaissance Revival Carnegie Library is one of fourteen municipal Carnegie libraries in the state of Alabama. Andrew Carnegie, steel magnate, as part of his philanthropy supported the construction of public libraries across the United States and Canada as well as the British Isles, Australia, and New Zealand. Over 2,500 Carnegie libraries were built over a period of fifty years, from 1883 to 1929. Andrew Carnegie was petitioned by Selmians to fund a library for the city. He provided a grant of $10,000, and the final cost came in at $11,785. The Selma Suffrage Association met at the Carnegie Library, now the Centre of Commerce, and from this group, Hattie Hooker Wilkins emerged as the first woman legislator in Alabama. In May of 1963 Patricia Swift Blalock became the director of the Carnegie Library. At this time African Americans in Selma checked out their books at the back door with the aid of a library maid. Patricia Blalock approached the library board concerning desegregating the library. Mrs. Blalock gradually won over the board, quietly integrating the library.[77]

FIGURE 2-223, Carnegie Library, 912 Selma Avenue, Photograph by Susan Besser, 2015

---

77. Fitts, *Selma: A Bicentennial History*, 239.

Designed by local architect Charles Henry Hopson and built of brick and stone, this Neo-Classical Revival one-story building has a dual-pitched hipped roof with a metal skylight at the apex of the roof. The impressive entrance pavilion is capped by a brick parapet leading to double doors with an arched stone enframed fanlight and sidelights with keystone lintels. Stone pilasters flank the entrance. Other details such as the dripstone course, cast-iron cyma-reversa denticulated cornice, and quoins at the corners exemplify this style.

Walton Theater/Larry D. Striplin Performing Arts Center
1000 Selma Avenue • *Constructed circa 1914*

The Walton Theater, currently Striplin Performing Arts Center , celebrated the grand opening of its theatorium on August 10, 1914. An advertisement in the *Selma Times-Journal* touted Mr. Hurlbert playing the famous Bartola organ by saying, "You Never Heard the Like Before." Admission was ten cents for adults and five cents for children under twelve. In 1932 the *Selma Times-Journal* described a complete renovation with a new Western Electric sound system, new seats, carpeting, draperies, and lighting effects when talking pictures made their debut and earned the the-ater national attention. In the late 1940s the Walton Theater staged amateur

FIGURE 2-224, Walton Theater/Striplin Performing Arts Center, 1000 Selma Avenue, Photograph by Susan Besser, 2002

nights that would include a feature movie, a local talent act, a newsreel, and a short comedy. By the 1970s the Walton Theater was in disrepair and had closed its doors. In the 1980s Anita Bryant, while a resident in Selma, along with Larry Striplin Jr., sponsored a benefit entitled "Stars Fell on Alabama" with Bob Hope and Ricky Skaggs as headliners, raising over $1 million. Under the leadership of Elizabeth Driggers, director of the Selma Planning and Development Department, who oversaw the rehabilitation, the Walton Theater reopened in May of 1985 as the Larry D. Striplin Performing Arts Center. In 1985 President Ford spoke at an event at the Center. In discussing its importance he said, "The rehabilitation of the Walton Theater will inevitably be a focal point of the expansion and the improvement of the city of Selma."[78] In the 1990s the theater again closed its doors. Partnering with J. David and Sharon Jackson, the city of Selma reopened the Walton Theater as a movie theater in January of 2012.

The Larry D. Striplin Performing Arts Center is a handsome brick-veneer, one-story, flat-roof building with a two-story entrance wing. A parapet wall enriches the façade and forms a geometric frieze formed by employing various brick patterns. The striking two-story primary entrance highlights the segmental arched stone enframed clerestory of geometric paned windows. The triangular-shaped parapet with arched ends has a double ranking stone cornice with paired corbels. Multilight double-leaf doors flank the original ticket window.

Selma-Dallas County Library • 1103 Selma Avenue
Constructed circa 1975 • Ed Neal of Bigger, Neal & Clark, Architect

The Selma-Dallas County Library resonates with the French influences of the Colonial Revival style. It is a two-story building in the raised plantation form. Two-story porticos project from the façade and are supported with piers on the first story and decorative cast-iron columns, frieze, and balusters on the second story. A circular stone staircase with cast-iron railing leads to either side of the main entrance. The fenestration features

---

78. Scott Bernarde, "Gerald Ford: His Message Rang Loud and Clear," *Selma Times-Journal*, September 13, 1985, 1.

FIGURE 2-225, Selma-Dallas County Library, 1103 Selma Avenue, Photograph by Susan Besser, 2015

double doors with glazing and sidelights surmounted by transoms on the first story and double doors with sidelights surmounted by transoms on the second story. The quintessential image of the raised plantation form is reinforced by the window configuration of six-over-six windows flanked by louvered shutters.

Downtowner Restaurant/Selma Steam Laundry
1114 Selma Avenue • *Constructed circa 1910*

The Selma Steam Laundry Building, built circa 1910, is constructed of cement block and during its tenure as a laundry in this location was completely electric. Managed by John C. Rennie, the establishment advertised the shafting process, which was conducted in the basement to eliminate the creation of dust and grease in the work room.[79] The laundry became the Downtowner Restaurant in 1984.[80]

---

79. *Selma Mirror*, June 28, 1911, 82.

80. Jeanette Berryman, "Renovation Efforts Bring New Businesses," *Selma Times-Journal*, March 18, 1984. 1.

FIGURE 2-226, Downtowner Restaurant/Selma Steam Laundry, 1114 Selma Avenue, Photograph by Bill Tomey, 2025

This one-story commercial block building is detailed with a corbel and dentil molding and has a shed-roof porch with standing-seam metal roof enriched with corner cast-iron brackets. The entry is composed of a single glass door flanked by sidelights surmounted by a fanlight.

First Christian Church/Blue Jean Church • 1209 Selma Avenue
Constructed 1906 • Attributed to Charles Henry Hopson
W. W. McKibbon, Contractor

First Christian Church was organized in 1852 and held meetings in the home of Mr. and Mrs. E. C. Lavender. The church had grown to thirty members by 1854 and decided to build a permanent building, which was located at the corner of Alabama Avenue and Green Street. The simple classic gable-front brick building with Gothic influences has an arched recessed entry with double doors leading into the sanctuary. The sanctuary is of the Neo-Gothic style, is one-and-one-half stories, and is constructed in the Akron Plan initially used in the First Methodist Church of Akron, Ohio. This plan was envisioned by philanthropist/Sunday school superintendent Lewis Miller, who was a part of the Chautauqua Move-ment; John Hyle Vincent; and architect Jacob Snyder. A domed sanctuary contains pews arranged in a semicircle with a sloping floor. Sunday school classes are placed around the perimeter of the assembly hall separated by folding doors. This affords additional worship space as the need arises. The exterior is of rough-faced cement block and a lantern with a polygonal roof with lancet dormer windows pierces the hipped roof of red asphalt shin-gles. Two corner entrances have double-leaf entry doors surmounted by an arched transom. Note the large Tudor windows on the south and east elevations, each composed of five smaller lancet stained-glass windows and three stained-glass rose windows.

FIGURE 2-227, First Christian Church/Blue Jean Church, 1209 Selma Avenue, Photograph by Susan Besser, 2015

First Christian Church is similar to J. Wesley Smith Memorial Church in Halifax, designed by Charles Henry Hopson, in the massing and placement of the corner entry as well as the Gothic Revival influences.

Additionally, Evergreen Baptist Church by Hopson in Evergreen, Alabama, has similar massing. Hopson is known for his mastery of ecclesiastical architecture.

Cumberland Presbyterian Church/Selma Avenue Church of Christ
1315 Selma Avenue • *Constructed circa 1890*

FIGURE 2-228, Cumberland Presbyterian Church/Selma Avenue Church of Christ, 1315 Selma Avenue, Photograph by Susan Besser, 2002

Selma Avenue Church of Christ is a one-story building with hipped roof of pressed metal shingles and is of the Romanesque Revival period. A Syrian arch supported by cushion capitals on plinths leads to an integral porch and double-leaf two-panel doors. Multilight windows are above the arch. The front tower has a pyramidal roof covered with pressed metal shingles. The second story of the tower features triple arched vents which aid in air circulation.

Alabama Avenue

Philpot-Walker House • 603 Alabama Avenue
Constructed circa 1852

Stone steps lead to this one-story Greek Revival raised cottage with a full-width hipped-roof porch of standing-seam metal graced with six square columns and an iron balustrade fashioned in a diamond pattern. The dwelling has three bays and flush board on the façade. Double-leaf doors of two panels each with an eight-light transom and four-light sidelights form the entry. Fenestration is composed of six-over-six windows placed symmetrically as is typical of the Greek Revival period.

FIGURE 2-229, Philpot-Walker House, 603 Alabama Avenue, Photograph by Susan Besser, 2023

While Robert Philpot was away on an extended business trip, Mrs. Philpot supervised the building of the house assisted by their enslaved workers. Mr. Philpot owned an iron foundry in Selma, was an elder at St. Paul's Episcopal Church, and was a founding member of the City National Bank, which is presently known as AmSouth. According to local historians the house survived the ravages of the Battle of Selma due to Mrs. Philpot's insistence the house be protected. Its close proximity to the Arsenal placed the house at great risk. Union General Wilson posted guards, who formed a bucket brigade from the Alabama River to keep the house wet throughout the Battle, thus saving the house. Unfortunately, Mr. Philpot died in the Battle of Selma.

612 Alabama Avenue • *Constructed circa 1890*

FIGURE 2-230, 612 Alabama Avenue, Photograph by Susan Besser, 2002

Illustrating a simpler form of the Queen Anne Spindlework style is this symmetrical one-story, hipped-roof with cross gable residence with shed-roof porch and spindlework frieze with turned columns and bracket capitals. Other elements typical of this style are double doors with glazing and transom flanked by paneled stiles and the variegated shingles enriching the cross gable.

613 Alabama Avenue • *Constructed circa 1890–1897*

Maud St. John Philpot Hooper and her husband, John J. Hooper, conveyed the lot for this dwelling to Edward S. Gatchell, a merchant and

FIGURE 2-231, 613 Alabama Avenue, Photograph by Susan Besser, 2002

druggist. The Gatchells built the house sometime between 1890 and 1897 and then sold the property in 1897 to Dr. John S. Peake for $4,500. Dr. William Jenkins Reynolds, a prominent dentist in Selma, purchased the property from heirs of Dr. Peak in 1903. Nancy Reynolds Bennett owned the property between 1983 and 1995, when she sold it to Micki Beth Stiller. A charming wrought-iron fence surrounds this one-story, four-bay dwelling of Queen Anne and Stick influences. To the west is the gable-front bay with two-over-two windows and cutaway bays. Applied stickwork enriches the frieze and fish-scale shingles enhance the gable end. Lathe-turned columns support the hipped-roof porch that has a geometric pattern balustrade.

614 Alabama Avenue • *Constructed circa 1890*

This vernacular two-and-one-half-story Queen Anne has a hipped roof with cross gables, beaded weatherboard, and a spindlework frieze around the main wraparound porch and second-story balcony. The north-facing gable front has cutaway bays and a multi-paned stained-glass window as

FIGURE 2-232, 614 Alabama Avenue, Photograph by Susan Besser, 2002

well as imbricated shingles in the gable end. There are two chimney clusters indicating five fireplaces in the interior.

618 Alabama Avenue • *Constructed circa 1880*

FIGURE 2-233, 618 Alabama Avenue, Photograph by Susan Besser, 2002

Reflecting influences of the late nineteenth century, this one-story, three-bay house has a side-gable roof with standing-seam metal and centered front gable with scroll-sawn vergeboard. Paired eave brackets enrich the cornice. The central entry portico has a front gable with cornice return and is supported by simple square columns and leads to a single-leaf door flanked by multi-pane sidelights.

619 Alabama Avenue • *Constructed circa 1900*

FIGURE 2-234, 619 Alabama Avenue, Photograph by Susan Besser, 2002

Built circa 1900, this one-story, five-bay Queen Anne–influenced vernacular dwelling is a side-gable form with centered cross gable. The shed-roof porch has columns set on wood piers, a flat-cut balustrade, and bracketed capitals. Early residents of the dwelling were John and Claudia Paisley. John was president of Paisley-Stewart, an insurance company.

626 Alabama Avenue • *Constructed circa 1900; alterations circa 1920*

FIGURE 2-235, 626 Alabama Avenue, Photograph by Susan Besser, 2002

Illustrating change over time is this one-story, Queen Anne L-plan with cutaway bays on the front gable. The residence retains the gable roof of pressed metal shingles. Circa 1920 it was modified with a Craftsman-era shed-roof porch with battered columns on brick piers.

Devotie House • 627 Alabama Avenue
Constructed circa 1850

FIGURE 2-236, Devotie House, 627 Alabama Avenue, Photograph by Susan Besser, 2002

This dwelling was once the home of Noble Leslie Devotie. Devotie graduated as valedictorian of the 1856 class of the University of Alabama and went on to Presbyterian Theological Seminary, graduating in 1859. He became pastor of First Baptist Church in Selma. In 1861 he joined the Confederate forces as a chaplain stationed at Fort Morgan. At the young age of twenty-three Devotie became an early casualty of the Civil War when, while attempting to board a Confederate ship, he slipped and drowned in Mobile Bay. In 1916 the house was listed as a business school run by Mrs. Minnie Miller. Devotie House is an I-house form two-story, five-bay brick building and has a side gable roof of standing-seam metal. A full-width first-story porch and second-story balcony with flat-cut balustrades and bracket capitals reflect the Italianate influence.

630 Alabama Avenue • *Constructed circa 1865*

FIGURE 2-237, 630 Alabama Avenue, Photograph by Susan Besser, 2002

Built circa 1865, this raised cottage of Greek Revival influences is a one-story, four-bay dwelling with a handsome full-width hipped-roof porch with square columns and simple balustrade. Nine-over-nine windows with louvered shutters flank the entry doors. A wide band of trim follows the cornice. Notable are the single six-panel doors which form two separate entries.

The reasoning for the separate doors was to provide separate entrances for the public and private spaces. One door led to the keeping room, which contained the fireplace and eating area. The other door led to the more formal living area or parlor.

700 Alabama Avenue • *Constructed circa 1890*

FIGURE 2-238, 700 Alabama Avenue, Photograph by Susan Besser, 2002

Indicative of the Queen Anne influences and Italianate influences of the nineteenth century is this one-story, five-bay cottage with side-gable roof with centered cross gable of pressed metal shingles. A full-width shed-roof porch covered with standing-seam metal has bracketed columns and flattened-arch frieze with scroll-sawn foliate detail that enhances the handsome edifice.

Stack Building • 706 Alabama Avenue
Constructed circa 1965

FIGURE 2-239, Stack Building, 706 Alabama Avenue, Photograph by Susan Besser, 2002

The Stack Building is a one-story commercial building with a flat roof and brick veneer exterior. The austerity of the façade is relieved by reveals of stack-bond brick between sections of brick and the distinctive glass block with geometric designs to the east. The primary entry is a plate-glass door, facing east and covered by a cantilevered roof.

Keith House • 711 Alabama Avenue
Constructed circa 1884 • Attributed to Michael J. Miller, Architect[81]

Keith House is a textbook version of the Carpenter Gothic Revival style. Alexander Jackson Davis and Andrew Jackson Downing, who were proponents of the Gothic style, popularized the style for domestic and public buildings in their influential mid-nineteenth century publications such as *Rural Residences* and *The Architecture of Country Houses*. It is rare to see this style in an urban setting. The two-story, four-bay L-plan with

---

81. *Selma Times-Journal*, September 30, 1880, 3.

FIGURE 2-240, Keith House, 711 Alabama Avenue,
Photograph by Susan Besser, 2002

board and batten exterior with cusp detail incorporates elements such as Tudor arch windows on the first story and lancet arch windows on the second story. The Tudor arch entrance features a wood door and sidelights with stained glass surmounted by an arched stained-glass transom with the numbers "711." Details such as a through-cornice dormer with lancet arch, a hipped-roof porch with braced arches enriched with bracket capitals, modified cluster columns, and delicately detailed vergeboards contribute to the exquisite design of the dwelling. A carriage house of the period is associated with the property. The house contains three full bathrooms, one of which has a rib-cage shower.

Georgette Apartments • 718 Alabama Avenue
Constructed circa 1910; porch circa 1980

The Georgette Apartments, built circa 1910 and of the Renaissance Revival style, are a three-story, brick-veneer edifice. Defined by polygonal bays with corner quoins of stone, the bays splay to reveal a handsome

FIGURE 2-241, Georgette Apartments, 718 Alabama Avenue, Photograph by Susan Besser, 2002

glass-door entrance with sidelights and transom. A parapet wall conceals the flat roof and is embellished with stone detail. Egg-and-dart molding enriches the cornice. A flat-roof entry porch with metal columns is a later addi-tion, circa 1980.

724 Alabama Avenue • *Constructed circa 1925*

This unique two-story stucco house has a one-story flat-roof porch supported by square piers that extend and form a balcony for the second story. The first-story porch has a solid balustrade and is enclosed with glass. A hipped roof with a cross gable forms the roofline. The second-story balcony has double doors with multi-panes with a blind fanlight. The fenestration of the first and second stories has casement windows. This site was the home of Edmund Winston Pettus. He was a United States senator and resided here from 1866 to 1907, when he passed away.

FIGURE 2-242, 724 Alabama Avenue, Photograph by Susan Besser, 2021

In the 1930s and 1940s this was the parsonage for the First Baptist Church. Dr. John A. Davison resided here from the 1930s until his passing in 1947.

808 Alabama Avenue • *Constructed circa 1920*

FIGURE 2-243, 808 Alabama Avenue, Photograph by Susan Besser, 2002

This Craftsman-era residence features a symmetrical façade with a partial-width porch with front gable enclosed by pent roof supported by battered columns set on brick piers. A single door with sidelights creates an inviting entrance.

Riggs-Morgan House • 816 Alabama Avenue
Constructed circa 1843

FIGURE 2-244, Riggs-Morgan House, 816 Alabama Avenue, Photograph by Frances Benjamin Johnston, Library of Congress

The Riggs-Morgan House is a one-story, brick, four-bay Greek Revival in a side-gable roof form with stepped parapet walls. Double-hung windows have a nine-over-nine window configuration. The full-width porch has square Doric columns and square Doric pilasters at corners of the façade. Two separate entries contain louvered weather doors surmounted by stone lintels. The separate doors provided separate entrances for the public and private spaces. One door led to the keeping room, which contained the fireplace and eating area. The other door led to the more formal living area.

Berry House • 900 Alabama Avenue
Constructed circa 1880

FIGURE 2-245, Berry House, 900 Alabama Avenue, Photograph by Frances Benjamin Johnston, Library of Congress, 1939

Located at the corner of Church Street and Alabama Avenue, the Berry House is named for the family who occupied the dwelling for many years. Built by Dr. John A. McKinnon, it is a brick hipped-roof, two-story, three-bay, side-hall-plan building. Embellished by an elaborate two-story gallery of cast ironwork manufactured in Selma, this handsome building has an entry of double-leaf doors with glazing and segmental arched transom. Four-over-four segmental arched windows to the north and south flank a central entry on the second story consisting of a four-panel door with segmental arched transom. The wide overhanging eaves are enriched with a dentil band and modillions. Frances Benjamin Johnston (1864–1952) was a groundbreaking female photographer and took this photograph in 1939, which was included in her documentation of buildings and gardens known as the *Carnegie Survey of the Architecture of the South*.

Parrish Building • 902 Alabama Avenue
Constructed circa 1900

FIGURE 2-246, Parrish Building, 902 Alabama Avenue, Photograph by Susan Besser, 2002

This early twentieth-century two-story, three-bay, brick building has a flat roof with shaped parapet. The recessed entry is to the east and has double-leaf doors with full glazing and transom. A brick arch with label stops frames the entry. To the west are two-over-two double-hung wood sash windows with arched lintel and radiating brick voussoirs. The second story has two-over-two windows with arched lintel and radiating brick voussoirs elongating into a lintel course. The center of the parapet has a triangular design recessed into the brick with projecting brick courses forming rectangles to either side. On either end of the parapet are cross shapes recessed into the brick. Stone coping caps the top course of the brick parapet. Over the years this commercial building has served as the offices for professionals such as Dr. B. C. Fowlkes, Dr. J. S. Chisholm, Dr. Samuel Kirkpatrick, and Dr. M. L. Rutland.

Federal Court House, NRHP 1976 • 910 Alabama Avenue
Constructed circa 1909 • James Knox Taylor, Architect

FIGURE 2-247, Federal Court House, 910 Alabama Avenue, Photograph by Susan Besser, 2002

Before James Knox Taylor's appointment as supervising architect, federal government buildings were constructed in the Romanesque Revival style. Architects were calling for a style of architecture that would reflect the country's status as a world leader. Taylor is credited for this Beaux Arts design, which is influenced by the exhibition buildings of the World's Columbian Exposition in Chicago. The imposing three-story, five-bay edifice is of cut limestone and yellow brick and has rusticated limestone on the first story. Double-leaf doors with glazing and segmental arched transom define the entry. To the east and west are paired one-over-one windows with transom and flat arch. Dominating the façade are the central bays of paired one-over-one windows with transom enriched with entablature and surmounted by a window hood and oculus. Stone arches have a keystone console and label stop, and pilasters with capitals define the bays. The second-story bays to east and west are one-over-one windows with segmental arched transom and stone surround with segmental arch and keystone. Third-story windows on either end are paired one-over-one windows with stone surround with keystone. The cornice is embellished with a modillion course and roofline stone balustrade with stone piers. Several important court cases relating to the Civil Rights Movement occurred in this courthouse under the direction of Judge Frank Johnson.

1001-1003 Alabama Avenue • *Constructed circa 1870; altered circa 1907*

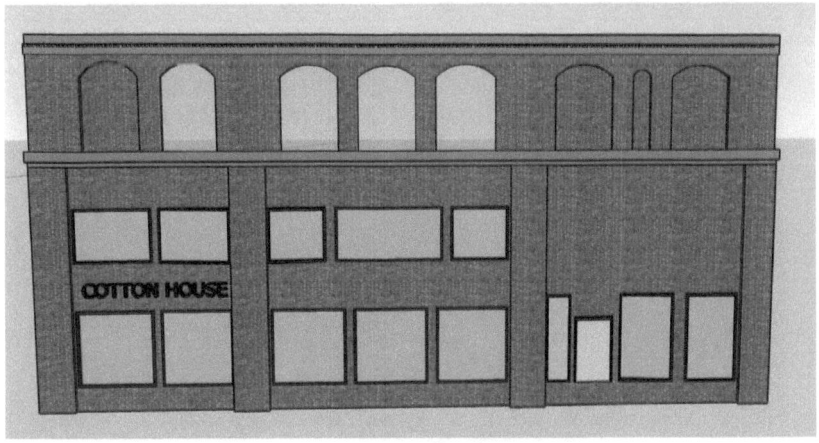

FIGURE 2-248, 1001-1003 Alabama Avenue,
Drawing by Carley Cabral, November 2023

This building has a fascinating history. It began as St. Paul's Episcopal Church in the 1870s. After the new building on Church Street for St. Paul's was completed, the older building was deeded to Temple Mishkan Israel in 1879. "The stranger who, in the future, shall visit our city and shall notice its different objects of interest, will depart feeling that of the places of worship to be found here, the synagogue is the most tasteful, elegant, comfortable and conveniently located. It was bought by the Jews of the Episcopalians of Selma, by whom it had been used since the war as a place of worship." M. J. Miller is noted as doing the woodwork for the building.[82] The exterior of the church remains behind the brick veneer. An armory was located in the building in 1903. The Sanborn map of 1907 indicates this was a two-story building with a wholesale clothing store occupying the space. The Mitchell-Snyder Drug Co. with an up-to-date soda fountain was located in this building in 1911. A sign for Mitchell-Snyder is embedded in the sidewalk.

FIGURE 2-249, 1001 Alabama Avenue, Photograph Courtesy Bill Tomey

This one-story brick, two-part commercial block building has a gable roof from the original church partially hidden by the parapet. Two bays are separated by brick piers and fixed-glass display windows rest on brick bulkheads. A denticulated cornice runs along the top of the parapet and

---

82. *Southern Argus*, June 13, 1879, 3.

creates the division between the parapet and storefront. Segmental arched openings are bricked except for the four facing Alabama, revealing the roof trusses of the original building.

Melvin Heinz Building • 1006 Alabama Avenue
Constructed circa 1908 • Charles H. Hopson, Architect

FIGURE 2-250, Melvin Heinz Building, 1006 Alabama Avenue, Photograph by Susan Besser, 2002

As technology for making glass improved and structural techniques using high-strength steel became more accessible, commercial buildings such as this three-story, enframed window wall were more prevalent in downtown Main Street settings. Note the yellow brick laid to create a rusticated effect, attached flat-roof canopy, and double door at the angled entrance. Pilasters define entry and enframe a multi-pane fixed central window. The wide overhanging modillioned cornice takes its cue from the Renaissance Revival era.

Robinson Building • 1007-1009 Alabama Avenue
Constructed circa 1885

FIGURE 2-251, Robinson Building, 1007-1009 Alabama Avenue, Drawing by Mary Peterson, November 2023

Embodying the Renaissance Revival influences is this three-story, two-bay, two-part commercial block building, circa 1885. Employing the cast-iron storefront fashioned into panel stiles, the display windows are set on a brick bulkhead and the transoms have stained glass that is nearly intact. Three entries, including one to the upper stories, are of plate glass with metal trim. Transoms surmount the doors; two have metal trim, one is the original wood trim. An angled display window with transom faces the alley. The second story's fenestration reveals two-over-two windows with a stone lintel course with keystone. Between the second and third stories and below the windows is a dogtooth brick patttern.

Creating an intricate stone lintel with keystones the fenestration of the original windows consists of single camber and segmental arched tripartite openings. Pilasters define the bays and a wide band of trim surmounts the pilasters. Originally, the building featured an elaborate continuous cornice finished with cor-bels with bulb finials at either end. A wide band of trim featured blind arches inset with horseshoe arches and separated by cartouche elements. Early occupants of this building were Brislins Bicycle Hospital and Brislins Selma Shoe Surgery and then I.J. Hix Jewelry and Sherwin Williams Paint Company in the 1920s.

1110-1112 Alabama Avenue • *Constructed circa 1900*

FIGURE 2-252, 1110-1112 Alabama Avenue,
Drawing by Giuila Ware, November 2023

This two-story stucco building has a unique transom configuration with Gothic overtones. The second-story windows are camber arched windows. The proposed rehabilitation of the storefront returns the symmetry of the building. The east and west entries feature the typical display windows and transoms. The uniqueness of this façade is exemplified by the Gothic tracery transoms. The two-story, three-bay stucco commercial block building has a wood bulkhead. The rendering reveals the original fenestration.

The second story indicates segmental arched windows with arched lintels with a brick relieving arch.

W. M. Hinson Furniture Co. • 1113 Alabama Avenue
Constructed circa 1916 • John W. McKeil, Architect
Thomas Purvis, Contractor

FIGURE 2-253, W. M. Hinson Building, 1113 Alabama Avenue, Photograph by Susan Besser, 2002

The three-story artfully designed W. M. Hinson Building was built as an enframed window wall and was constructed during the period when daylight was maximized by the use of large transoms above first-story display windows. The first story of display windows of the historic wood storefront splays to double doors with glazing. An enframed signboard of brown tile with a white field creates a division to the third story. Two rows of stone torus molding with a fillet create a narrow band that enframes the window wall brickwork. Full entablature with projecting cornice embellished with paired modillions lends a distinctive classic air to the façade.

In the periodical *Industrial Development and Manufacturers' Record of 1916,* John W. McKeil is listed as the architect of record with the building completed at a cost of $9,000. Defining the entrance is inlaid tile which reads "W. M. Hinson Furniture Co." The interior of the building is intact and retains the pressed tin ceiling, historic office configuration, and mezzanine.

1115 Alabama Avenue
Constructed circa 1890; Carrara glass addition circa 1930

FIGURE 2-254, 1115 Alabama Avenue, Old Depot Museum Archives

Note the initials "IBS" above the second-story windows, indicating the owners of the building in the 1930s—I. Bendersky & Sons. Mr. Bendersky had elevated himself from a junk dealer located at 501 Water Avenue in 1906. Previous to this the building housed Ike's Saloon (1906) and Elite Theatre (1913) for African Americans. Refaced circa 1930, the Carrara glass in black and cream creates a distinctive contrast to the early twentieth-century brick streetscape. In 1906 Penn-American Plate Glass Company began manufacturing white and black Carrara glass, so named due to the resemblance to white Carrara marble. It was a popular material to cover existing buildings in the 1920s to 1940s.

1118 Alabama Avenue
Constructed circa 1872; storefront circa 1950
A. Von Fichert, Architect

FIGURE 2-255, 1118 Alabama Avenue, Photograph by Susan Besser, 2019

Originally known as Gillman's Hall, Barton's Department Store occupied this handsome building at the corner of Alabama Avenue and Washington Street, a two-story, two-bay brick component of a two-part commercial block. This has a decidedly classic influence reflecting the Renaissance Revival era. The fenestration of the second story is a tripartite division of two segmental arched openings with relieving arch flanked by three arched openings. The elegant pediment exhibits brick corbelling, a dentil band, and a shaped parapet incorporating finials and a shell ornament.

Eagles Department Store • 1119-1121 Alabama Avenue
Constructed circa 1890

FIGURE 2-256, Eagles Department Store, 1119-1121 Alabama Avenue, Drawing by Kate Allen, 2023

The Eagle family owned Eagles Department Store on the corner of Alabama and Washington and were the original occupants of the building. The name is inscribed in the sidewalk. It is a two-story, commercial brick building in the Renaissance Revival manner. The display window on marble bulkhead splays to off-center entrances. Six-over-six windows are capped with a flat lintel. The original cast-iron pilasters are intact. Cast-iron cornice lintels cap second-story windows.

Sullivan Building • 1220 Alabama Avenue
Constructed circa 1915

FIGURE 2-257, Sullivan Building, 1220 Alabama Avenue, Photograph by Dr. Carroll Van West, NRHP 2013

Positioned on the corner of Alabama Avenue and Franklin Street, the Sullivan Building with its original metal awning creates an imposing presence. During the Civil Rights era it was the headquarters for the Student Nonviolent Coordinating Committee. The Courageous Eight along with J. L. Chestnut, Margaret Moore, and Louretta Wimberly also held Voting Rights meetings in the Sullivan Building in the 1960s. Horace B. Sulllivan and his son, H. Stanley Sullivan, built the building. Crocheron & Lewis, African American undertakers, owned and occupied the Sullivan Building after the death of Mr. Sullivan. A fine early twentieth-century commercial building constructed circa 1915 featuring a variation of the Chicago window, a large fixed-glass pane with double sash windows on either side. One of the primary considerations of the Chicago window was allowing maximum light to the interior. In this case the third-story windows are arched and segmental arched and artfully linked with a continuous lintel. This three-story building displays dichro-matic brickwork and multiple brickwork patterns. Multiple dentil bands are surmounted by a handsome parapet composed of triangular-shaped piers.

City Hall/Cecil C. Jackson, Jr. Public Safety Building
1300 Alabama Avenue • *Constructed circa 1941*
Raymond Sizemore, Architect • *Forcum-James, Contractor*

FIGURE 2-258, City Hall, Cecil C. Jackson, Jr. Public Safety Building, 1300 Alabama Avenue, Photograph by Susan Besser, 2002

The Public Safety Building, originally the city hall, was constructed as part of the recovery program of the depression era. Martin Luther King Jr. was housed in its jail in February of 1964, penning the influential "Letter from Selma Jail," which was published in *The New York Times*. During the Civil Rights Movement era Rep. John R. Lewis was jailed here for two weeks for picketing for voting rights at the Dallas County Courthouse.[83]

---

83. John Lewis, "Six Month Report (July-December)," SNCC, PDF available at http://www.crmvet.org/docs/6312_sncc_lewis_rpt.pdf.

This three-story brick building, designed by Raymond Sizemore, reflects the Neoclassical influences of the period. A stone balustrade surmounts the monumental two-story porch with Doric columns and pilasters. A stone drip course embellishes the façade. The classical surround has a triangular broken pediment surmounted by inscribed scroll stonework. To the west and east are fixed-glass windows. The smaller windows have a stone surround and cornice lintel and the larger windows of the first story have a crossetted surround. Third-story windows are simpler with a flat lintel with keystone. The parapet wall is enriched with a molding of fascia and cyma reversa. Band molding caps the top course of brick.

Arsenal Place

701 Arsenal Place • *Constructed circa 1925*
Frank Lockwood, Architect

FIGURE 2-259, 701 Arsenal Place, Photograph by Susan Besser, 2002

This Colonial Revival two-story features a six-panel door with blind wood fanlight, triangular pedimented entry portico with classical columns, banks of casement windows, and denticulated cornice. Designed by Frank Lockwood of Montgomery, Alabama, the dwelling cost $20,000 and was built for Dr. Monroe Maas.[84]

Eagles Nest • 707 Arsenal Place
Constructed circa 1925 • H. J. Koski, Architect

FIGURE 2-260, Eagles Nest, 707 Arsenal Place, Photograph by Susan Besser, 2002

The Eagles Nest is a two-story, stucco-exterior multidwelling in the Spanish Eclectic style and is associated with the Eagle family, who owned Eagles Department Store at 1119 Alabama Avenue. Indicative of the period is the shaped parapet wall and colonnaded first-story porch of square piers and arcaded second-story porch. A single arched wood door defines the entry. Note the decorative vigas, a distinctive Spanish Eclectic element,

---

84. "Extraordinary Amount of Building Activity Going on in Selma, Store Rooms and Residences in All Parts," *Selma Times-Journal*, July 26, 1925, 8.

along the shaped parapet. The building cost $35,000 to create four apartments of eight rooms each.

711 Arsenal Place • *Constructed circa 1925*

FIGURE 2-261, 711 Arsenal Place, Photograph by Susan Besser, 2002

The arched entry portico supported by smooth Doric columns dominates this one-story, three-bay Colonial Revival cottage. The central entry is a twelve-light door flanked by four-light sidelights. Note the fenestration, which is composed of full-height windows of nine-over-nine with narrow windows of three-over-three. Mrs. Clytie McCulley, a stenographer at City National Bank, rented out rooms to board here in the 1920s and 1930s. This was a trend during that time, especially the Depression Era.

712 Arsenal Place • *Constructed circa 1925*

This two-story brick Foursquare of Prairie style influences with a low-pitched hipped roof and wide overhanging eaves features square columns on piers and Doric columns supporting a hipped-roof, full-width porch. The symmetrical plan has a central entry with a multi-paned door flanked by Chicago-style windows. The second story windows are eight-over-one

FIGURE 2-262, 712 Arsenal Place, Photograph by Susan Besser, 2002

configuration. Mrs. Rosa Dunklin, a neuropath, resided in this dwelling in the 1930s.

715 Arsenal Place • *Constructed circa 1925*

FIGURE 2-263, 715 Arsenal Place, Photograph by Susan Besser, 2002

Built circa 1925, the one-story, three-bay dwelling is indicative of the Craftsman style with its full-width porch with porte cochère and multigable roof. Tapered columns set on brick with a solid brick balustrade anchor the dwelling. Triangular knee braces enhance the gable ends of the porches. Issie and DuBose Cole began their married life in this dwelling in 1933.

719 Arsenal Place • *Constructed circa 1925*

FIGURE 2-264, 719 Arsenal Place, Photograph by Susan Besser, 2002

This Colonial Revival dwelling with Craftsman influences is a two-story, three-bay dwelling with low-pitched hipped roof making a grand statement with its triangular pedimented entry porch supported by smooth Doric columns set on brick piers. Characteristic of the Craftsman style are the large expanses of windows with four-over-one sash windows on the first and second stories and exposed rafters and knee brackets within the porch pediment. The louvered door central entry has multi-paned sidelights and transom.

720 Arsenal Place • *Constructed circa 1925; porch alteration 1980*

Built in the Craftsman style, this front-gable, one-and-one-half-story, three-bay dwelling has drop siding and full-width, hipped-roof porch supported by classical columns, circa 1980. Tapered pilasters on the façade indicate the style of the original columns. Oftentimes with Craftsman buildings, as here, a louvered weather door acts as the entry. Paired nine-over-one windows are to the east and a single nine-over-one window is to the west. Triangular knee braces embellish the eaves.

FIGURE 2-265, 720 Arsenal Place, Photograph by Susan Besser, 2002

The Johnson Apartments • 722-724 Arsenal Place
Constructed circa 1927

FIGURE 2-266, The Johnson Apartments, 722-724 Arsenal Place, Photograph by Susan Besser, 2022

Built in a U-shaped configuration, this apartment complex embodies Spanish Colonial Revival influences with the two-story arcaded integral porches embellished with polychromatic brick in stack-bond and common-bond patterns. Windows are four-over-one double hung and entries are twelve-light doors. The Johnson Apartments were built by Horis Johnson aided by his sons Ellis, James Allen, and Glen.

723 Arsenal Place • *Constructed circa 1925*

FIGURE 2-267, 723 Arsenal Place, Photograph by Susan Besser, 2002

This Colonial Revival two-story, frame duplex with low-pitched hipped roof with cross gable has a triangular pedimented entry porch with pent roof supported by fluted classical columns on brick piers. Louvered entry doors are surmounted by multi-pane transoms. The window configuration is eight-over-one double hung sash.

725 Arsenal Place • *Constructed circa 1930*

FIGURE 2-268, 725 Arsenal Place, Photograph by Susan Besser, 2002

This one-story stucco Craftsman hip roof with clipped gable has been modified to enclose the porch with fixed windows. A brick tile landing leads to an offset entrance consisting of a six-panel door with multilight sidelights and transom. Exposed rafters enrich the eaves.

813 Arsenal Place • *Constructed circa 1935*

FIGURE 2-269, 813 Arsenal Place, Photograph by Susan Besser, 2002

Indicative of the Craftsman style is the square pier support of the side entry porch. Built circa 1935, this L-plan one-story, three-bay dwelling has a low-pitched hipped roof. The front bay has triple four-over-one windows and is enframed with square piers with a decorative stonework detail. Atypical of this style is the boxed cornice. A dormer with clipped gable features triple windows that follow the eave line of the dormer.

815 Arsenal Place • *Constructed circa 1935*

FIGURE 2-270, 815 Arsenal Place, Photograph by Susan Besser, 2002

The clinker brick used in this Craftsman one-story, three-bay bungalow is closely associated with the Craftsman movement but is relatively uncommon in the South. The dark purple color that characterizes clinker brick occurs when the bricks are close to the fire in the firing process. Initially such bricks were discarded, but architects and builders of the Arts and Crafts era found them to be a distinctive addition to the exterior. Note the one-story front gable roofed porch with solid brick balustrade that displays the clinker brick as well as the paired colonettes on battered piers and the exposed rafters at the eaves.

816 Arsenal Place • *Constructed circa 1930*

FIGURE 2-271, 816 Arsenal Place, Photograph by Susan Besser, 2002

This one-story, three-bay brick Tudor Revival has an asymmetrical plan that features a unique front-gabled porch with an arched entry with buttress detail and radiating voussoirs and keystone. Paired three-over-one double-hung windows with stone lintels are visible through the arched entry. Three-over-one windows with stone lintels flank a front exterior brick chimney. To the east is a side integral porch with arched openings of brick radiating voussoirs.

Lamar Avenue

503 Lamar Avenue • *Constructed circa 1910*

FIGURE 2-272, 503 Lamar Avenue, Photograph by Susan Besser, 2002

This handsome Prairie-style hipped-roof, two-story, three-bay dwelling has a weatherboard and stucco exterior. Decorative eave brackets enrich the wide overhanging eaves. The hipped-roof dormers have four-light windows. Piers covered with weatherboard and stucco support the full-width arcaded porch. A single door with sidelights and broken transom constitutes the entry. Windows are double hung and have trellis panes over three lights.

Lamar-Guy House • 508 Lamar Avenue
Constructed circa 1850; Queen Anne renovation circa 1890; Craftsman renovation circa 1925

Lamar-Guy House, circa 1850, represents the continuum of architectural evolution. Although portions of the dwelling date to the antebellum period, the façade presents influences of the Queen Anne and Craftsman periods. It is a two-story, three-bay brick exterior with hipped roof with

FIGURE 2-273, Lamar-Guy House, 508 Lamar Avenue, Photograph by Susan Besser, 2002

cross gables. To the east is a projecting bay with cutaway bays enriched with corner brackets. The two-over-two windows have an arched lintel with a brick relieving arch. The full-width, flat-roof porch has a brick balustrade, is supported by square brick columns (circa 1925), and is embellished with a dentil course. Double-leaf, single-light doors with a two-light transom provide the entry. Other elements of the Queen Anne influence are the multilight windows on the first and second stories and the imbricated shingles of the gable ends. Dent Lamar and Elizabeth Law Lamar resided here in the 1860s.

Notable Buildings

Charles Henry Hopson House • 22 View Street
Constructed circa 1905 • Charles Henry Hopson, Architect

Charles Henry Hopson, who designed this house in the early twentieth century, was an architect who trained in Reading, England, with Joseph

Greenaway. He moved to Halifax, Nova Scotia, in 1888 and was an assistant to Edward Elliott. He worked in Boston and also in Washington as a designer of government buildings until 1895. In 1894 he married Mary Groves, a Selma native, and practiced in Selma from 1903 until 1911, when he moved to Atlanta, Georgia. He is acknowledged for his ecclesiastical designs, most notably Peachtree Christian Church in Atlanta, Georgia, which is on the National Register of Historic Places.

FIGURE 2-274, Charles Henry Hopson House, 22 View Street, Photograph by Susan Besser, 2018

Hopson designed in many architectural styles. For his own house he chose the Mission style, reflected here in the shaped parapets with coping, tile roof, arched porch supports, and wide overhanging eaves. The two-story stucco dwelling has an attached full-width hipped roof and one-story arcaded porch. The defining feature of the west elevation is a through-cornice shaped parapet at the second story. To the north is a two-story ell that contains the porte cochère leading to the double-door primary entrance of leaded glass in an overlapping arch design. The gable roof of the ell terminates in a shaped parapet.

Methodist Orphanage • 1712 Broad Street
Constructed circa 1908; alterations circa 1955
Reuben Harrison Hunt, Architect • Thomas Purvis, Contractor

FIGURE 2-275, Methodist Orphanage, 1712 Broad Street, Postcard Collection of Susan Besser

The administration building of the orphanage is a Neoclassical-influenced two-story brick building with partial-width, full-height gable front portico with four Doric columns and dentil molding delineating the pediment. The fenestration consists of eight-over-eight windows to the north and south. The bays are defined by a shouldered architrave brick detail with keystone, which is a nod to the Greek Revival. Beneath the portico are six-over-six windows with two-over-two windows to either side. The entry features an elliptical fan light and sidelights and is surmounted by a bracketed cornice, giving a nod to Early Classical Revival. The building began as a three-story building with a cross gable centered over the façade above the portico.

In 1908 the building was designed by Rueben Harrison Hunt for the Presbyterian Church and was called the Selma Military Institute. The school was considered to be a Presbyterian school for boys. Hunt also designed First Presbyterian Church on Broad Street, whose members donated the majority of the funds. Previously the school had been located in a section of the Vaughan/Smitherman Building.

In 1911 the building and grounds were purchased for $15,000.00 by the Methodists to serve as an orphanage. Over one hundred children plus staff were housed in the building. From 1948 to 1952 cottages were built for the children. In 1955 a ceremony was held removing the cornerstone from the building that had designated it for the Selma Military Institute. At that time the third-floor wings were removed, and the third floor was reconfigured and converted into a skating rink. The portico was redesigned by removing the balustrade and changing the roofline. The building was painted white, and the interior was renovated for offices, dining hall, and kitchen.[85]

Alabama Baptist Hospital • 15 Riverview Avenue
Constructed circa 1922 • Frank Lockwood, Architect

FIGURE 2-276, Alabama Baptist Hospital, 15 Riverview Avenue, Photograph by Susan Besser, 2016

---

85. "Removal of Cornerstone Marked by Ceremonies," *Selma Times-Journal,* April 10, 1955, 22.

Frank Lockwood is listed as the architect of record for Alabama Baptist Hospital in the October 1920 edition of *Manufacturer's Record*. The budget for the building was $150,000 and Lockwood received a $25,000 fee for his design. Dr. Louis J. Bristow was the director of what was originally the Alabama Baptist Hospital and Good Samaritan Hospital on Voeglin Avenue. He was a member of the Southern Baptist Hospital Commission and was a renowned figure in Baptist hospitals. In 1927 he published a book, *Healing Humanity's Hurt*.[86]

Alabama Avenue Methodist Church • 2259 Alabama Avenue
Constructed circa 1904
Gillenwater Contractors and Builders, **Contractor**

FIGURE 2-277, Alabama Avenue Methodist Church, 2259 Alabama Avenue, Photograph by Susan Besser, 2015

---

86. Stephen McNair, PhD, interview, August 4, 2018.

The Gothic Revival vernacular is the inspiration for the L-shaped plan intersected with a two-story tower. Note the triangular arched Gothic windows with lozenge panes that dominate the south façade and east elevation. Triangular arched lintels with diamond-shaped keystones delineate the windows. The entrance tower features decorative buttresses harkening back to the Gothic vocabulary of the medieval time period.

The beginning of Alabama Avenue Methodist stemmed from the Church Street Methodist congregation with a land donation on Water Avenue and $500 to construct a wood-frame building in 1861. Early meetings were sporadic. W. S. McDaniel became the pastor in 1869 and gave the church much needed vitality. The congregation thrived under his leadership with the organization of a Sunday school providing outreach to the community.

A building program began in 1901 with the purchase of property at Vine and Alabama. Gillenwater Contractors and Builders oversaw the construction. The first services were held on April 14, 1904.

In 1978 the congregation relocated to west Selma on Barret Road forming Barret Road United Methodist Church. The building was sold to Sylvan Street Church of God in 1980.[87]

Alabama Avenue Presbyterian Church • 1817 Alabama Avenue
Constructed 1907 • Attributed to Charles Henry Hopson, Architect

This congregation, sponsored by First Presbyterian Church, held services in a small wooden building on Alabama Avenue. A revival was held in 1872 led by Rev. James Watson and in 1873 the Alabama Avenue Presbyterian Church was officially launched. In May of that year the second pastor, Rev. Peter Gowan of Charleston, assumed the leadership of the church. With the donation of land on the north side of Alabama Avenue by a Mrs. Weaver, the members constructed a wooden-frame church dedicated on September 28, 1875, known as "the Oldside Presbyterian Church." The present brick building was constructed under the leadership of Rev. E. B.

---

87. *Fitts, Historic Churches of Selma Prior to 1925*, 23.

Robinson after he became pastor in 1906. Estimated construction costs were between $10,000 and $12,000.

FIGURE 2-278, Alabama Avenue Presbyterian Church, 1817 Alabama Avenue, Photograph by Susan Besser, 2015

The front-gabled façade features a bay with intricate stained-glass windows. Side entries with Tudor arches lead to cloisters and on into the sanctuary. Corner brackets beneath the eaves and half-timbering in the gable ends of the front and side elevations are characteristic of this style. Note the steeple with a crown element. Owing to the distinctive details of this one-and-one-half-story brick church, such as the half-timbering, the bay window featuring stained glass, and the cloistered side entry, the work appears to be that of a trained architect. Although there are no records crediting the architect, the church exhibits influence of the English Arts and Crafts, designs typical of English ecclesiastical architect Charles Henry Hopson, was who responsible for the Tudor Revival Rock Springs Presbyterian Church in Atlanta, Georgia, and resided in Selma, Alabama.

Silent Night Guest House • 2201 Broad Street
Constructed circa 1890

FIGURE 2-279, Silent Night Guest House, 2201 Broad Street, Postcard Collection of Susan Besser

This impressive Neoclassical dwelling was known as the Silent Night Guest Home and began as a Queen Anne house. Note that the cutaway bays on the south side exterior and the columns were added at a later date. Guests would have a perfect view of Broad Street from the cast-iron balcony on the second story. Semicircular porch columns with ionic capitals, one-over-one windows with porch brackets, and bay window to the south complete the overall effect of the Neoclassical style.

CHAPTER 3

Water Avenue Historic District

Given the proximity of Water Avenue to the Alabama River and access to steamboats and ferry, the siting of this commercial district on the river bluffs occurred as a natural outgrowth of the topographical setting. The location of the city wharf along the bank near the St. James Hotel in close proximity to the turnstile bridge provided necessary access to cotton plantations, warehouses, and wholesale merchants. Historically, a secondary wharf servicing a flour mill and warehouse stood near the site of the present Selma Masonic Lodge in Old Town Historic District. Crucial to the county's economic viability, the export of cotton necessitated the establishment of trading centers for cotton and receipt of consumer goods. Within the district is one of the few remaining river hotels in the southeast; the St. James Hotel, circa 1837, pivotal to Selma's growth as a river town presently operates as an historic hotel. The turnstile bridge no longer spans the Alabama River, but the Bridgetender's House on Lafayette Park testifies to the importance of a bridge to the local and regional economy.

The St. James Hotel functioned as a hotel until 1892 when competition from the Hotel Albert proved to be insurmountable; however, the building continued to function in other commercial endeavors. Another hotel, the three-story brick Greek Revival building at 1308-1318 Water Avenue, circa 1855, known historically as the Edistone Hotel, exemplifies the restrained denticulated cornice and six-over-six windows with cast-iron lintels of the era. The building retains the original French doors.

According to Alan Gowans the purpose of commercial architecture "from the 1850s onward . . . was to promote an image of businesses associated with culture."[1] The architecture of the buildings in the Water Avenue Historic District from 1860 through 1930 reflects the awareness of commercial vernacular throughout the continent and, consequently, represents a continuum of western architectural heritage.

The north side of the 1200 block of Water Avenue has experienced the loss of important circa 1860–1870 buildings. Two buildings remain and have a high degree of integrity. The two-story Italianate at 1223-1225 Water Avenue has an elaborate pediment of pressed metal and keystone arches beneath a wide cornice. Displaying engaged fluted columns of cast iron, 1203 Water Avenue illustrates the manner in which cast-iron-front technology adapted to the commercial building.

The proximity of textile mills to cotton plantations near Selma in the 1880s created a business climate that supported numerous commercial enterprises; consequently, Selma experienced a boom period in their economy relative to a rebuilding of Water Avenue Historic District. This presented an opportunity for expression of architectural form such as the Italianate and Renaissance Revival. The two-story commercial buildings of the 1100 block of Water Avenue illustrate Selma's prominence as a cotton market and distribution center. Designed in the Italianate style with deep bracketed cornices, 1118-1124 Water Avenue exhibits French doors with full arched transoms surmounted with stone hood molds. Hallmarks of the Italianate style are the elaborate bracketed cornice and pilasters that flow from the first story to denticulated molding as depicted on 1112 Water Avenue. The Italianate style as interpreted on 1110 Water Avenue presents

---

1. Alan Gowans, *Styles and Types of North American Architecture: Social Function and Culture Expression* (New York: IconEditions, 1992), 179.

a unifying element of an arcaded pediment treatment within the parapet. The Selma Times-Journal Building, 1014 Water Avenue, embodies the essence of the Italianate movement. A resplendent projecting bracketed cornice with triangular pediment embellishes the façade. Italianate buildings fill the block with details such as the projecting bracketed cornice modulating to a triangular pediment on the Woolsey Building. At 1010 Water, cast-iron gates with segmental arched detailing augment the primary entrance's fifteen-pane door with transom and sidelights.

The Renaissance Revival style resonates in the three-story Harmony Club Building, circa 1909. Characteristic of the style is the arcaded loggia and paired arched windows with arched stone archivolt. Historically, the building displayed a two-story porch enhanced with delicate cast-iron balustrade and spandrels. The high architectural style evidences the mercantile success of the builders of the edifice—the Jewish population in Selma. Initially, the first wave of Jewish settlers came upriver from Mobile; many had immigrated from Europe to the West Indies during the Inquisition before moving there. Two more waves of immigration, in the 1840s and the 1880s, strengthened their numbers. Known for their expertise in merchandising the Jewish community established many businesses in Selma, notably Tepper's, Kayser's, and Lilienthal's. Their presence in Selma led to the establishment of the Reform Congregation in 1870, ultimately building Temple Mishkan and the Harmony Club.

A second building, at 1008 Water Avenue, circa 1873, exemplifies the Renaissance Revival style in the dichromatic masonry and stone detailing above the entrances and windows. This is building has a denticulated cornice below a stepped parapet surmounted by stone coping. Windows are enhanced with rock-faced stone lintels.

Selma's prominence as a distribution center is due in large part to the railway system established before the Civil War and expanded during and after Reconstruction with numerous lines connecting in Selma. Within the expanded district is the only remaining train depot in Selma, once a part of the Louisville & Nashville Railroad, a Romanesque Revival brick edifice with stone detailing exhibited in a wide stone belt course enriched with cyma reversa molding. Details such as a denticulated cornice embellished with brackets and shaped parapet are hallmarks of the style. A two-and-one-half-story tower with bell-shaped roof gives prominence to the building.

Water Avenue

The Harmony Club • 1007 Water Avenue
Constructed circa 1909 • Thomas Purvis, Contractor

FIGURE 3-1, Harmony Club, 1007 Water Avenue, Photograph by Susan Besser, 2002

The Harmony Club, one of the most established social clubs in Selma, previously held their social functions on the second floor of the Selma National Bank at 30 Broad Street. The Renaissance Revival style resonates in the three-story Harmony Club Building circa 1909. Benjamin J. Schuster, a local merchant, supervised the project. Characteristic of the style is the arcaded loggia and paired arched windows with arched stone archivolt. Historically, the building displayed a two-story porch enhanced with del-icate cast-iron balustrade and spandrels. The high architectural style evi-dences the mercantile success of the builders of the edifice—the Jewish population in Selma. Insurance agent J. B. Ellis of Georgia Casualty occu-pied the first story. The *Selma Mirror* in 1911 touted the credentials of Mr. Ellis, "who knows land values in this section better than any one man."[2] A restaurant and lounge were located on the second floor. The third floor con-tained a ballroom where movies were shown and where the annual Beaux Art Ball was held. The Elks Club occupied the building from the 1930s to 1960s. In 1999 David Hurlbut, an industrial designer, purchased the prop-erty and rehabilitated the building. The *New York Times* did a feature article of the project in December of 2010.

1008 Water Avenue • *Constructed circa 1873*

FIGURE 3-2, 1008 Water Avenue, Photograph by Bill Tomey, 2024

---

2. "Ellis Insurance and Investment Company," *Selma Mirror*, June 28, 1911, 32.

Attorney A. M. Pitts occupied this building in the 1920s. This two-story, two-part Renaissance Revival commercial block building is brick with stone detailing and has a stepped parapet with stone coping and denticulated cornice. Entry to the second story is through an arch opening. To the east and west are bays with single doors with transom and display windows set on brick bulkheads. Second-story windows are one-over-one configuration with a rock-faced stone lintel course. A modillion course surmounts the sign "Established 1873."

1010 Water Avenue • *Constructed circa 1870*

FIGURE 3-3, 1010 Water Avenue, Photograph by Susan Besser, 2002

In the 1910s insurance agent Charles A. Patterson as Aetna Life Insurance Co. of Hartford, Connecticut; Globe & Rutgers Fire Insurance Co. of New York; Massachusetts Bonding & Insurance Co. of Boston, Massachusetts; and Hartford Steam Boiler Inspection & Insurance Co. of Hartford, Connecticut, occupied the second story, as did Central City Building & Loan Association. This two-story, two-part commercial block building is brick with a scored stucco exterior and has a flat roof with parapet. Cast-iron gates with segmental arched detailing to the west lead to the second story. Double metal doors are to the east. Paired windows to the east are surmounted by a transom. The entrance consists of a fifteen-pane door with transom and sidelights. The second-story fenestration consists of two-over-two windows. Visible beneath the stucco are segmental arched hood molds. The building was the original site of the National Voting Rights Museum & Institute, established in 1991.[3] In the 1960s it had been the headquarters of the White Citizens Council.

Woolsey Building • 1012 Water Avenue
Constructed 1889

The Woolsey Building acquired its historic name from Woolsey and Sons cotton factors, who were the first occupants of this two-story, two-part commercial block building of the Italianate period. A projecting bracketed cornice modulating to a triangular pediment enriches the parapet. A corbel table combined with band molding enriches the field of brick above the windows. Fenestration of the first story is composed of double-leaf doors with glazing and display windows on a wood panel bulkhead. Fluted cast-iron columns and cast-iron fluted pilasters add a classical element.

FIGURE 3-4, Woolsey Building, 1012 Water Avenue, Photograph by Susan Besser, 2002

---

3. Rose Sanders, "National Voting Rights Museum Growing with Community Support," *Selma Times-Journal*, March 3, 1993, 4.

Selma Times-Journal Building • 1014 Water Avenue
Constructed circa 1870

FIGURE 3-5, Selma Times-Journal Building, 1014 Water Avenue, Photograph by Susan Besser, 2002

The Selma Times-Journal Building embodies the essence of the Italianate movement. Fenestration of the five-bay building is composed of French doors surmounted by fanlights and embellished Gibbs surrounds. Second-story windows with elaborate bracketed hood molds characterize the Eastlake style. A resplendent projecting bracketed cornice with triangular pediment surmounts the façade. Quoins enrich the corners of the building.

1110 Water Avenue • *Constructed circa 1880*

FIGURE 3-6, 1110 Water Avenue, Photograph by Susan Besser, 2002

Brislin Brothers Funeral Chapel occupied this building in 1924 and also had a house-furnishing business. Attorneys J. H. Berry, Reese & Reese, and W. W. Quarles also occupied this building in 1924. This two-story brick Italianate is within a two-part commercial block. The Italianate style presents a unifying element of an arcaded pediment treatment within the parapet that is indicative of the style. Multiple pairs of French doors provide access to the cast-iron gallery.

1112 Water Avenue • *Constructed circa 1880*

FIGURE 3-7, 1112 Water Avenue, Photograph by Susan Besser, 2002

In 1924 Southern Clothing & Notion Co. occupied this building. This two-story brick Italianate has hallmarks of the style such as the elaborate bracketed cornice and pilasters that flow from the first story to the denticulated molding above the second-story windows. The first story's fenestration consists of double-leaf doors with two-pane glazing surmounted by arched hood molds with corbeling. Second-story fenestration indicates two window openings with arched hood molds would have surmounted windows, now covered. Two central windows have two-over-two configuration with window crowns. An arched canopy with slender cast-iron posts shelters the first story.

1118-1124 Water Avenue • *Constructed circa 1857*

FIGURE 3-8, 1118-1124 Water Avenue, Photograph by Susan Besser, 2002

Believed to predate the Civil War, the building was occupied by Liverpool and London and Globe Insurance Company as well as the New York Life Insurance Company. A grocer, T. H. Rosser, had his business on the first floor. The building functioned as an exchange, most likely for cotton as I. Yaretzky and Co. had offices in the building in the 1910s. Former C.S. Gen. Joseph E. Johnston was the agent for New York Life after the Civil War and had offices in Selma from 1868 to 1871. This two-story, seven-bay brick Italianate is a two-part commercial block building with a deep bracketed cornice and French doors with full arched transoms surmounted with stone hood molds. Slender cast-iron columns support an attached shed-roof canopy. A modillioned cornice typical of this era crowns the building.

St. James Hotel/Brantley Hotel/Planters Hotel/ Troupe House/Riverside Hotel
1200 Water Avenue • *Constructed circa 1838; restoration 1997*

The St. James Hotel, completed in 1838 by H. J. Brantley, now a fine historic hotel, provided lodging for guests brought by steamboat and overnight lodging for Dallas County landowners for oversight of the distribution of the cotton crop. Purchased for $800, the hotel site Lot 29 was part of the Selma Town Land Company's holdings. An article in the *Selma Free Press* of February 17, 1838, notes steady progress of the building. A subsequent article announced the opening of the hotel with rates published at $20 and $25. The St. James functioned as a hotel until 1892 when competition from the Hotel Albert, no longer extant, proved to be insurmountable; however, the building continued to function in other commercial endeavors. The St. James Hotel catered to plantation owners, cotton brokers, and riverboat travelers. The first floor of the hotel functioned for businesses while the second and third floors offered spacious rooms each with a fireplace. In 1907 the hotel operated as the Riverside Hotel.

FIGURE 3-9, St. James Hotel, 1200 Water Avenue, Photograph by Susan Besser, 2002

Selma's location on the Alabama River in close proximity to cotton plantations provided the impetus for the area as a shipping center via steamboat, thus creating the need for upscale lodgings along the river such as the St. James. According to John Hardy the citizens of Selma experienced the innovation of the steamboat with a mixture "of fear and astonishment, and but few could be persuaded to go aboard and examine the works of the 'belching craft.'"[4] As the steamships proved their worth in the transport of people and goods, the refinement of technology resulted in the production of fine steamboats traveling through Selma, such as the *Clipper*, *Sallie Spann*, *Fairfield*, and *Stonewall Jackson*. Steamship travel and shipping continued to dominate until the development of the rail system.

Dr. James T. Gee operated the hotel before he enlisted in the Confederate Army and placed his former slave, Benjamin Sterling Turner, African American, in charge of the hotel during his absence. After the war Turner operated a livery stable and in 1870 became the first African American from Alabama to hold a seat in Congress. His objectives while in Congress were amnesty for Confederate leaders and civil rights.

The notorious James brothers were once guests of the hotel, with manager James Dedman telling the story of playing pool with them. They had listed their names as "Williams" and according to Dedman were "perfect gentlemen." The James brothers' cousin, John Green Norris, resided in the area, and as Norris was a city council member felt they should use discretion during their stay.

The three-story building of masonry construction covered with stucco has penciling detailing to simulate ashlar stonework. Stepped parapet walls conceal the gable standing-seam roof. A two-story hipped-roof gallery is supported by an elaborate cast-iron foliated design around the second story. Double-leaf doors with glazing provide entry to the hotel on the Water Avenue elevation and Washington Street elevation.

---

4. John Hardy, *Selma: Her Institutions and Her Men* (Spartanburg, SC: Reprint Company), 168.

FIGURE 3-10, St. James Hotel, 1200 Water Avenue, HABS, Library of Congress

A $6 million restoration project in 1997 directed by Elizabeth Driggers of the City Government Development Office and Patty Sexton, director of Main Street, revived this hotel, which had sat dormant for nearly a century. The project included adding rooms to the river side of the hotel and creating an elegant courtyard with a fountain as the focal point. The hotel closed in 2019 but reopened in 2021.

1203 Water Avenue • *Constructed circa 1860–1870*

This brick, three-story, three-bay brick Italianate component of a two-part commercial block has a cast-iron front with engaged fluted columns as piers. The central entrance has been converted to a window. Double-leaf six-light doors with five-light transoms are symmetrical. Two-light transoms surmount display windows that rest on a wood bulkhead. The original

FIGURE 3-11, 1203 Water Avenue, Photograph by Susan Besser, 2002

cast-iron two-story gallery has been removed. Evidence of a second-story balcony is the central entry of the second story with double-leaf doors with glazing and a camber transom. Three four-over-four windows with cast-iron lintels are to the east and west of the entry. Foliated cast-iron vents enhance the refined design while a dentil band forms the frieze. Stone coping caps the top course of brick.

Adler Furniture • 1223-1225 Water Avenue
Constructed circa 1860–1870

According to the *Selma Mirror* Lee C. Adler and Arthur Leob operated Adler Furniture, a retail and wholesale business, at this site located at the corner of Franklin Street and Water Avenue. They were sole agents for Baldwin refrigerators and ice chests with porcelain interiors. In the 1920s it was the location for Creagh and Smith, a business that sold Hood Rubber Tires. The Italianate edifice is a two-story, two-bay brick component of a two-part commercial block. The first story exhibits brick patterns forming rusticated piers set on plinths. To the west is an entrance of double-leaf doors with eight lights each surmounted by transom. The second entrance has been

FIGURE 3-12, Adler Furniture, 1223-1225 Water Avenue, Photograph by Susan Besser, 2002

modified to incorporate doors not of the period with a single transom surmounted by a five-light transom. Four fixed display windows of nine lights on wood bulkheads complete the first story. An intricate two-story gallery with cast-iron frieze, supports, posts, and balustrade wrapping around the corner was removed circa 2020. Second-story fenestration is symmetrical and exhibits a central door with glazing and segmental transom with three four-over-four windows surmounted by segmental stone lintels to the east and west of the entry. The elaborate pediment displays a pressed metal cornice of brackets and keystone arches beneath a wide cornice. Cast-iron quoins define the building corners.

Confederate Naval Foundry & Iron Works • Water Avenue
Constructed circa 1862

The transformation of Selma into a center for military provisions included the conversion of the cotton warehouses into an arsenal for the production of cartridges, powder, and armament. The arsenal, located in the Old Town Historic District, employed approximately ten thousand workers, including some skilled German artisans but mostly enslaved people, women, and children. It consisted of twenty-four buildings on Church Street on the Alabama River and ran west two blocks to Union Street and north to Alabama Avenue. The women of Selma worked in the arsenal rolling cartridges and were also called upon to provide a most necessary component—chamber lye for the processing of gunpowder.

Spearheaded by Colin J. McRae, an Alabama representative to the Provisional Congress, the Confederate Naval Foundry was formed in Selma from the Alabama Manufacturing Company, founded in the 1850s. McRae was successful in purchasing the foundry and obtaining contracts. Unfortunately, he struggled with labor shortages of qualified mechanics to provide the technical support to the foundry. McRae was asked to accept a commission to Europe for procurement of funds for the Confederacy. He accepted the position with the provision that a suitable successor be obtained. Subsequently, the War Department and Navy Department purchased the foundry and appointed Colonel George W. Rains to take over the operations. Rains's assignment proved to be a poor choice as he did not support the location of the foundry in Selma.[5]

At this juncture the Navy appointed Commander Catesby ap R. Jones to take control of the Foundry. Upon his arrival at Selma Jones realized the foundry had not yet begun production. Jones set out to find the most experienced metallurgist available and was able to persuade George Peacock of England and formerly of the iron works of Columbiana, Alabama, to come on board. The addition of Peacock to oversee production was instrumental in the full startup of the foundry.

Still in the experimental stage, the first Brooke rifle was produced in July of 1863. In January of 1864 the foundry produced the first gun for use in combat. During the course of the war approximately one hundred naval guns were assembled in the foundry.[6] In addition to the Brooke rifles, ironclad ships and cannons were produced here.

With the establishment of the Confederate Naval Foundry and numerous railways providing supplies for the war effort, Selma gained a reputation

---

5. William N. Still, "Selma and the Confederate States Navy," in *From Civil War to Civil Rights: Alabama 1860–1960*, ed. Sarah Woolfolk Wiggins (Tuscaloosa: University of Alabama Press, 1987), 22–23.

6. Still, "Selma and the Confederate States Navy," 22–23.

as an industrial and distribution center. The Foundry and the involvement of Commander Catesby ap R. Jones increased Selma's stature as a strategic center for the Confederacy.

FIGURE 3-13, Confederate Naval Foundry & Iron Works, Water Avenue, Photograph by Susan Besser, 2002

The remaining ruins of the Confederate Naval Foundry & Iron Works are three buildings of brick construction with a gable roof of standing-seam metal. Windows are six-over-six pane with brick relieving arch. Brick buttresses alternate with windows and terminate in a corbeled cornice. A gable-roof clerestory follows the ridge of the roof.

It is significant to note the loss of the Confederate Foundry on April 2, 1865, and its support of the Confederate War effort. The war ended just a week later at Appomattox, Virginia, on April 9 with Lee's surrender of the Confederate troops.

Edistone Hotel (1890), Florence Hotel (1865), Ackerman Hotel (1870), Central City Hotel (1884), Hotel Sullivan (1889) 1308-1318 Water Avenue • *Constructed 1855*

Built circa 1855, the Edistone Hotel has gone through several name changes over time and is a Greek Revival, three-story, five-bay brick building with a denticulated pediment. Fenestration of the first story to the east reflects double-leaf doors with glazing that provided entry into the hotel. A cast-iron balustrade embellishes the west bay of the second story. Stone lintels over the window openings are intact. The Freedmen's Bureau, a United States government agency that assisted African Americans, occupied the hotel during Reconstruction from 1865 to 1872.[7] Various businesses occupied the first story, such as the Exchange in 1907 and W. M. Hinson Furniture. Physician T. E. Lockhart hung his shingle there in the 1920s. The land on which the hotel stands previously held a three-story frame building whose purpose was a market for the enslaved population. The frame building was removed in 1854 by Dent Lamar.[8]

FIGURE 3-14, Edistone Hotel, 1308-1318 Water Avenue, Drawing by Caitin Kadlec, November 2023

"The one thing that makes the hotel very special and highly significant within the state context and of the two hotels the St. James and the Edistone, what makes it really important is its interior is so intact."[9] The St. James Hotel interior was modified during its renovation in 1997.

---

7. Will Whaley, "A Look at the Latest Project from the Selma-Dallas County Historic Preservation Society," *Selma Times-Journal*, April 5, 2019, https://www.selmatimesjournal.com/2019/04/05/a-look-at-the-latest-project-from-the-selma-dallas-county-historic-preservation-society/.

8. Hardy, *Selma: Her Institutions and Her Men*, 16.

9. Robert Gamble, quoted by James Jones, "Edistone Hotel: The Unknown Historic Hotel," *Selma-Times Journal*, March 27, 2023, https://www.selmatimesjournal.com/2023/03/27/edistone-hotel-the-unknown-historic-hotel/.

Martin Luther King, Jr. Street

Old Depot Museum/Louisville & Nashville Railroad Depot
4 Martin Luther King Street • *Constructed circa 1891*
Albert Fink, Architect

Selma's expansive Romanesque Revival Louisville & Nashville Railroad Depot resonates from the architectural spirit of the time but also reflected the Jim Crow laws requiring segregation with large, expansive spaces for white passengers and smaller, less ornate spaces for African American passengers. The new building bristled with a charged electricity of the fast-paced environment. One of the restaurants that operated there in the 1920s was Crescent News & Hotel Co.

Presently housing the Old Depot Museum, the two-story brick building has an off-center primary entrance of double-leaf four-panel doors with a transom. Large triangular brackets support an attached hipped-roof canopy. A wide stone belt course is enriched with cyma reversa molding and a denticulated cornice is embellished with brackets that terminate at the shaped parapet. Within the parapet, radiating voussoirs surmount triple arches. Large triangular braces support wide overhanging eaves. To the east is a secondary entrance of double-leaf four-panel doors originally designated for African Americans. To the west is a two-and-one-half-story octagonal tower with a bell-shaped roof topped by a finial.

The history of the railroads coming to Selma is complex. Leaders such as Senator Jesse Beene had recognized that transportation of manufactured goods and raw materials such as coal and iron ore as well as exportation of cotton enhanced the profitability of their state. Consequently, the capitalists looked to more modern transportation to facilitate shipment rather than steamboats and stagecoaches.

The first railroad in Selma had its genesis as the Selma and Tennessee Rivers Railroad. A charter was granted to the railroad on December 22, 1836, and promoted by Senator Jesse Beene and Rep. James M. Calhoun. Local merchants William Johnson and P. J. Weaver pledged $100,000 toward the necessary $500,000 funding. By March of 1837 the railroad was organized with the goal to install track to Montevallo.[10] The Panic of 1837 brought the operations to a halt.[11] However, in 1838 John Lapsley and Col. Thornton B. Goldsby were able to obtain a new charter for the railroad under the name of the Alabama and Tennessee Rivers Railroad.[12]

FIGURE 3-15, Old Depot Museum/Louisville & Nashville Railroad Depot, 4 Martin Luther King Street, Photograph by Dr. Carroll Van West, NRHP 2013

The Selma and Gulf Railroad Company was incorporated in January of 1858 as Selmians sought to connect the city with the Gulf of Mexico. The impetus for this connection was the transport of coal, iron ore, and limestone from Shelby County. Initially, the line was intended to run from

---

10. Alston Fitts III, *Selma: A Bicentennial History* (Birmingham: University of Alabama Press, 2017), 21-22.

11. Fitts, *Selma: A Bicentennial History*, 24.

12. Fitts, *Selma: A Bicentennial History*, 38.

Uniontown to Cahawba. The leadership of Cahawba refused to support the project, which created the opportunity for Phillip J. Weaver and Thornton B. Goldsby to take this to the legislature.

Although the necessary steps were taken in the next two years, such as issuing stock and setting the interest rate, with the advent of the Civil War the Selma and Gulf Railroad was temporarily halted.[13]

With Selma's prominence as a transportation and manufacturing center the Confederacy looked to the city to further develop the transportation and industrial base. A third railroad, the Alabama and Mississippi Rivers Railroad, had been incorporated in 1850. Due to the importance of the line to the transportation of troops, munitions, provisions, and the public mails, Confederate President Jefferson Davis lent his support, with the line being opened on December 18, 1862.[14]

After the war the Southern states had little capital to fund improvements to the railroad equipment and consequently were supported by Northern capitalists who took over the operations. The Alabama and Tennessee Railroad consolidated with two other lines, Georgia and Alabama Railroad and Dalton and Jacksonville Railroad, and became a part of the Selma, Rome and Dalton Railroad. A shortfall of $91,000 caused the bankruptcy of this railroad, after which it became part of the East Tennessee, Virginia and Georgia Railroad Company in 1881.[15] Southern Railroad assumed administration of what was originally the old Alabama and Tennessee Railroad.[16]

---

13. Fitts, *Selma: A Bicentennial History*, 40-41.

14. Alston Fitts III, *Selma: Queen City of the Black Belt* (Selma, AL: Clairmont Press 1989), 49-50.

15. Walter M. Jackson, *The Story of Selma* (Birmingham: Birmingham Printing Company, 1954), 117-120.

16. Jackson, *The Story of Selma*, 121.

Lafayette Park

Bridgetender's House • 2 Lafayette Park
Constructed circa 1884

FIGURE 3-16, Bridgetender's House, 2 Lafayette Park,
Photograph by Susan Besser, 2002

Bridgetender's House is an L-shaped one-and-one-half-story Queen Anne with weatherboard exterior, front and side gable roof of standing-seam metal, and a brick foundation. The exterior of the façade is flush board. A full-width, flat-roof entry porch is embellished with a scroll-sawn frieze, turned columns, and flat-cut balustrade and railings. The original screen door fronts a wood door with stained glass and creates an inviting entry. A two-over-two window is to the north of the entry. Scalloped trim enriches the gable end and side elevations.

This building provided lodging for the bridgetender who was charged with operating the turnstile bridge, also built in 1884, replacing the ferry. The turnstile bridge, which was built by Milwaukee Bridge Works for $55,000, had three spans, two fixed spans and one swing span. The swing span would allow river traffic to pass. Opening and closing the span and collecting tolls was a 24-7 job performed by the bridgetender. A typical toll for the period would be five cents for a pedestrian and twenty-five cents for a one-horse buggy. The cornerstone for the bridge can be seen from the downstairs porch of the Bridgetender's House. This bridge was replaced with the Edmund Pettus Bridge completed in May of 1940.

CHAPTER 4

Boyntons Street

This area was considered a 1950–1960 Civil Rights strategy center with residents of homes and stores highly involved. Specific homes such as the Amelia Boynton Robinson House, the R. B. Hudson House, and portions of Selma University are included in this area. This area was discussed in Dr. Carroll Van West's National Register of Historic Places Multiple Property Documentation Form from 2013. These select residences show the grassroots foundation of the Civil Rights Movement.

Amelia Boynton Robinson House • 1315 Boyntons Street
Constructed circa 1920

Amelia Boynton Robinson along with S. W. Boynton were key figures of the Selma Voting Rights Movement. A Savannah native, Amelia came to Selma in the 1930s as a county home extension agent, her role being to educate rural Dallas County in homemaking and in particular food processing. She met Samuel Boynton through the county extension office, where he also worked as an agent, and they married in 1936. She and Samuel focused on making the lives of sharecroppers better. Boynton cofounded the Dallas County Voters League and participated in African American voter registration for decades before the seminal Voting Rights Movement began in Selma.

FIGURE 4-1, Amelia Boynton Robinson House, 1315 Boyntons Street, Photograph by Dr. Carroll Van West, NRHP 2013

This dwelling is a pyramid-roofed Craftsman form with a front-gable wing to the left. Brick piers for the porch are still intact. The house is significant for the time period of the Civil Rights Era as it was the site for much of the strategic planning and meetings for the Movement. Mr. Boynton passed in 1963 and did not live to see the successes of the Movement. Amelia Boynton participated in the March from Selma to Montgomery in 1965 and was in fact wounded during the event. Amelia passed away in 2015.

Benjamin F. Hudson House • 1401 Boyntons Street
Constructed circa 1910

This unique Craftsman bungalow has a full-width porch. The dominant feature is the cluster porch columns set on plinths that rest on brick piers on the brick balustrade. The porch supports are arched and feature half-timbering. The fenestration consists of four-over-one windows, and a single door is flanked by sidelights. Decorative eave brackets enrich the wide overhanging eaves. A cross-gable dormer has decorative knee brackets.

FIGURE 4-2, Benjamin F. Hudson House, 1401 Boyntons Street, Photograph by Dr. Carroll Van West, NRHP 2013

Mr. Hudson worked as assistant cashier at the Alabama Penny Savings Bank. He was the father of Richard B. Hudson Jr., who became a prominent leader in the Civil Rights Movement.

George Williams House • 1403 Boyntons Street
Constructed circa 1910

FIGURE 4-3, George Williams House, 1403 Boyntons Street, Photograph by Dr. Carroll Van West, NRHP 2013

This one-story Minimal Tradition house has a central entry flanked by unique windows of one-over-one configuration. The entry is a paneled door with glass above. The roof is hipped with cross gable and the flat-roof porch is supported by iron railings.

R. B. Hudson House • 1420 Boyntons Street
Constructed 1907; addition 1910 • Wallace A. Rayfield, Architect

The R. B. Hudson House is two-story gable front and wing with Stick details in the gable ends. The house features a wraparound porch and exposed rafters. The Sanborn map of 1907 indicates that the house was originally one story and had a wraparound turreted porch. The dwelling was modified with a second story with square columns supported by brick piers, circa 1910. It was designed by African American architect Wallace A. Rayfield.

FIGURE 4-4, R. B. Hudson House, 1420 Boyntons Street, Photograph by Dr. Carroll Van West, NRHP 2013

R. B. Hudson, a graduate of Selma University and a proponent for education for African American children, was instrumental in establishing Clark Elementary School, which was originally located in a portion of Sylvan Street Hall. Hudson was the administrator for forty years, and during his tenure a permanent structure was built on Lawrence Street, circa 1894, no longer extant. R. B. Hudson Middle School, formerly R. B. Hudson High School, was named in his honor.

1427 Boyntons Street • *Constructed circa 1940*

FIGURE 4-5, 1427 Boyntons Street, Photograph by Dr. Carroll Van West, NRHP 2013

This one-story gable-front commercial brick building has a central entry flanked by one-over-one windows with a flat-roof addition that has a door to the south with a large single-pane window to the north. It is a typical commercial building for the African American vernacular architecture.

Foster Memorial Hall (Selma University Historic District)
1501 Boyntons Street • *Constructed 1910*
Wallace A. Rayfield, Architect

FIGURE 4-6, Foster Memorial Hall, Selma University, 1501 Boyntons Street, Photograph by Dr. Carroll Van West, NRHP 2013

This two-story simplified Neoclassical brick building on a raised basement was a girls' dormitory and features a bracketed hood with scroll brackets at the primary entrance. The architect Wallace A. Rayfield used modulation from first story to second story and first story to a raised basement, as a means of giving more prominence to the first floor and providing balance and proportion to the building. The original parapet and flat roof were removed and replaced with a low-pitched, front-gabled roof.[1] The building was named in honor of Susie C. Foster, president of the Women's Convention in the early 1900s.

---

1. Keith S. Hebert, Selma University National Register Nomination, 2023, 7.

Dinkins Memorial Chapel (Selma University Historic District)
1501 Boyntons Street • *Constructed 1903; rebuilt 1921*
Robert Robinson Taylor & Leo Persley, Architects

This three-story red-brick Renaissance Revival–influenced building is embellished with tan brick quoins and belt course. The hipped roof with wide overhanging eaves is supported by eave brackets. The primary entrance of double doors with transom and sidelights has a hipped bracketed hood. Above the entrance is brick detailing featuring four sections of header-course red bricks outlined with tan brick. Double arched windows on the third floor are flanked by the same brick detailing. The building was destroyed by fire and rebuilt in 1921.

FIGURE 4-7, Dinkins Memorial Chapel, Selma University, 1501 Boyntons Street, Photograph by Dr. Carroll Van West, NRHP 2013

The building was named for C. S. Dinkins, who was president of Selma University from 1893 to 1901. Robert Robinson Taylor was the first college-educated African American architect and the first African American graduate of MIT. He is noted primarily for his work at Tuskegee, where he worked with Booker T. Washington designing many of the campus buildings and teaching architectural drawing. One of his most noteworthy buildings is the Carnegie Library on the Tuskegee campus.

Stone-Robinson Library (Selma University Historic District)
1501 Boyntons Street • *Constructed 1960*

FIGURE 4-8, Stone-Robinson Library, Selma University, 1501 Boyntons Street, Photograph by Dr. Carroll Van West, NRHP 2013

The Stone-Robinson Library honors Alabama State Missionary Baptist leader Susie Stone (Hardy), corresponding secretary of the Alabama Women's State Convention, and Dr. U. J. Robinson, who was president of the Convention during the 1960s. This modernistic one-story, yellow-brick, gable-front building has an arched covered entrance to the east with double doors, transom, and sidelights. The building is noteworthy for the distinctive raised grid pattern on the façade.

Pollard Hall (Selma University Historic District)
1518 Boyntons Street • *Constructed circa 1916*

Built during R. T. Pollard's tenure as President of Selma University, Pollard Hall served as the dwelling for university presidents, a center for visitors, and at times a men's dormitory. The edifice has a hipped roof with wide overhanging eaves and asymmetrical floor plan. The primary entrance has a single-leaf door with sidelights and transom. R. T. Pollard was recognized

FIGURE 4-9, Pollard Hall, Selma University, 1518 Boyntons Street, Photograph by Dr. Carroll Van West, NRHP 2013

as a stirring orator, and speaking of the University's future in 1906 Pollard notes, "We begin work, I am glad to say, under the most encouraging conditions; except that the way is dark when we raise the question from what source may we secure money to meet our many needs? If ever we needed the help of those interested in Christian education, we need it now."[2]

1605 Boyntons Street • *Constructed circa 1900; modified circa 1920*

The origins of this side-gabled dwelling with cross-gable wings appear to be from the Queen Anne era as indicated by the imbricated shingles in the gable end to the left of the dwelling. The partial-width porch was modified circa 1920 with brick columns.

---

2. R. T. Pollard, *Baptist Home Mission Monthly* 27–28 (1905–1906): 416, cited at "Alabama Baptist Colored University, Selma, AL," Baptist History Homepage, http://baptisthistoryhomepage.com/alabama.bapt.colored.univ.html.

FIGURE 4-10, 1605 Boyntons Street,
Photograph by Dr. Carroll Van West, NRHP 2013

The Reverend David V. Jemison, pastor of Tabernacle Baptist Church, and his wife, Henrietta, resided in this dwelling. Jemison oversaw the construction of Tabernacle Baptist Church and was active in the church from 1902 through 1954. He was president of the National Baptist Convention from 1940 to 1953.

Pollard-Brown House • 1609 Boyntons Street
Constructed circa 1900

FIGURE 4-11, Pollard-Brown House, 1609 Boyntons Street,
Photograph by Dr. Carroll Van West, NRHP 2013

This dwelling was at one time the residence for R. T. Pollard, president of Selma University from 1916 to 1929. His wife, Eliza Pollard, led the Baptist's Women's State Convention. It exhibits elements of the Queen Anne style such as the bay window in the right bay and the hipped roof with multiple cross gables. A partial-width hipped-roof porch is supported by cast-iron decorative posts. The single-door entry is surmounted by a transom and three-over-one windows form the left bay.

1616 Boyntons Street • *Constructed circa 1940*
George Wilson, Architect

FIGURE 4-12, 1616 Boyntons Street,
Photograph by Dr. Carroll Van West, NRHP 2013

Utilizing a combination of brick and molded concrete blocks, George Wilson created this unique house on Boyntons Street. During this era, molded concrete blocks were a frequent form of building material with the blocks created on-site from molds. This pyramidal-roof house has a cross-gable entry porch with brick pillars. The three-bay house has two-over-two windows. Mrs. Gertrude Danzy, a teacher at Clark Elementary School, resided here in the 1950s.

Wilson-Odom House • 1620 Boyntons Street
Constructed circa 1940 • George Wilson, Architect

George Wilson, local architect, is credited with building and designing approximately forty residences as well as approximately twelve commercial buildings in Selma. He constructed this Tudor Revival for himself and his wife, Anna T. Wilson, a teacher at Knox Academy. His most widely recognized building was the Franklin Street community center, presently named to honor him—George D. Wilson Selma Community Center.

FIGURE 4-13, Wilson-Odom House, 1620 Boyntons Street, Photograph by Dr. Carroll Van West, NRHP 2013

The one-story brick cottage is entered through an arched vestibule. Curved steps form the stoop of the vestibule. Indicative of the style are two cross gables, with one cross gable flaring out to create a roof for the vestibule.

1621 Boyntons Street • *Constructed circa 1900*

One of the older houses on the street, this vernacular Queen Anne has a hipped roof with cross gables, arched vent, and imbricated shingles in the

FIGURE 4-14, 1621 Boyntons Street, Photograph by Dr. Carroll Van West, NRHP 2013

gable ends. To the south is an inset porch with shed roof. Windows are two-over-two, segmental arched. The Reverend Charles Smedley, the original resident, was listed as pastor of Morning Star Baptist Church in the 1913 city directory. Coincidentally, he was also a carpenter.

1625 Boyntons Street • *Constructed circa 1925*

FIGURE 4-15, 1625 Boyntons Street, Photograph by Dr. Carroll Van West, NRHP 2013

The Craftsman style was very popular in middle-class neighborhoods. This side-gable, one-story bungalow has an attached hipped-roof porch supported by square columns set on brick piers. The Reverend Nathan M. Carter, assistant dean at Selma University, lived here in the 1950s with his wife, Lillie.

CHAPTER 5

African American Historic Sites

For African Americans, religion in the antebellum period and during Reconstruction offered the sense of community and a means to cope and express their deepest longings. According to Wilson Fallin Jr. in his work *Uplifting the People*, "by singing together, eating together, praying together, and engaging in other forms of fellowship in their church, Black Baptists maintained a sense of community. As a social institution, the church offered relief from the physical stress of life through church suppers, picnics, and carnivals."[1] This sense of community continued, and during the Civil Rights Movement churches became a place to hold meetings and often strategize.

The importance of education to African Americans cannot be overemphasized as it provided a means to better their standard of living and during the Civil Rights Movement played a major role in inspiring teachers and students alike. One of the heroes of the African American educational

---

1. Wilson Fallin Jr., *Uplifting the People: Three Centuries of Black Baptists in Alabama*, Religion and American Culture (Tuscaloosa: University of Alabama Press, 2007), 62.

system was Rosa Young. Rosa was an Alabama native, born in Rosebud, Alabama, the fourth child in a family of ten children. She attended classes in Selma and after receiving her degree from Payne University was able to purchase land by fundraising in African American and white communities. On this land she built Rosebud Literary and Industrial School.[2] Rosa was instrumental in helping to establish Concordia College, which originated on Green Street in Selma as Alabama Luther College with its main purpose to educate preachers, teachers, and missionaries for the Lutheran Church.[3]

In studying the African American building tradition, many African Americans learned these skills from their fathers and grandfathers. One need only look to the antebellum plantation houses to acknowledge that these builders were true craftsmen. Two of these architect/builders appear to be self-taught—A. J. Farley and David T. West.

First Colored Baptist Church on M. L. K., Jr. Street, NRHP 1979
709 Martin Luther King, Jr. Street • *Constructed 1894*
David Benjamin T. West, Architect

The Gothic Revival–influenced First Baptist Church was considered to be the "finest colored church edifice in Alabama" at the time of its construction and is built in a cruciform plan with the sanctuary and chancel located within the steeply pitched front gable. The front gable features a large Tudor arched window flanked by smaller Tudor arched windows detailed with stucco drip molds that reinforce the Gothic style. Towers are located to the north and south. Before a tornado in 1978 that nearly destroyed the church, the tower to the south was surmounted by a tall wood spire set atop a crown roof. Presently, the two-story pyramidal roofed north tower has a double-leaf door entrance with Tudor arch transom and louvered vents

---

2. Rosa Young, *Light in the Dark Belt*, rev. ed. (St. Louis: Concordia Publishing, 2014), 64-70.

3. Alston Fitts III, *Selma: A Bicentennial History* (Birmingham: University of Alabama Press, 2017), 189-190.

FIGURE 5-1, First Colored Baptist Church on M. L. K, Jr. Street, 709 Martin Luther King, Jr. Street, Photograph by Susan Besser, 2013

surrounded by corbeling. The shorter south tower has a single-leaf entrance with Tudor arch transom and louvered vents with Gothic arch detail. A stucco belt course connects the Tudor and lancet arched windows and adds definition to the fenestration.

The establishment of this church was the culmination of African Americans seeking to create their own worship experience. After having shared a worship space with whites before emancipation, the congregation formed the First Colored Baptist Church on Phillip Street in 1866. The congregation was very involved in the formation of Selma University during the Reconstruction era. The architect for the church, David Benjamin T. West, also designed buildings for the university. First Baptist Church figured prominently in the Civil Rights Movement. Meetings of the Student Nonviolent Coordinating Committee were held in the church.

FIGURE 5-2, First Colored Baptist Church, Photograph from *The Cyclopedia of the Colored Baptists of Alabama*, https://docsouth.unc.edu/church/boothe/boothe.html

In 1965, in preparation for the Voting Rights Movement, it was the site of training sessions led by Martin Luther King and Ralph Abernathy for the youth of Selma.[4]

Mount Zion Primitive Baptist Church • 1306 Union Street
Constructed circa 1912

Mt. Zion Primitive Baptist Church's front-gable form embellished with stone quoins displays a central entrance three-storied brick tower topped by

---

4. Fitts, *Selma: A Bicentennial History*, 3.

a pyramidal roof of pressed metal shingles. Arches on the first story of the tower form the entry of Mt. Zion. Embracing the Gothic Revival vernacular, triple arched lancet windows on the west façade and north and south elevations create a light-filled sanctuary.

FIGURE 5-3, Mount Zion Primitive Baptist Church, 1306 Union Street, Photograph by Dr. Carroll Van West, NRHP 2013

Established in 1898, Mt. Zion Primitive Baptist Church follows the practices of the National Primitive Baptist Convention but differs from other Primitive Baptist churches in its incorporation of Sunday School and use of instruments in the service. Foot-washing is one of the rituals taken from Primitive Baptists. Mount Zion first met in a wood-frame building at the present location. The growth of Primitive Baptists throughout the country in the early 1900s was also a factor in the growth of Mt. Zion.

In 1912 the Gothic Revival–inspired sanctuary was completed. In the 1930s two other Primitive Baptist Churches grew from Mt. Zion—Little Canaan and Union Grove. Formed in the late 1800s, Mt. Zion and First Baptist Church reflected the achievement of African Americans in Selma and offered safe havens for the Civil Rights Movement, as well as providing leadership for the movement. On June 23, 1963, the church hosted one of the first mass meetings of the Civil Rights Movement.

Little Canaan Baptist Church • 1326 Eugene Street
Constructed circa 1933

FIGURE 5-4, Little Canaan Baptist Church, 1326 Eugene Street, Photograph by Dr. Carroll Van West, NRHP 2013

This front-gable brick church has a double-door central entrance with the gable roof overdoor. Stained-glass windows that feature a cross design are on either side of the entrance. The windows on the east and west façades also feature the cross design. A simple cross of tan brick in located in the upper portion of the façade. A wood cupola with a hipped roof is a remnant of the 1933 wood frame building, covered in brick in 1985. The Reverend S. B. Acuff was the pastor in the 1960s when the congregation was very involved in the Civil Rights Movement.

Burwell-Dinkins House, NRHP 2022 • 700 L. L. Anderson Avenue
Constructed 1898; addition 1909 • *Wallace A. Rayfield, Architect*

This two-and-one-half-story Craftsman, with wraparound porch supported by brick columns, features a single entry with transom and sidelights, wide overhanging eaves with modillions, and a polygonal bay. It was designed by preeminent African American architect Wallace A. Rayfield. A triangular pedimented dormer with tripartite windows to the west pierces the pyramidal roof. The residence was built for Dr. L. L. Burwell, who was a Selma University graduate and obtained his medical degree at Leonard Medical College in

FIGURE 5-5, Burwell-Dinkins House, 700 L. L. Anderson Avenue, Photograph by Dr. Carroll Van West, NRHP 2013

Raleigh, North Carolina, graduating as valedictorian of both schools. Seeing a need for medical facilities for African Americans he opened Burwell Infirmary on Philpot Avenue (extant) and a drugstore at 2014 Franklin Avenue. Burwell served as secretary of the Board of Trustees of Selma University. Initially, Dr. Burwell used the parlor of this dwelling for his office.

It was also the residence for Dr. William Dinkins, president (1932–1950) of Selma University. Dinkins served in World War I as an officer. Dr. Dinkins's daughter, Dr. Pauline E. Dinkins, was a physician in Selma and served as a medical missionary in Liberia. After her return she created a children's book with Effie Newsome called *African Folk Tales*. Rev. L. L. Anderson, pastor of Tabernacle Baptist Church and influential Alabama Civil Rights leader, also resided here with his wife, Pauline Dinkins Anderson. The city directory of 1954 shows that the building was serving as a private school.

Morning Star Missionary Baptist Church
408 Buckeye Avenue • *Constructed 1923*

FIGURE 5-6, Morning Star Baptist Church, 408 Buckeye Avenue, Photograph by Susan Besser, 2023

This brick-veneer church is surprising for its contemporary design in the 1920s. The soaring height of this two-story building creates a dramatic sanctuary that is lit within by a stained-glass window framed by a brick course on either side and corbeling below and is located in the projecting façade. Brick balustrades on either side of the projection complete the façade. The steeply pitched gable roof is surmounted by a cupola and topped with a steeple. Morning Star Missionary Baptist Church dates to 1915 when it was pastored by Reverend J. H. Skinner. It was rebuilt in 1923 with R. A. Daniel as the pastor. The Reverend I. C. Acuff is noted as being supportive of the Civil Rights Movement.

Lord's Tabernacle, Church of Holiness
815 Minter Avenue • *Constructed circa 1900*

FIGURE 5-7, Lord's Tabernacle, Church of Holiness, 815 Minter Avenue, Photograph by Dr. Carroll Van West, NRHP 2013

This Pentecostal church was documented by Sara J. Duncan in 1905 as one of twenty-two African American churches in Selma.[5] Ms. Duncan was an activist who was president of the African Methodist Episcopal Church Women's Home and Foreign Missionary Society. The church is a one-and-one-half-story front-gable frame building with a two-story pyramidal roofed tower to the west. Tudor arched louvers are in the second story of the tower. Arched windows flank the double-door entry, which has a gable roof overdoor.

Ward Chapel A.M.E. Church • 811 Philpot Street
Constructed 1925; alterations 1949

FIGURE 5-8, Ward Chapel A.M.E. Church, 811 Philpott Street, Photograph by Dr. Carroll Van West, NRHP 2013

Ward Chapel is a one-story, front-gable brick building. The entry is composed of double doors and framed with a Tudor arch. Tudor-arched windows are on either side of the entry. A cupola is original to the 1925 structure and is located to the west of the building and has a pyramidal roof

---

5. Carroll Van West, Amber Clawson, Jessica French, and Abigail Gautreau, "The Civil Rights Movement in Selma, Alabama, 1865-1972," National Register Multiple Property Nomination, 10, https://npgallery.nps.gov/NRHP/.

with flared eaves. Ward Chapel A.M.E. Church was originally located at 403 Young Street according to the 1913 Sanborn map.

At the time of Ward Chapel's construction, Reverend C. J. L. Rumph was the pastor. The congregation of Ward Chapel was very involved in the Civil Rights Movement in the 1950s with Rev. M. S. Hasty as the pastor. Payne University, a historic Black college no longer in operation, supported the beginnings of the congregation.

Tabernacle Baptist Church, NRHP 2013 • 1431 Broad Street
Constructed 1922 • David T. West, Architect

FIGURE 5-9, Tabernacle Baptist Church, 1431 Broad Street, Photograph by Susan Besser, NRHP 2013

Rev. Edward M. Brawley, president of the Alabama Baptist and Theological School, now Selma University, recognized that the students and faculty of the school should have their own church. In 1885 several members of First Baptist and Saint Phillip Street Baptist Church formed a new congregation under the name Tabernacle Baptist Church with the University's chapel serving as the first meeting place. The first permanent building was located on Minter Avenue next to the present building. In order to finance the building, Rev. Brawley mortgaged his library and, sadly, lost the library in a public auction. Tabernacle Baptist Church was designed by local African American architect David T. West and is noteworthy for the Neoclassical style of the two-story brick building. It dominates the corner of Broad Street and Minter Avenue with two façades of full-height pedimented porticoes supported by Doric columns, which is a defining characteristic of the style. The church is a modified Akron plan and features a domed roof clerestory creating a light-filled space. Defining the corners of the façades are four towers, which feature stained-glass windows on the second and third stories. Surmounting the multilight doors is a transom indicating the year the church was established, 1866, and the year of construction, 1922. Looking closely at the Broad Street façade one notes that one of the towers is red brick. These bricks were salvaged from the original church and used to build the tower.

FIGURE 5-10, Tabernacle Baptist Church, Photograph by Billy Brown

The African American population during this era was experiencing a measure of success, both financially and in leadership in international church organizations. The church was built under the direction of Rev. David V. Jemison. During the beginnings of the Civil Rights Movement, Rev. L. L. Anderson opened the church for the first mass meeting of the Student Nonviolent Coordinating Committee. It was at this meeting that

James Forman, executive director of SNCC, encouraged the students to stand up for their voting rights.[6]

St. Edmund's Memorial Chapel, St. Elizabeth's Catholic Church
1417 Broad Street • *Constructed circa 1940*

Originally known as St. Elizabeth's Catholic Church, this gable-front brick building features clinker brick and skintled mortar indicative of the Arts and Crafts movement. The dark purple color that characterizes clinker brick occurs when the bricks are close to the fire in the firing process. Skintled mortar is a technique used by masons to create the effect of mortar squeezed out of the joints. The double-door entry is defined with a soldier course of bricks. A large Tudor arch covered with plaster enframes the entry and the Gothic window is flanked by narrow windows.

FIGURE 5-11, St. Edmund's Memorial Chapel, St. Elizabeth's Catholic Church, 1417 Broad Street, Photograph by Dr. Carroll Van West, NRHP 2013

---

6. West et al., "Civil Rights Movement in Selma," 35.

This church is associated with the Fathers of St. Edmund, a Catholic order that began their mission work in Selma in July of 1937 when Father Frank Casey and Father John "Barney" Paro arrived in Selma responding to the mission of Pope Pius XI to spread Catholicism to poor African Americans. They worked alongside the Sisters of St. Joseph who came in 1940 serving African Americans through the Good Samaritan Hospital and St. Elizabeth's School. In 1947 Father Nelson Ziter formed the Don Bosco Club, which worked with African American young men as a boy's club.[7] Father Maurice Ouellet, pastor during the Civil Rights era, was supportive of the Movement and the Selma to Montgomery March.[8]

Good Samaritan Hospital • 1107 Voeglin Avenue
Constructed 1964 • Tom Brown Kirkland, Architect

The original hospital, a small frame building no longer extant, was established in 1922 as Baptist Good Samaritan Hospital and operated by the Southern Baptist Hospital Commission. Local physicians assumed operation of the facility in 1937. The Edmundite Fathers led by Father Francis Casey, S.S.E., acquired the original building in 1944. Substantial renovations were made to the original building in 1947 and 1957. Together with the sisters of St. Joseph, the Edmundite Fathers served the African Americans of Selma for many years.[9]

The present Good Samaritan Hospital had been on the drawing board for five years and was completed in 1964. The architect, Tom Brown Kirkland, from Montgomery Alabama, along with Father Eymard P. Galligan and Sister Louis Bertrand Dixon, envisioned this project, which would bring a hospital with modern facilities to the African Americans of the

---

7. West et al., "Civil Rights Movement in Selma," 17.

8. "The Selma Civil Rights Trail: 50 Landmarks for a 50th Anniversary," brochure, Center for Historic Preservation at Middle Tennessee State University, https://irp.cdn-website.com/2c253136/files/uploaded/3507SelmaCivilRightsBrochurePages.pdf.

9. "Edmundite Missions," Smithsonian National Postal Museum, https://postalmuseum.si.edu/exhibition/america's-mailing-industry-industry-segments-nonprofit-organizations/edmundite-missions.

FIGURE 5-12, Good Samaritan Hospital, 1107 Voeglin Avenue, Photograph by Dr. Carroll Van West, NRHP 2013

region. The four-story Mid-Century Modern brick building was built at a cost of $1,000,000, had 45,000 square feet, and was air-conditioned.[10] Most notable is the fenestration, which is comprised of double casement windows with flat roof overhangs. Limestone panels create divisions between the double windows.

Good Samaritan Hospital is recognized locally as a Civil Rights resource as African Americans as well as whites were treated here on Bloody Sunday.[11]

Ebenezer Missionary Baptist Church • 1548 F. D. Reese Street
Constructed circa 1960

Ebenezer Missionary Baptist Church is a Colonial Revival gable-front brick building with full-height portico supported by four Doric columns. The corners are embellished with brick quoins and there are two

---

10. "Good Samaritan Hospital Has Long History," *Montgomery Advertiser*, December 14, 1964, 15.

11. West et al., "Civil Rights Movement in Selma," 14.

FIGURE 5-13, Ebenezer Missionary Baptist Church, 1548 F. D. Reese Street, Photograph by Dr. Carroll Van West, NRHP 2013

double-door entrances surmounted by broken pediments. The triple-tiered steeple features arched windows on the second tier.

Ebenezer Baptist Church was pastored by the Rev. Frederick Douglas Reese, who was one of the Courageous Eight during the Voting Rights Movement. His congregation was involved in the Voting Rights Movement.

F. D. Reese House • 1566 Marie Foster Street
Constructed circa 1918 • Wallace A. Rayfield, Architect

A cast-iron fence leads to the F. D. Reese House, which was designed by Wallace Rayfield and dates to the early part of the twentieth century. Earlier residents of the dwelling were H. A. Barnes and his family. Barnes was a teacher at Payne University. The two-story frame L-plan house features a front gable with a polygonal bay with a four-over-four window configuration. The porch has a brick balustrade with brick piers supporting cast-iron supports and leads to a single-leaf door with transom and two windows of two-over-two configuration to the south. A cast-iron balustrade enhances the roofline of the porch. Six-over-six windows complete the fenestration of the second story.

FIGURE 5-14, F. D. Reese House, 1566 Marie Foster Street, Photograph by Susan Besser, 2022

Rev. Frederick Douglas Reese, pastor of Ebenezer Baptist Church and former public-school teacher, was a member of the Courageous Eight of the Civil Rights Movement. Reese's letter to Martin Luther King in December of 1964 inviting him to Selma was instrumental in propelling the movement forward. Rev. Reese and his wife, Allin, along with their five children, lived in this dwelling for over fifty years.

Northern Heights Presbyterian Church • 1575 Marie Foster Street
Constructed circa 1950

FIGURE 5-15, Northern Heights Presbyterian Church, 1575 Marie Foster Street, Photograph by Dr. Carroll Van West, NRHP 2013

The Reverend Ernest M. Bradford served at Northern Heights Presbyterian Church from 1962 until 1970 during the height of the Voting Rights Movement. Rev. Bradford, along with his congregation, joined the Selma to Montgomery March in 1965. This simple two-story, gable-front gold-brick building has a one-story portico supported by brick columns leading to the entrance flanked by two narrow stained-glass windows on either side. The simplicity of the façade is accentuated by the glass block cross of the second story. Stained-glass windows are on the north and south elevations of the building and offset the austerity of the exterior.

St. Paul C.M.E. Church • 808 Minter Street
Constructed circa 1940

St. Paul C.M.E. was established in 1891. The church has been associated with the Civil Rights Movement since 1963. The Reverend T. R. Harris was instrumental in bringing new energy to the movement for a short period as pastor in 1964. The congregation hosted meetings even after he left, one in particular by the Southern Christian Leadership Conference in March 1966, which was documented by journalist Jim Peppler from the *Southern Courier*. White Episcopal minister Jonathan Daniels gave a sermon at St. Paul C.M.E.[12]

FIGURE 5-16, St. Paul C.M.E. Church, 808 Minter Street, Photograph by Dr. Carroll Van West, NRHP 2013

This impressive two-story building of masonry construction has two Tudor arched entrances with keystones containing double doors. Pyramidal roofed twin towers are to the east and west of the entrance. Blind arches create interest on the façade. Tudor-arched stained-glass windows are on the east and west elevations of the building. This sanctuary is an excellent

---

12. West et al., "Civil Rights Movement in Selma," 37.

example of the powerful presence of African American churches in the twentieth century.

Lannie's Bar-B-Q Spot • 2115 Minter Avenue
Constructed circa 1940; addition 1998

FIGURE 5-17, Lannie's Bar-B-Q Spot, 2115 Minter Avenue, Photograph by Dr. Carroll Van West, NRHP 2013

The original building is a one-story frame hipped-roof building with screened-in porch entrance. The commercial one-story brick building with metal soffit and shed roof was attached circa 1998.

Lula Hatcher continues the tradition of Lannie's Bar-B-Q Spot started by her father, Lannie Moore Travis, and his brother, Will, beginning in a cinder-block pit near Lannie's home. It features authentic smoked pork cooked on-site.

Lannie's is noted as the only restaurant that served whites and African Americans during the Civil Rights Movement. "We were the only place that wasn't segregated," Lula Hatcher remarked. "White, black, whoever

. . . they were welcome, anybody that came. They were comfortable."[13] It was also a meeting place for Voting Rights activists who gathered there frequently as well as the local police officers, state troopers, and National Guard. In that regard it was considered a safe haven.

Clark Elementary School • 405 Lawrence Street
Constructed 1918 • Warren & Knight, Architect

FIGURE 5-18, Clark Elementary School, 405 Lawrence Street, Photograph by Dr. Carroll Van West, NRHP 2013

Clark Elementary School's main building is a one-story brick building with a parapet capped with alternating vertical and horizontal stretcher brick courses and stone coping. The arched entrance leads to double doors. On either side of the entrance are five double-hung windows. It was built at a cost of $9,868.55. The original building was a six-room brick school constructed in 1894 with a contribution of $5,000 from the city council. This

---

13. Bethune, Meredith, "A Lifetime of Barbecue in Selma," *Gravy*, Fall 2016, https://www.southernfoodways.org/a-lifetime-of-barbecue-in-selma/.

building is notable in that it was the first public school for African American children in Selma. The school bears the name of Clark Elementary in honor of Dr. Courtney J. Clark, who championed the cause of education for African Americans. R. B. Hudson was the first principal.[14] This was also the site where a group of local teachers in January of 1965 gathered before marching to the Dallas County Courthouse to register to vote, led by Frederick Douglas Reese.[15]

R. B. Hudson Middle School • 1701 Summerfield Road
Constructed 1949 • Raymond Sizemore, Architect
S. J. Curry, Contractor

This was the first public African American high school in Selma, built at a cost of $400,000 by S. J. Curry and designed by Raymond Sizemore. It was originally R. B. Hudson High School, named in honor of educator R. B. Hudson. He was the principal of Clark Elementary School for forty-one years. Soldiers returning from World War II completed their high school education here while on the G. I. Bill. Before the passage of the Civil Rights Act of 1964 and Voting Rights Act of 1965, students at R. B. Hudson High School participated in demonstrations supporting these efforts. The school's name was changed in 1970 to Westside Junior High School and then to Chatt Academy in 2000. In May of 2012, the school was reestablished as a memorial to Hudson when it was renamed R. B. Hudson Middle School.

The building is a two-story brick Mid-Century Modern design. The two-story entry is recessed set between one-story blocks and has a metal shed roof supported by four brick columns with stone caps. The austerity of the fenestration, which consists of three-pane awning windows, is relieved by recessed brickwork. Stone coping defines the roofline.

On January 22, 1965, in his role as a science teacher at R. B. Hudson School, Dr. Frederick Douglas Reese led over one hundred teachers to the Dallas County Courthouse in order to attempt to register to vote, an

---

14. Fitts, *Selma: A Bicentennial History*, 145.

15. "Selma Civil Rights Trail."

FIGURE 5-19, R. B. Hudson Middle School, 1701 Summerfield Road, Photograph by Dr. Carroll Van West, NRHP 2013

activity that jeopardized their positions—it was a pivotal moment in the Voting Rights Movement.

West Trinity Baptist Church • 310 L. L. Anderson Avenue
Constructed circa 1953 • C. R. Smyley, Architect

This church exhibits elements of the Romanesque Revival. The double-door arched entry has a limestone surround with keystone. Stained-glass arch windows are to the north and the south. Two multi-pane arched stained-glass windows with hood molds are just above the entry with a stone inset engraved with "Welcome West Trinity Baptist Church" in the center of the façade. An arched louvered vent is in the gable end of the front gable. Towers are on either side of the façade, which are a carryover from the Romanesque of the Medieval time period. The corners of the tower are embellished with quoins in a random design.

West Trinity Baptist Church (originally West Selma Baptist Church) was established in 1895, funding a permanent sanctuary in 1910, which due to steady growth was enlarged in 1920. Its importance in the Alabama Baptist Convention is shown by its being the host church for the Southwest

FIGURE 5-20, West Trinity Baptist Church, 310 L. L. Anderson Avenue, Photograph by Dr. Carroll Van West, NRHP 2013

District Convention in 1921. In 1924 the congregation purchased this lot at 310 L. L. Anderson Avenue. In 1947 Rev. I. C. Ravizee was asked to lead West Trinity Baptist Church. For five years he led a fund-raising drive for a new sanctuary. C. R. Smyley was the architect of record.[16] Dr. D. V. Jemison officiated the dedication of the building in March of 1953.[17]

Clinton Chapel A.M.E. Zion Church • 615 Green Street
Constructed 1975

Clinton Chapel A.M.E. Zion Church was established in 1866 led by the Reverend James Wadsworth. The Reverend C. C. Hunter, one of

---

16. Carroll Van West, Amber Clawson, Jessica French, and Abigail Gautreau, "The Civil Rights Movement in Selma, Alabama, 1865-1972," National Register Multiple Property Nomination, 18, https://npgallery.nps.gov/NRHP/.

17. "West Trinity Opens Newly-Built Church," *Selma Times-Journal*, March 15, 1953, 19.

the Courageous Eight, assumed leadership in the 1960s, and in 1963 the church was associated with the Dallas County Improvement Association, which was a more moderate civil rights group. Clinton Chapel was a location for Civil Rights Movement meetings.

FIGURE 5-21, Clinton Chapel A.M.E. Zion Church, 615 Green Street, Photograph by Dr. Carroll Van West, NRHP 2013

The original church was built in 1889 with this sanctuary built in 1975. The church has strong Colonial Revival stylist elements such as the temple front entrance with engaged square columns leading to an inset porch. The double-door entry is enhanced by transom and flanking sidelights and surmounted with a Greek Revival–influenced entablature. To either side of the entrance are arched multi-pane windows. A tall spire gives prominence to the building.

Shiloh Baptist Church • 1416 Selma Avenue
Constructed circa 1965

This impressive two-story brick church is located on Selma Avenue and is a front-gable form. This is the second location of the church. The original

FIGURE 5-22, Shiloh Baptist Church, 1416 Selma Avenue, Photograph by Susan Besser, 2022

location is on Mechanic Street. The form has three recessed entrances, the middle entrance having a triangular pediment. The other entrances are surmounted by a simple entablature. Windows are located above the entrances to the east and west. Leading up to the church are brick steps with a brick cheek wall to either side. Creating the sense of a courtyard is a low brick planter fronting Selma Avenue.

Shiloh Baptist Church, Original • 110 Mechanic Street
Constructed circa 1900

Shiloh Baptist Church was founded in 1899 at the corner of Range and Water Streets. The church began with only ten members under the

FIGURE 5-23, Shiloh Baptist Church, 110 Mechanic Street, Photograph by Dr. Carroll Van West, NRHP 2013

leadership of the Reverend Elmore. The Reverend J. E. Noble, who became pastor in 1954, oversaw changes to the exterior over the next seven years and established a building fund for new development. Shiloh Baptist Church welcomed the Rev. R. L. Flowers as its new minister in 1963 and was a center for meetings during the Civil Rights Movement. As recounted in a church history, "Under his leadership, we are enjoying working together in beautifying our church. We have added oak floors, fine paneled the inside, added a kitchen, dining room, secretary room, classrooms, enlarged the choir room and pastor's study, added new years and bricked the church."[18] The one-story gable front brick veneer church features a gable-roof porch leading to double-leaf doors. Tudor arched stained-glass windows are to the east and west of the entry. A steeple graces the roofline. The congregation moved to a new location on Selma Avenue in 1965.

---

18. "Shiloh Baptist Church, Second Family & Friends Days, May 27, 28, & 29, 1988," church pamphlet, quoted in West et al., "Civil Rights Movement in Selma," 37-38.

Mt. Ararat Baptist Church • 120 North Division Street
Constructed circa 1981 • Charles Moss, Contractor

FIGURE 5-24, Mount Ararat Baptist Church,
20 North Division Street, Photograph by Susan Besser, 2022

Mt. Ararat Baptist Church, which was established in 1888, is a one-and-one-half-story brick building distinctive for the projection of four brick walls that support the overhang of the front gable. The projections create a portico that leads to two sets of double doors with three narrow vertical windows. Stained-glass windows define the second story. A large cross is located midway on the center of the second-story façade. On the north and south elevations are brick buttresses and narrow twelve-pane windows. To the north is a side gable one-story education building with a central-gable roof and full glass entrance. The church is surmounted by a wood frame cupola.

Claude C. Brown Branch YMCA • 1133 Minter Avenue
Constructed circa 1960

FIGURE 5-25, Claude C. Brown Branch YMCA, 1133 Minter Avenue, Photograph by Dr. Carroll Van West, NRHP 2013

This is a one-story brick minimalist Mid-Century building with a one-and-one-half-story gymnasium attached to the west. The branch was the offshoot of two boys' clubs as envisioned by Father Nelson B. Ziter and Reverend Claude C. Brown as they observed the lack of organized activity for African-American males. Father Ziter set up a club known as the Don Bosco Boys Club. Claude C. Brown, pastor of Reformed Presbyterian Church, set up the Ralph Bunche Club, named after an African-American diplomat. These two clubs had a fierce rivalry for many years. Ultimately, the Bunche Club became a branch of the YMCA, known as the George Washington Carver Branch. It was later named the Claude C. Brown Branch.[19]

---

19. Fitts, *Selma: A Bicentennial History*, 214.

St. Elizabeth's School • 1211 Church Street
Constructed circa 1952

This one-story Mid-Century Modern building was constructed in 1952. The entrance is to the east and consists of double doors with a single pane each and sidelights. To the west of the entrance are double awning windows. Two banks of seven awning windows are to the west and are delineated by a belt course that terminates at the entry.

FIGURE 5-26, St. Elizabeth's School, 1211 Church Street, Photograph by Susan Besser, 2018

Recognizing the need for educational facilities for African American children, the Edmundite Brothers and the Sisters of St. Joseph from Rochester, New York, worked together to create a Catholic school beginning in 1940, adding a grade each year until 1948.[20]

Temple Gate Seventh Day Adventist Church
1601 Franklin Street • *Constructed 1959*

The original portion of this church was built in 1959. As with many African-American churches in this era, additions and changes were made as the congregation grew. The addition to the north reflects the modernistic architecture of the 1960s and 1970s. Most notable from the front is the

---

20. West et al., "Civil Rights Movement in Selma," 17.

FIGURE 5-27, Temple Gate Seventh Day Adventist Church, 1601 Franklin Street, Photograph by Dr. Carroll Van West, NRHP 2013

high pitch of the front gable indicating a large vaulted worship center in the addition. Temple Gate, under the guidance of Elder F. O. Jones, was involved in the Civil Rights Movement in the 1960s.

Second Missionary Baptist Church • 2809 Hardie Avenue
Constructed 1976 • Rev. J. Jackson Sr., and Ledger Rutledge, Architects

FIGURE 5-28, Second Missionary Baptist Church, 2809 Hardie Avenue, Photograph by Dr. Carroll Van West, NRHP 2013

A steeple surmounts a front gable vaulted ceiling in this one-story gray-brick building. Notable are the four windows that project to the eaves. A one-story gable front entrance is to the north creating a front portico entrance supported by columns. The architects were R. J. Jackson Sr. and Ledger Rutledge. Rutledge was chair of the church building committee. The black Baptists who formed First Colored Baptist Church began to divide into a new congregation during Reconstruction, with the creation of Second Baptist Church in 1869.[21]

Brown Chapel A.M.E. Church, NHL and NRHP 1982
410 Martin Luther King, Jr. Street • *Constructed 1908*
A. J. Farley, Architect

After the emancipation Black Methodists of Selma met in the basement of the Hotel Albert. African Methodist Episcopal missionary John Turner in August of 1867 proposed that the congregation consider linking with the African Methodist Episcopal Church. A year later the first conference of the A.M.E. Church was held in Selma with Bishop John Mifflin Brown officiating.

The congregation purchased property on Sylvan Street in 1869 with the original church being wood frame. Built to honor Bishop Brown, the present sanctuary was constructed in 1908 with Rev. A. J. Hunter overseeing the project. The form of this Romanesque Revival Church with Mission and Byzantine influences is reminiscent of the mission churches of California, especially San Juan Capistrano. The design for the building is credited to A. J. Farley, an African American architect/builder. Very little is known about Farley and his background. He appears to have been self-taught. Local architect John McKeil, originally from Nova Scotia, offered drafting lessons during this period and it is possible that Farley may have been instructed by McKeil.

A triple-arcaded entrance that references the triumphal arch of Early Romanesque churches is surmounted by a stained-glass rose window with

---

21. West et al., "Civil Rights Movement in Selma," 3.

two vertical and two horizontal mullions. A shaped parapet owing to Mission influences outlined with stone coping crowns the central bay. Flanking the entrance are four-story towers. The two lower stories of the towers are outlined with stone quoins. The third story of the towers features Gothic-influenced louvered vents with the fourth story of the tower an octagonal domed lantern. The experience of entering the beautiful sanctuary is enhanced by a soaring, vaulted coffered ceiling. A Henry Pilcher pipe organ was added circa 1925.

FIGURE 5-29, Brown Chapel A.M.E. Church, 410 Martin Luther King, Jr. Street, Photograph by Susan Besser, 2022

The church leaders knew education was paramount to the African American ability to thrive and purchased property for Payne Institute, which was located at 1525 Franklin Street. The college remained here until 1922, moving to Birmingham, where it was known as Daniel Payne

Institute. A devastating tornado destroyed much of the campus in 1977 and the college closed in 1979.

The church figures prominently in the Civil Rights Movement with the initial meeting of the Voting Rights Movement in Selma taking place in the church, despite Circuit Court Judge James Hare's injunction against mass meetings. Brown Chapel was the site where the three Selma-to-Montgomery marches began.[22]

George Washington Carver Homes • 410 Martin Luther King, Jr. Street
Constructed 1951

FIGURE 5-30, George Washington Carver Homes, 410 Martin Luther King, Jr. Street, Photograph by Dr. Carroll Van West, NRHP 2013

Built in 1951 as Federal housing for low-income families, the two-story gable-roof buildings with one-story entry porticos were significant for the contextual history of housing activists associated with the Selma to Montgomery March during the heart of the Civil Rights Movement in Selma. The site became the "Face of the Civil Rights Movement" as many of the activists, including Dr. Martin Luther King Jr., members of the Southern Christian Leadership Conference, and members of the Student Nonviolent Coordinating Committee, would dine and live with the families.

---

22. West et al., "Civil Rights Movement in Selma," 29.

Louretta Wimberly House • 1423 Eugene Street
Constructed circa 1940

FIGURE 5-31, Louretta Wimberly House, 1423 Eugene Street, Photograph by Dr. Carroll Van West, NRHP 2013

Louretta Wimberly was very involved in the Civil Rights Movement. She was sometimes met with the potential of violence from the white community.[23] She was involved in the Black Heritage Council and was a great resource during this time. She assisted in the fieldwork of property assessment.[24] This frame house has a hipped roof with a central entry flanked by six-pane windows and has a brick foundation. The inset porch is supported by iron posts.

Edmund Pettus Bridge, NHL, NRHP 2013
U.S. Highway 80 • *Constructed 1940*

In 1938 construction on a new bridge across the Alabama River marked the end of an era of the turnstile bridge in Selma and connected the city's

---

23. West et al., "Civil Rights Movement in Selma," 27.
24. West et al., "Civil Rights Movement in Selma," 51.

FIGURE 5-32, Edmund Pettus Bridge, U.S. Highway 80, Photograph by Susan Besser, 2023

southern boundary. In order to accomplish this monumental task, it was necessary to demolish late nineteenth-century buildings on Water Avenue perpendicular to Broad Street. Congressman Sam Hobbs was instrumental in obtaining funding for the bridge. Although the project suffered from setbacks such as flooding, it was completed in two years and ushered in new potential for economic progress for the city. The opening ceremony was held Friday, May 24, 1940. The Edmund Pettus Bridge is a steel through-arch bridge with a central span of 250 feet and is supported by nine concrete arches. The design was by Selma native Henson Stephenson, who was a graduate of American Polytechnic Institute, and was named for Edmund Pettus, who was a Confederate officer and United States senator. It was designated a National Historic Landmark on March 11, 2013, due to its importance during the Voting Rights era of the Civil Rights Movement in Selma.

CHAPTER 6

Lost Buildings of Selma

Why do we grieve the loss of historic buildings . . . why does preservation matter? Twenty years ago, I traveled to Selma, Alabama, to determine if I would participate with the City of Selma in the resurvey of the Old Town Historic District and the Water Avenue Historic District. I was so taken by the beautiful setting and with Selma that I felt I needed to be part of this project. I came to realize quickly there were buildings that had been lost when I would see many empty lots and compare my findings to the previous survey and Sanborn maps. Many of these buildings were high style, designed by an architect or master builder and lost in the name of progress. It is apparent that Selma experienced the highest level of growth from the 1890s to the 1920s. Many of the buildings that were lost were built during that time. What is important to realize is that the buildings tell the story of how the city developed. Additionally, it is not just the high-style architecture that has been lost but also the working-class cottages and houses. Any time a working-class neighborhood is lost the city is not only losing the historic buildings, they are losing affordable housing. What was evident is that entire streets had been lost since the original survey of these districts. Many of these would have been shotgun houses and worker cottages. These neighborhoods would have provided a sense of community. So the loss of architecture in Selma is tragic not only for the story it would have told but also for the story of the families that would have been housed in these buildings and the loss of community. This list is not all inclusive but gives a sense of the magnitude of the loss.

In 1979 Nicholas H. Holmes Jr., an architect out of Mobile, Alabama, created a study called "What's Good About Downtown." It is subtitled "The Handbook for the Economic and Aesthetic Revitalization of Downtown Selma." He discusses how he and his team spent hours researching to determine how these buildings looked before they were altered or suffered from demolition by neglect. It is an excellent way to see how towns can be reenvisioned and returned to their former glory. Some of the recommendations have been followed through with, such as changes to the Gothic Revival building at 30 Broad Street. The original was primarily rehabilitated except for the parapet. It cannot be overemphasized that downtowns and their Main Streets are vital to our nation's economy. Selma has the potential to be revitalized and benefit from cultural tourism due to its prominence as a Civil Rights site and its architectural legacy. As part of the development of these plans the St. James Hotel was renovated and made into a Historic Hotel. Recently purchased by Hilton Hotels, St. James has been newly renovated. This renovation will certainly bring renewed vigor to Selma's downtown.

Lee-Bender-Butler House • 401 Church Street
Constructed circa 1843 • Thomas Helm Lee, Architect

The Greek Revival style owes its beginnings to the increased interest in the architectural heritage of ancient Greece and was popularized by pattern books of architects such as Alexander Jackson Davis. The Lee-Bender-Butler House was built by Thomas Helm Lee, cousin of Robert E. Lee and owner of the Selma Lumberyard as well as builder of Sturdivant Hall. The Lee family occupied this house until Lee's death in 1857. Lee was the son of Miller Lee, who was from Buckingham County, Virginia. He married Mary Jane Blanks, who was from Cahawba, in 1839. The house was sold "at

FIGURE 6-1, Lee-Bender-Butler House,
401 Church Street, Photograph by Susan Besser, 2002

public outcry" to W. H. Bender in 1866. Local history sources state that it was later the home of "Miss Annie," a piano teacher to many Selmians until 1947. Miss Annie willed the house to Miss Mary Butler, an educator at Dallas Academy, who sold the property to her brother, Roger C. Butler Sr. The house remained in the Butler family. Exemplifying the epitome of the southern interpretation of the Greek Revival was this five-bay, L-shaped, two-story dwelling with a monumental porch supported by square columns and a second-story balcony with balustrade. Entry is composed of a full glass door with sidelights flanked by pilasters with an entablature. A wide band of trim with dentil molding at the cornice is a distinguishing characteristic of the style. The house was lost to a fire on November 14, 2017.

500 First Avenue • *Constructed circa 1930*
George Wilson, Architect

Formerly located at the corner of First Avenue and Summerfield Road, this one-part commercial block building functioned as a grocery store managed by white tenants in the front part. The corner entrance faced Hudson

FIGURE 6-2, 500 First Avenue, Photograph by
Dr. Carroll Van West, NRHP 2013

High School and had parapet walls at the double-door entrance and the walls facing Lapsley Street and First Avenue, which was typical of commercial buildings of the era. During the Civil Rights era a letter by the Courageous Eight asking Dr. Martin Luther King Jr. to aid Selma in the Voting Rights Movement was formulated in one of the back rooms used by SNCC. Another back room functioned as offices for George Wilson's architect and construction business.

1201 Water Avenue • *Constructed 1860*

Isaac Blauner operated a dry-goods store in the 1910s and Joseph Rosenburg operated a dry-goods/retail store in 1924 in this location. Situated at the corner of Water and Washington, this brick three-story component of a two-part commercial block had a corner entrance of double-leaf wood

FIGURE 6-3, 1201 Water Avenue, Photograph by Susan Besser, 2002

doors with glazing. On the Water Avenue side and Washington Street side were display windows with transoms. The display windows were circa 1950 and set on brick bulkheads. A metal canopy covered the perimeter of the building. On the second story above the entry were fixed-glass windows, circa 1990. To the east was a fixed-glass window with a stone lintel. On the Washington Street elevation second story were two one-over-one windows with stone lintels. On the third story above the entrance were two one-over-one windows with cast-iron cornices. To the east was a one-over-one window with cast-iron cornice. On the Washington Street elevation were four one-over-one windows with cast-iron cornices. A stepped parapet and a stepped signboard set off with header bricks relieved the austerity of the building pediment. This was demolished circa 2020.

1207-1211 Water Avenue • *Constructed circa 1860*

The tragic loss of this building in 2006 along with the Phoenix Building façade was recorded in the *Selma Times-Journal* in June of 2006. Boley & Reed Refrigerator and Appliance were occupying the building at the time and Wayne Reed narrowly escaped the building collapse.[1]

---

1. "Water Avenue Building Collapses," *Selma Times-Journal*, June 7, 2006, 12.

FIGURE 6-4, 1207-1211 Water Avenue, Photograph by Susan Besser, 2002

The Greek Revival two-story, two-bay, brick two-part commercial block had cast-iron pilasters and double-leaf doors with glazing surmounted with ten-pane transoms. Four-pane display windows rested on a brick bulkhead. The second-story fenestration was composed of four-over-four windows with window crowns. A denticulated pediment capped the building. Few storefronts incorporating wood double doors remain of this era, and that makes this loss all the more unfortunate.

Phoenix Façade • 1217-1221 Water Avenue
Constructed circa 1886 • W. W. Walker, Architect

This Italianate façade was a two-story, three-bay, cast-iron construction with a pressed metal cornice of Tudor arch detail and eave brackets. The two-story gallery had a lacy cast-iron frieze, balustrade, and porch supports indicative of the French Colonial Revival influence. The windows of the second story were segmental arched. The Phoenix building burned in 1886 and was rebuilt with W. T. Walker acting as the architect. In June of 2006 the building to the west collapsed and the Phoenix façade also collapsed at that time.

FIGURE 6-5, Phoenix Façade, 1217-1221 Water Avenue, Photograph by Susan Besser, 2002

Hotel Albert • Broad Street
Constructed circa 1860–1870 • James E. Street, Architect
J. G. Barnwell, Architect, 1890s
John W. McKeil, Architect, 1919 Additions

Modeled after the Doges Palace in Venice and designed by architect James E. Street, construction on the Hotel Albert began in 1860 just before the Civil War. The Venetian-inspired façade featured a second-story arcade of fourteen columns. Crowning the building was an octagonal observation tower. Work on the building stopped during the War and the building was used as a stable for Union and Confederate cavalry. The National Hotel Development Company of Selma purchased the property in 1866 and continued the project, completing the first- and second-floor guest rooms. "One of the outstanding features of the first-floor lobby was a broad open stairway which curved to the right and the left leading to the second floor. The stairway was fronted with large stained-glass windows."[2] Albert G. Parrish purchased the property in 1891 and was instrumental in the completion of the top two floors. In recognition of his involvement, the Hotel bore his name. The architect for the interior during that period was J. G. Barnwell of Rome, Georgia, who oversaw the completion of the ground-floor retail spaces as well. The official opening was in 1893.

FIGURE 6-6, Hotel Albert, Broad Street, Postcard Collection of Susan Besser

It is noted by the *Selma Times-Journal* in 1919 that architect J. W. McKeil prepared plans to convert a dining room into ten rooms, each with a private bath. The plans included a conversion of a rear addition with two additional stories to be twenty-four rooms with bathrooms attached.[3] The hotel was the site of debutante balls and hosted celebrities such as Sara

---

2. James Frederick Sulzby, *Historic Alabama Hotels and Resorts* (University of Alabama Press, 1989), 10.

3. "The Hotel Albert Decides to Resume Building of Additional Facilities," *Selma Times-Journal*, September 17, 1919, 1.

Bernhardt, Maurice Chevalier, and Jeanette McDonald. The Academy of Music was adjacent to the property and provided the venue for these noteworthy performers. The Hotel Albert was threatened by demolition in 1963 and saved by the Downtown Development Corporation, but sadly was demolished six years later in 1969. The hotel gained national recognition during the Civil Rights Era when Martin Luther King Jr. registered as a guest.

The Wilby Theatre • Corner of Broad Street and Selma Avenue
Constructed circa 1880; remodeled 1938 • Oscar Cobbs, Architect

FIGURE 6-7, The Wilby Theatre, Corner of Broad Street and Selma Avenue, Photograph Credit Alabama Archive

Originally known as the Academy of Music, the theatre opened in November of 1885. The Milan Italian Opera Company was the opening act. Others who appeared included the Ziegfeld Follies, Will Rogers, Lillian Russell, Lillie Langtry, Jeanette McDonald, and Nelson Eddy. Broadway plays and operas would come from New York, stopping first in Atlanta, then Selma and on to New Orleans, traveling by train. There was a rail spur that went from the Broad Street Depot to the rear of the Academy.

It was also a movie house. The theatre was remodeled in 1938 with a new façade and interior furnishings. The name was changed to The Wilby at this time. Many celebrities such as Gene Autry, Hank Williams Sr., and Minnie Pearl graced the stage. Unfortunately, the building was lost to fire on June 8, 1972.

Marx-Leva, H. G. Pattillo House • 801 Dallas Avenue
Constructed circa 1850

FIGURE 6-8, Marx-Leva, H. G. Pattillo House, 801 Dallas Avenue, Photograph by Frances Benjamin Johnston, Library of Congress, 1939

This Classical Revival house with a gracious full-width two-story portico was dismantled in order to build the Liberty National Life building in the 1960s. Eugene Rush reconstructed the house on his farm north of Selma on Highway 22 East.

Benjamin H. Craig House • 15 Union Street
Constructed circa 1850

This Italianate dwelling with beautiful cast-iron friezes was the dwelling of Benjamin Craig, who was a member of the Alabama state legislature

FIGURE 6-9, Benjamin H. Craig House, 15 Union Street, Photograph by Frances Benjamin Johnston, Library of Congress, 1939

and was a proponent of women's suffrage. Oddly, his wife was not in favor of women's suffrage. The house was demolished and the site is now the location of the River Oaks Apartments, located on Union Street.

Marks House • 415 J. L. Chestnut, Jr. Street
Constructed circa 1840

FIGURE 6-10, Marks House, 415 J. L. Chestnut, Jr. Street, Library of Congress

This Greek Revival plantation house was in the cross fires of the Battle of Selma on April 2, 1865, when a cannon ball landed on one of the columns. It was demolished in 1960 and a supermarket was built on the site. Four columns were incorporated into the portico of Shiloh Baptist Church, Sardis, Alabama.[4]

Lamar Mansion • 723 Alabama Avenue
Constructed circa 1860

FIGURE 6-11, Lamar Mansion, 723 Alabama Avenue, Photograph Courtesy of Joe McKnight

This house is believed to have been built circa 1860 by William Johnson, who owned the entire block. The house passed to Daniel Partridge, then to Smith Robbins, and then to Joe and Bessie Lamar in April of 1916. It is hard to imagine that a post office is located on the site of this once beautiful Classical Revival house. It is thought to have been built before the

---

4. Robert Gamble, *The Alabama Catalog: Historic American Buildings Survey; A Guide to the Early Architecture of the State* (University of Alabama Press, 1987), 222.

Civil War and was remodeled in the early twentieth century with the addition of the Ionic columns and new façade. Sadly, it was demolished in 1961.

First Christian Church Parsonage • 207 Franklin Street
Constructed circa 1855

FIGURE 6-12, First Christian Church Parsonage, 207 Franklin Street, HABS, Library of Congress

This two-story Greek Revival was documented by the HABS Project in the 1930s. It is tragic that this building with its beautiful two-story Doric portico and flat scroll-sawn balcony were lost to redevelopment. The building was demolished circa 1960.

Elks Home • Corner of Water Avenue and Lauderdale Street
Constructed 1904 • Charles Henry Hopson and John McKeil, Architects
Thomas Purvis, Contractor

FIGURE 6-13, Elks Home, Corner of Water Avenue and Lauderdale Street, Postcard Collection of Susan Besser

Constructed by Thomas Purvis at a price of $16,150.00, this home for the Selma Elks would have overlooked the Alabama River. The Renaissance Revival two-story brick building featured a three-story tower with a hip roof and arcaded third story. A two-story porch would have provided sweeping views of the river.

L. B. Pitts House • 504 Broad Street
Constructed circa 1850

FIGURE 6-14, L. B. Pitts House, 504 Broad Street, HABS, Library of Congress

This house was documented by the HABS Project and reflects the Greek Revival and Italianate influences of the 1850s. It is not known when the house was demolished and currently the site is an empty lot.

California Cotton Mill, Estelle Mill, Sunset Mill, Rabell Cotton Mill, Lewis Cigar Company, Bayuk Cigars
218 Morgan Avenue • *Constructed 1897*
C. A. Praray, Architect

FIGURE 6-15, Selma Cotton Mill, 218 Morgan Avenue, Photograph by Jet Lowe, Historic American Engineering Record, Library of Congress

To understand the economy of Selma one must look to the cotton industry and the components of this industry. A mill located in close proximity to the production of cotton was an essential part of this economy. C. A. Praray designed this state-of-the-art building, one of five using this system, which began operation in 1897, the design having recently being patented by Praray in 1894. The Mill featured triangular bays composed of windows that offered superb natural light. The unique construction featured support columns and walls built on separate foundations, which resulted in the walls being non–load bearing. A water tank providing water pressure to the mill was located on the top floor of the three-story tower dominating the façade. The risks of fire in a cotton mill due to the cotton fibers in the air made fire protection foremost in their design. This protection was offered by reservoirs located in front of the building and a 750,000-gallon water tank to the east of the building. Steam boilers served to operate the cotton looms and provided heat. Large bay windows were opened during the summer months to create ventilation. The mill was located on a railroad spur essential for convenience in delivery of cotton bales as well as coal to heat the building. In 1997–1998 the Department of the Interior sent a team to study this structure that was state of the art for its time. The building was demolished in 2014.

Arcadia Hotel • 325 Broad Street
Constructed 1902

FIGURE 6-16, Arcadia Hotel, 325 Broad Street,
Postcard Collection of Susan Besser

Originally a four-room, one-story residence built in 1888 by Marx Leva, this grand building served Selma for forty-four years as a hotel. In 1902 R. R. Kornegay had the house remodeled into a forty-three-room, three-story, multi-layered Queen Anne with turrets, bay windows, and a one-story wraparound for his brother, J. B. Kornegay. At that time, it was known as the Kornegay Hotel. When the hotel was sold to Mr. and Mrs. David Vaughan, Mrs. Joseph Lumpkin, and Miss Minnie Kennon, the hotel became Arcadia Hotel. The hotel had an excellent reputation, being known for its flavorful cuisine.

Belle-Marie Flats • 100 Alabama Avenue
Constructed 1910 • Charles Henry Hopson, Architect

FIGURE 6-17, Belle-Marie Flats, 100 Alabama Avenue, Postcard courtesy of Jonathan Chappelle

Constructed in 1910, the Belle-Marie Flats boasted of such elements as a skylight in the center of the Y-shaped plan that gave daylighting to the interior apartments and apartments containing six rooms each in addition to kitchen and bathrooms. Sadly, the Belle-Marie Flats, designed by Charles Henry Hopson and located at 100 Alabama Avenue, were demolished in 1978 for the Court House Annex located at the corner of Church Street and Alabama Avenue. The three-story Classical Revival had a rooftop enriched with a balustrade providing the occupants with a place to grow plants. It is described as having "magnificent large reception halls" and was constructed of concrete to create a fireproof building.[5]

---

5. "New Flats Now Near Completion," *Selma Times-Journal*, May 1, 1910.

Lamar Court • 622 Dallas Avenue
Constructed circa 1920

FIGURE 6-18, Lamar Court, 622 Dallas Avenue,
Postcard Collection of Susan Besser

Lamar Court, a three-story brick structure, had a prominent place on Dallas Avenue providing fine apartment living for its residents. The U-shaped plan allowed for a courtyard in the center as a place to wish your neighbor a good day. Unfortunately, the complex was severely damaged by fire in September of 1987 and demolished in 1988.

819 Jeff Davis Avenue (now the corner of J. L Chestnut, Jr. Boulevard and Church—southwest corner)
Constructed circa 1860

FIGURE 6-19, 819 Jeff Davis Avenue (now J. L. Chestnut Boulevard), HABS, Library of Congress

The home of Horace H. Stewart, city clerk, and his wife, Josephine, who lived here in 1903, this fine Italianate two-story dwelling had a projecting pavilion with a full-width porch and decorative eave brackets. On the north and south elevations was a polygonal bay with a balcony on the second floor. Delicate cast iron provided porch supports. In 1913 Houston F. Cooper and his wife, Bama, resided here. Mr. Cooper was a cashier at Peoples Bank & Trust, moving up to president in the 1930s. This photograph was taken in the 1930s as part of the HABS project.

Purnell House • 711 J. L. Chestnut, Jr. Boulevard
Constructed circa 1850

FIGURE 6-20, Purnell House, 711 J. L. Chestnut, Jr. Boulevard, Photograph by Frances Benjamin Johnston, Library of Congress, 1939

This gracious Greek Revival–influenced one-and-one-half-story weatherboard house had a portico supported by Doric columns. The operable shutters would have offered protection against the elements. The photograph is by Frances Benjamin Johnston, a groundbreaking female photographer, working during the Depression era.

Old Christian Church • Alabama Avenue and Green Street
Constructed 1854

This simple classic gable-front brick building had an arched recessed entry with double doors leading into the sanctuary. Flanking the entry were windows covered with Tudor arch shutters.

410 A Field Guide to Selma's Architectural Legacy

FIGURE 6-21, Old Christian Church, Alabama Avenue and Greene Street, Photograph by Frances Benjamin Johnston, Library of Congress, 1939

The congregation was formed in 1852 and met in the home of E. C. Lavender at the southwest corner of Broad Street and Dallas Avenue, led by Rev. Pickney B. Lawson. Fortunately, the church was able to survive the Civil War. In 1880 Rev. J. S. Kendrick became the pastor, splitting his time between Selma, Cambridge, and Richmond. The Rev. Sherman B. Moore became the full-time pastor in 1885 and grew the congregation quickly. In 1905 the church purchased property on the corner of Selma Avenue and Franklin Street and began the present sanctuary.[6]

The 1913 Sanborn map indicates that this building served as B'Nai Abraham Synagogue. Newspaper accounts indicate the congregation was formed in 1908.[7]

---

6. Alston Fitts III, *Historic Churches of Selma Prior to 1925* (City of Selma, 2006), 25.
7. "Big Crowds at Holiday Meeting," *Selma Times-Journal*, October 14, 1910, 1.

Law Lamar House • Church Street and Dallas Avenue
Constructed circa 1895

FIGURE 6-22, Law Lamar House, Church Street and Dallas Avenue, Old Depot Museum Archives

It is difficult to imagine that such an exquisite two-and-one-half-story Queen Anne house would be lost to demolition. So many details such as the turret and three-story polygonal wing with a conical roof project the essence of a castle. It was owned by Law Lamar and his family. Lamar was chairperson of the board of City National Bank and was a cotton commission merchant. In 1897 he proposed that there be a competition for ladies to create a dress from the "new cotton mill," which would have been the state-of-the-art California Cotton Mill. "The dresses would cost practically nothing and an evening of genuine pleasure could be derived from the rivalty [sic] between the ladies thus attired."[8] There was a follow-up story a few days later with several suggestions of categories including "consideration for

---

8. *Selma Times-Journal,* January 31, 1897, 2.

the less expensive dress."⁹ Mr. Lamar's business was located in the Adler Furniture building on Water Avenue.

City Hall • Southeast Corner of Franklin Street and Alabama Avenue
Constructed 1904 • W. Chamberlain Co., Architect

FIGURE 6-23, City Hall and Fire Station, Corner of Franklin Street and Alabama Avenue, Collection of Lannie Murphy

City governments are defined by their buildings, such as this grand structure, which was demolished when the present city building, a WPA project in 1937, was constructed. The three-and-a-half-story building with a shaped parapet defining the half story was designed by W. Chamberlain Co. with a Romanesque Revival influence as evidenced by the round arches of the first story and main entrance. The most dominant feature is the bell tower with its steeply pitched pyramid-shaped roof supported by four square columns. This facility also functioned as a fire station, and the bell tower was an integral part of life in the early twentieth century as it was the manner in which the town was alerted to a fire emergency. The *Selma*

---

9. "What the People Are Saying and Doing," *Selma Times-Journal*, February 2, 1897, 2.

Times was most eloquent in the praise of the building and the progress of the city: "But a change has come. Selma has eaten of the life giving fruit and it has wakened her sleeping energies. Her old men dream dreams and her young men see visions of wealth and progress and power. She still looks at the rippling river but with changed and quickened eyes."

Andrea Apartments • 11 Mabry Street
Constructed circa 1925

FIGURE 6-24, Andrea Apartments, 11 Mabry Street, Photograph by Susan Besser, 2002

This Spanish Revival two-story, three-bay, stucco building had a shaped parapet of Moorish arch and crenellation, a central entrance recessed into a two-story arch, a wood entrance door with glazing and arched transom, integral porches with arched openings, and a simple balustrade. The Andrea Apartments were lost to a fire in 2021.

Green Street Baptist Church • 1200 Green Street
Constructed circa 1922 • A. J. Farley, Architect

Architect A. J. Farley's Romanesque Revival cross plan with an eight-sided dome structure at the cross intersection featured distinctive

FIGURE 6-25, Green Street Baptist Church, 1200 Green Street, Photograph by Susan Besser, 2015

characteristics of the style as seen in the rows of double-hung windows surmounted by arched windows with arched keystone lintels. The front and side gables featured arched corbel tables. To the north was a four-story tower with a tent roof. The entrance of the tower featured a double-leaf door with arched stained-glass transom and arched keystone lintel. The second story had double arched windows with keystone lintels and the third story was embellished with corbel tables. The fourth was arcaded. The south tower had similar characteristics but only employed two stories.

Green Street Baptist Church was organized in 1881 and was once affiliated with First Baptist Church on Martin Luther King, Jr. Street. The Reverend John Blevins served as the first pastor. At this time, the congregation was meeting in a store on Green Street. The first church building was an austere wood-frame structure lit with three lanterns hung from the ceiling and was pastored by the Reverend Larry Brian. During his tenure, a brick church was dedicated in July 1892.

The Reverend J. A. Martin became the pastor in 1905. He was affiliated with the Alabama Baptist State Convention and was a trustee at Selma

University. Dr. Martin envisioned a larger, more imposing building that would reflect the economic status of the growing middle class in Selma. Rev. Martin approached A. J. Farley with his vision to bring this dream to a reality. The present building was dedicated in June 1922.

As part of its outreach program Green Street established a kindergarten in 1946. Green Street Baptist Church was the setting for a mass meeting in June of 1964 led by Rev. Ralph Abernathy of the Southern Christian Leadership Conference. Rev. Charles Lett was the pastor during this time. At this mass meeting members were met by violence from Sheriff Jim Clark's men. One of the most significant contributions during the Civil Rights era involved members of Green Street preparing meals and transporting those meals to activists during the Selma to Montgomery March.[10] The roof collapsed in 2016.

319 Selma Avenue • *Constructed circa 1890*

FIGURE 6-26, 319 Selma Avenue, Photograph by Susan Besser, 2002

---

10. Carroll Van West, Amber Clawson, Jessica French, and Abigail Gautreau, "The Civil Rights Movement in Selma, Alabama, 1865-1972," National Register Multiple Property Nomination, 33, https://npgallery.nps.gov/NRHP/.

Noteworthy details of the dwelling are the wraparound porch and second-story balconet with spindlework detail. This Folk Victorian two-story multi-dwelling was the home of Sophia Kingston, who founded East End Academy, also known as Little Knox School, a school for African Americans, built under her supervision and in use from 1904 to 1922. In the 1920s the city built a public school that brought in the students from East End Academy. Sophia also taught at Knox Academy, an African American private school, no longer extant. In 2005 East End Elementary was renamed Sophia Kingston Elementary School.

The Reformed Presbyterian Church • 627 J. L. Chestnut Street
Constructed circa 1878

Knox Reformed Presbyterian Church was established under Rev. Lewis Johnston to serve and educate the African-American community. The congregation was organized on May 21, 1875. The church was associated with Knox Academy, which was a private school for African Americans. It was brought into the public school system in 1937; however, the

FIGURE 6-27, The Reformed Presbyterian Church,
627 J. L. Chestnut Street, Photograph by Susan Besser, 2002

original building, which was located east on the church property, is no longer extant. The church was active in the Civils Rights Movement providing accommodations for visiting Civil Rights activists in the basement. It was also the headquarters for Concerned White Citizens of Alabama.[11]

Of the Gothic Revival vernacular, the building had a front-gable form on a raised basement to aid in air circulation. Double-leaf four-panel doors with Tudor-arch five-light transom formed the entry. A front-gable door hood with triangular knee brackets added presence to the façade. The six-over-six windows had triangular pedimented surrounds flanked by louvered shutters. Decorative truss and lancet arched louvered vent enriched the gable end. Originally, the church had a steeple with a bell. Reformed Presbyterian Church was destroyed during the January 12, 2023, tornado.

---

11. Fitts, *Historic Churches of Selma Prior to 1925*, 9.

CHAPTER 7

Looking to the Future of Selma

Selma is widely known for its Civil War history and Civil Rights history. However, the time between reflects a town that was one of the most flourishing in Alabama due to its cotton industry—not only did they grow cotton but they manufactured cotton oil and textiles as well. In the late 1900s and early twentieth century Selma was booming with a high level of residential and ecclesiastical architecture in both white neighborhoods and African American neighborhoods. It is difficult to fathom the thriving, successful Selma when driving through the streets of Selma today. The dichotomy of this is heartrending when so many Main Streets across the United States are thriving. Selma's economic woes are reflected in the underutilized storefronts and abandoned historic houses—the forgotten Selma.

In April of 2022, a charette was held to explore how Selma could be revitalized. "Reimagining Selma, Alabama" illustrated the potential of utilizing existing building stock and infrastructure to create a livable, walkable downtown.¹ The charette team noted the unique and eclectic mix of architecture in Selma that speaks to its once bustling downtown with beautiful Italianate, Renaissance Revival, and rare Gothic Revival architecture. The findings focused on the following: adaptive reuse of the buildings downtown that would accommodate the local residents and visitors, riverfront development, and redevelopment of the historic George Washington Carver Neighborhood, bringing those buildings up to contemporary public-housing standards and removing perceptual barriers. The team noted that various funding avenues are available for redevelopment.

Just as it looked as if Selma was on the upswing, disaster struck. On January 12, 2023, a tornado tore through Selma, damaging over 200 buildings in the historic districts and decimating the mature landscape of treasured streetscapes and antebellum mansions.

There are many heartwarming stories that center around rebuilding after the tornado. One such story centers on 626 Church Street, which was

FIGURE 7-1, 626 Church Street, Photograph by Bill Tomey, 2024

---

1. "Reimagining Selma, Alabama: A DesignPlace Report," DesignAlabama, April 2022, https://selma-al.gov/wp-content/uploads/2022/04/design-al-plan.pdf.

damaged by the tornado. Krystal Hardy Allen purchased the home telling her parents that she was going to rehabilitate it and resell it. Her parents actually participated in the rehabilitation. Her actual plan to was to gift the home to her parents. It was a lovely gesture that caught them totally by surprise.

The tornado destroyed the important Reformed Presbyterian Church noted for its African American heritage in religion and education.

FIGURE 7-2, Reformed Presbyterian Church, 627 J. L. Chestnut Street, Photograph by Susan Besser, 2002

Driving through Selma one is struck by the well-developed but underutilized commercial district and the number of vacant houses in the historic districts that appear to have been abandoned, some being significant resources in terms of their level of design and craftsmanship. One in Old Town Historic District at 509 Lapsley Street, known locally as the Ikerman House, has been vacant for some twenty years and, initially, it was felt the integrity remained. The tornado created damage from the force of trees that were blown against the front of this resource, and its ability to be renovated is less promising.

FIGURE 7-3, Ikerman House, 509 Lapsley Street, Photograph by Susan Besser, 2023

For those who are familiar with Selma the landscape figures prominently in the mystique of the city. One of the most revered buildings of Selma is Sturdivant Hall, considered one of the prime examples of Greek Revival architecture in the Southeast. The building itself received some damage that is repairable and there is a sense of gratefulness that it remains standing. However, the loss of this landscape—trees that were planted over 150 years ago—is impossible to quantify, something that adds to the sense of place. The photos below show before and after the tornado.

Each house in an historic district has importance as it becomes a timeline for the street showing the manner in which an area developed. Again consider Sturdivant Hall, which is on Mabry Street. The house retains outbuildings that help tell the story of the house. The rest of the story is how the street was subdivided over time to encompass buildings from the Queen Anne period, Colonial Revival period, and as late as the Prairie Style. At least one Queen Anne house sustained major damage and was demolished—leaving an empty lot and countless memories.

Selma is an architectural timeline from the 1820s through the Civil Rights Movement, and this is reflected in its historic resources. According to Dr. Carroll Van West, "The losses underscore what is precious and the important legacy of Selma." There are additional areas that were hard hit by the tornado. These areas, located north and east of the central business district along Highway 22, had great vernacular houses that would have had the potential of becoming an historic district.

Many of the occupants of these houses are renters and have few resources to deal with the aftermath. There is concern that people will be discouraged about the future of Selma and due to their own lack of resources or other options will leave Selma. Nearly one-third of Selma's residents live in poverty and struggle to feed their families. To illustrate this, each Thursday cars line up at Temple Gate Seventh Day Adventist Church to receive food supplies.

A number of the houses are being repaired and there is a sense of optimism from the local residents, who were touched that so many organizations and helpers came to Selma's aid when the storm had passed. But it is the Selmians themselves who have proved to be the most important helpers. Jo Taylor of Taylor's Studio 903 had a vision to create a mural from the

FIGURE 7-4, Sturdivant Hall, 713 Mabry Street,
Photograph by Susan Besser, 2002

FIGURE 7-5, Sturdivant Hall after tornado, Photograph by Susan Besser, 2023

remnants of the tornado. The mural is titled *Broken to Beautiful* and was designed by Linda Munoz. Mrs. Taylor was inspired by a similar mural that was crafted from remnants of things damaged by a tornado that came through Birmingham.

Mrs. Taylor noted that the sense of community after the storm was palpable. "Within 20 minutes after the tornado came through you could hear chainsaws." One of the residents, Steve Griswell, was interviewed by Kyle Gassiott of NPR as he stood on the porch of his 150-year-old home on Old Marion Junction Road that was soon to be demolished. He feels that this is the opportunity to improve race relations and noted that after the storm age or color did not seem important. "It wasn't a, well, he's with him or he's with him. They just walked across the yard to the next guy and started helping."[2]

There is hope for Selma. There are several projects that are being developed by Invictus Development out of Tampa, Florida—the Harmony Club,

---

2. Kyle Gassiott, "Selma Residents Are Still Recovering from January's Tornadoes," NPR, March 4, 2023, https://www.ideastream.org/2023-03-04/selma-residents-are-still-recovering-from-januarys-tornadoes.

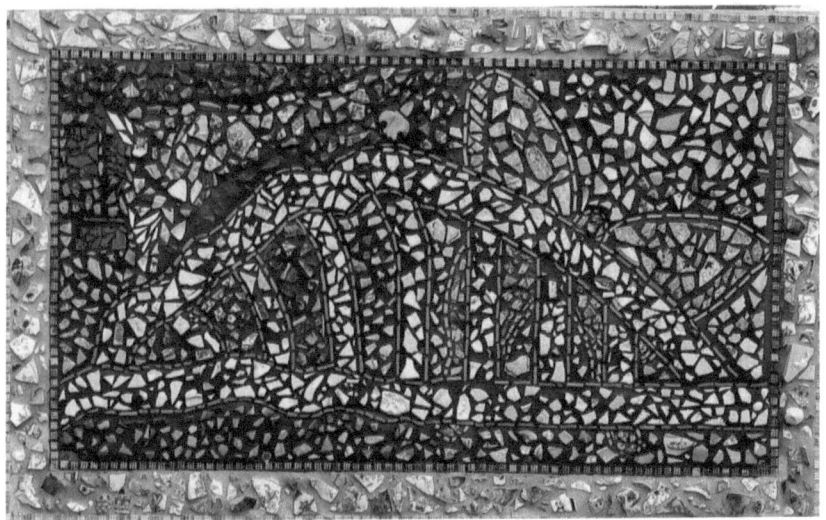

FIGURE 7-6, *Broken to Beautiful*, Photograph by Jo Taylor, 2024

the Adler Building, and the Dallas Academy. These mixed-use real-estate ventures bring the promise of more tourism and revitalization. According to Invictus Development, "The goal of these initiatives is to make Selma a destination, not just for the Bridge, but for the many stories that Selma holds, and its historic architecture and growing art community. Selma deserves investment; it is representative of the struggles and perseverance that can inspire change, a message that resonates around the world."[3]

Willa Mae Brown, a Selma native, has written a book about growing up in Selma, *My Selma: True Stories of a Southern Childhood at the Height of the Civil Rights Movement*. Brown has this to say about Selma's future: "People of all nations and genres or whatever, just come and let's build this together, a new Selma, and keep it that way."[4]

The architectural resources and the loss of the landscape will be difficult to replace. Some houses will be rebuilt, and new landscaping will be planted for future generations. For a city that has long been forgotten, this is an opportunity to create a new chapter one that opens Selma up to

---

3. "Selma Rising," Invictus Development, https://www.invictusdev.com/?page_id=1163.

4. Gassiott, "Selma Residents Are Still Recovering."

better race relations, more tolerance, and more community—and a sense of pride. Just as Selma rebuilt after the Civil War and showed the world its resilience during the Civil Rights Movement, the potential is there to come back stronger than before. Pastor Wilson of Temple Gate concurred with Brown's statement: "I think it's Selma's opportunity again, and I think the world is watching."[5]

---

5. Gassiott, "Selma Residents Are Still Recovering."

GLOSSARY

Arts and Crafts Influenced by the architecture of Greene and Greene and built during the early twentieth century, this style features low pitched roofs, large overhanging eaves with exposed rafter tails, and porches that were supported by square or tapered columns set on piers.

Baluster A single component of a balustrade, typically a column or flat wood or metal that supports the rail of a porch.

Balustrade A railing that is composed of balusters.

Bargeboard A decorative element attached to the gable end eaves, typically seen on a Gothic Revival or Queen Anne dwelling.

Bay A unit of a building defined as a window or door element.

Bay Window A window that projects from the building, typically with an angular configuration.

Beaux Arts (1885–1925) This style is characterized by a rusticated stonework, symmetrical façade, embellished surfaces with garlands, and medallions. Other defining characteristics are quoins, pilasters, and flat, low-pitched hip or mansard roofs.

Bellcast Roof A roof that terminates in a curve at the eave.

Belt Course A course of brick or stone that projects from the plane of the building and defines the location of the upper floors.

Capital The upper portion of a column that supports the entablature.

Carpenter Gothic A variant of Gothic Revival style that typically is noted by board-and-batten siding and wooden bargeboards and spindlework porches.

Cornice The molding located along the top of a building.

Corbel Any bracket, particularly of stone or brick, that serves as part of a corbel table.

Corbel Table A continuous row of corbels made up either of brick or stone that supports the eaves of the roof or cornice.

Cupola A circular or polygonal roof structure that functions as an observation point, often used as a decorative element.

Cutaway Bay A corner that is formed by the intersection of three walls and usually paired with corner brackets. Typically seen in Queen Anne style.

Dentil Molding Small square blocks along the cornice line that are typically seen in Greek Revival, Georgian, and Neoclassical styles.

Eaves The portion of the roof projecting from the walls.

Fanlight Semicircular window typically located above an entrance door.

Federal (1780–1830) Style characterized by a symmetrical façade, a semicircular fanlight, and a denticulated cornice.

Fenestration The arrangement of windows and doors on the exterior of a building.

Gable-Front-and-Wing A vernacular house form composed of a gable or upright section with a one-story ell.

Gothic Revival (1830–1880) Architectural style characterized by a steeply pitched roof with cross gables, ornamental bargeboards, hood molding over doors and windows, and Tudor or lancet arched windows. The style originates from medieval castles and cathedrals and was promulgated by the writings of Andrew Jackson Downing.

Greek Revival (1825–1860) Architectural style characterized by low-pitched gable or hip roof, pediments, and columns, with door openings flanked by sidelights and surmounted by a transom.

Hood Molding Molding over a window that protects the window from water and adds a decorative element.

Italianate (1840–1880) This style is characterized by paired eave brackets, full arched windows or segmental arched windows, and a low-pitched hip roof. This was the predominant style for downtown commercial main streets, incorporating arched windows, corbel tables, and eave brackets.

Klinker Brick Brick that is located the closest to the heat source when fired, resulting in deep rich colors.

Lancet Window A tall, narrow window with a pointed arch.

Mansard Roof A roof having two slopes on all four sides and associated with the Second Empire style. The roof derives its name from François Mansart.

Modillion Ornamental block or bracket to support the overhang of the roof.

Neoclassical Revival (1900–1940) Architectural style characterized by a two-story pedimented portico or porch supported by columns of the Doric or Ionic order. Typically, the doorway is centrally located, and the windows have a symmetrical pattern.

Palladian Window A three-part window consisting of an arched middle portion flanked by two rectangular windows, associated with André Palladio.

Parapet A wall that extends beyond the roofline and acts as a screen for the roof, often with decorative details.

Pediment A triangular form created by a horizontal element and two sloping elements.

Pilaster A square-shaped column with a base, shaft, and capital attached to the building.

Porte Cochère A covered entrance that allows exiting vehicles at the home entrance, developed for carriages and later for automobiles.

Portico A porch supported by columns.

Prismatic Glass Square pane of opaque glass that has one side smooth and the other textured, introduced in the 1890s. Given the lack of electricity during this time period it acted as a way to provide light to nineteenth- and early twentieth-century buildings.

Queen Anne Free Classic (1880–1910) Architectural style characterized by a steeply pitched irregular roof shape with porches supported by classic columns. Other elements of this style are patterned shingles and cutaway bays.

Queen Anne Spindlework (1880–1910) Architectural style characterized by a steeply pitched irregular roof shape with porches supported by spindlework detailing. Other elements of this style are patterned shingles and cutaway bays.

Quoins Rectangular pieces of stone, wood, or brick that are used to define the corners of a building. These may serve as a functional way of reinforcing corners of a building.

Romanesque Revival (1880–1900) An architectural style characterized by round arches over doors and windows, an asymmetrical façade, and conical roofs. Porches of this period have broad arches that spring from low piers. This style is also known as Richardsonian Romanesque after the architect Henry Hobson Richardson, who designed Trinity Church in Boston.

Second Empire (1855–1890) An architectural style characterized by a two-to-three–story building that has a mansard roof, eave brackets, ornamented hood molding, and arched windows and doors. This period emanated from the Baroque Style in France.

Segmental Arch An arch that is made of a half circle, typically seen in the Italianate style.

Spindlework A type of ornamentation that occurs in porch balustrades or friezes and is characterized by lacey decorative spandrels. This was typically seen in Queen Anne architecture.

Tower of the Winds Column Column that has a square abacus and a simplified form of the Corinthian capital.

Tudor Arch Flat arch that is used in doors, door surrounds, and windows, typically seen in Gothic Revival– and Tudor-style buildings.

Transom A rectangular-shaped window over a door or window.

Vernacular A term used in architecture to define the use of regional materials and craftsmen in the construction of a dwelling.

BIBLIOGRAPHY

Books and Journal Articles

Ayers, Edward L. *Promise of the New South: Life After Reconstruction.* New York: Oxford University Press, 1992.

Boothe, Charles Octavius. *The Cyclopedia of the Colored Baptists of Alabama: Their Leaders and Their Work.* Birmingham: Alabama Publishing, 1895.

Bower, Alice Meredith. *Alabama Architecture: Looking at Building and Place.* Tuscaloosa: University of Alabama Press, 2001.

Bro, Harmon Hartzell. *A Seer Out of Season: The Life of Edgar Cayce.* New York: Penguin Books, 1989.

Brooks, Daniel Fate. "The Faces of William Rufus King." *Alabama Heritage* 69 (Summer 2003): 14-23.

Durough, Allen R. *The Architectural Legacy of Wallace A. Rayfield, Pioneer Black Architect of Birmingham.* Tuscaloosa: University of Alabama Press, 2010.

Fallin, Wilson, Jr. *Uplifting the People: Three Centuries of Black Baptists in Alabama.* Tuscaloosa: University of Alabama Press, 2007.

Fitts, Alston, III, "Built on Faith." *Spanish Moss,* Winter 2011.

Fitts, Alston, III. *Historic Churches of Selma Prior to 1925.* City of Selma, 2006.

Fitts, Alston, III. *Selma: A Bicentennial History*. Birmingham: University of Alabama Press, 2017.

Fitts, Alston, III. *Selma: Queen City of the Black Belt*. Selma, AL: Clairmont Press, 1989.

Gamble, Robert. *The Alabama Catalog: Historic American Buildings Survey: A Guide to the Early Architecture of the State*. University of Alabama Press, 1987.

Gamble, Robert. *Historic Architecture in Alabama: A Primer of Styles and Types, 1810-1930*. Tuscaloosa: University of Alabama Press, 1990.

Gamble, R., C. Cooper, and H. Knopke. *Silent in the Land*. Tuscaloosa: CKM Press, 1993.

Gowans, Alan. *Styles and Types of North American Architecture: Social Function and Cultural Expression*. New York: IconEditions, 1992.

Grayson, Claude C. *Yesterday and Today: Memories of Selma and Its People*. New Orleans: Pelican Press, 1948.

Hale, Jennifer. *Historic Plantations of Alabama's Black Belt*. Charleston, SC: History Press, 2009.

Hammond, Ralph. *Ante-bellum Mansions of Alabama*. New York: Bonanza Books, 1978.

Hardy, John. *Selma: Her Institutions and Her Men*. Spartanburg, SC: Reprint Company, 1978.

Hebert, Keith S. "Selma University Historic District." National Register of Historic Places Nomination Form. 2023.

Keenan, Jerry. "Wilson's Selma Raid." *A Civil War Times Illustrated Extra*, January 1963.

Landau, Sarah Bradford. *Edward T. and William A. Potter: American Victorian Architects*. New York: Garland, 1979.

Massey, James, and Shirley Maxwell. *House Styles in America: The Old House Journal Guide to the Architecture of American Homes*. Dovetail Publishers, 1996.

McAlester, Virginia, and Lee McAlester. *A Field Guide to American Houses: The Definitive Guide to Identifying and Understanding America's Domestic Architecture*. Rev. ed. New York: Knopf, 2015.

Morgan, Carl C. "Craig Air Force Base: Its Effect on Selma, 1940-1977." *Alabama Review*, April 1989.

Rieff, Daniel. *Houses from Books: Treatises, Pattern Books, and Catalogs in American Architecture, 1738-1950, A History and Guide*. University Park: Pennsylvania State University Press, 2001.

Rifkind, Carole. *Main Street: The Face of Urban America*. New York: Harper Colophon, 1978.

Robb, Frances Osborn. *Shot in Alabama: A History of Photography 1839-1941*. Tuscaloosa: University of Alabama Press, 2016.

"Selma, Alabama: A Charming Southern Winter Resort." Pamphlet. 1893; reprint, Selma Printing, 1999.

Still, William N. "Selma and the Confederate States Navy." *Alabama Review*, January 15, 1962.

Still, William N. "Selma and the Confederate States Navy." In *From Civil War to Civil Rights: Alabama 1860-1960*. Edited by Sarah Woolfolk Wiggins. Tuscaloosa: University of Alabama Press, 1987.

Sulzby, James Frederick. *Historic Alabama Hotels and Resorts*. University of Alabama Press, 1989.

Thole, Lou. *Forgotten Fields of America: World War II Bases and Training Then and Now*. Vol. 2. Missoula, MT: Pictorial Histories Publishing, 1999.

The Tradesman 63 (1910).

Weerts, Christine. "Selma, Alabama's First Black Church Is Still Going Strong: Take a Look at Its Amazing Legacy." *The Federalist*, February 26, 2020, 4.

Weiss, Ellen. *Robert R. Taylor and Tuskegee: An African American Architect Designs for Booker T. Washington*. Montgomery: NewSouth Books, 2012.

West, Carroll Van, Amber Clawson, Jessica French, and Abigail Gautreau. "The Civil Rights Movement in Selma, Alabama, 1865-1972." National Register of Historic Places Multiple Property Nomination Form. 2013.

Wiggins, Sarah Woolfolk, ed. *From Civil War to Civil Rights: Alabama 1860-1960*. Tuscaloosa: University of Alabama Press, 1987.

Willkens, Danielle S., Heather M. Haley, and Junshan Liu. "Race, Space, and Digital Interpretation at Selma's Old Depot Museum." *Arris: The Journal of the Southeast Chapter of Architectural Historians* 31 (annual 2020): 108+. https://link.gale.com/apps/doc/A654984215/AONE?u=tel_oweb&sid=googleScholar&xid=ca6bf82b.

Wright, Gwendolyn. *Building the Dream: A Social History of Housing in America*. Cambridge, MA: MIT Press, 1981.

Young, Rosa. *Light in the Dark Belt*. Rev. ed. St. Louis: Concordia Publishing, 2014.

Newspapers

Alabama Citizen
The Anniston Star
The Cleburne News
The Montgomery Advertiser
The Selma Mirror
The Selma Times
The Selma Times-Journal

Interviews

Jean Martin, in person, September 7, 2001.
Stephen McNair, by text, PhD, August 4, 2018.

Websites

"Alabama Baptist Colored University, Selma, AL." Baptist History Homepage. http://baptisthistoryhomepage.com/alabama.bapt.colored.univ.html.

Bethune, Meredith. "A Lifetime of Barbecue in Selma." *Gravy*, Fall 2016. https://www.southernfoodways.org/a-lifetime-of-barbecue-in-selma/.

Birmingham Museum of Art. "Magic City Realism: Richard Coe's Birmingham." Exhibition, March 24–June 17, 2018. https://www.artsbma.org/exhibition/magic-city-realism-richard-coes-birmingham/.

Causey, Donna R. "Biography: L.L. Burwell, October 25, 1867, African-American." Alabama Pioneers, 2021. https://www.alabamapioneers.com/31173-2/.

"Edmundite Missions." Smithsonian National Postal Museum. https://postalmuseum.si.edu/exhibition/america's-mailing-industry-industry-segments-nonprofit-organizations/edmundite-missions.

Gassiott, Kyle. "Selma Residents Are Still Recovering from January's Tornadoes." NPR, March 4, 2023. https://www.ideastream.org/2023-03-04/selma-residents-are-still-recovering-from-januarys-tornadoes.

Harris, Mark. "The Elusive Mr. Richard B. Coe: Part Two." Dixie Art Colony Foundation, April 23, 2020. http://dixieartcolony.org/2020/04/23/richard-coe-3/.

ABOUT THE AUTHOR

Susan became fascinated with Selma, Alabama in her work as an architectural historian. Her background is an interior designer and architectural historian. She earned a BFA degree in Historic Preservation from O'More College of Design, is a Tennessee Registered Interior Designer and has LEED AP certifications. Her Master of Arts is in Historic Preservation from Middle Tennessee State University. At O'More College of Architecture and Design at Belmont University she was a long time professor of Historic Preservation and Interior Design History. She has served on the Franklin Historic Zoning Commission and acted as Chairwoman for five years. As an architectural preservationist she works to bring the architectural style and cultural history together.

Susan has two children, Jackie and Joe, and three grandchildren, Eddie, Frank and Sam. Her husband, John, has had several successful careers and is now a professor teaching college chemistry.

www.ingramcontent.com/pod-product-compliance
Lightning Source LLC
Chambersburg PA
CBHW030246010526
44107CB00031B/1342/J